823.8 S874F   FV
FARSON
THE MAN WHO WROTE DRACULA :
A BIOGRAPHY OF BRAM STOKER
                 3.98

St. Louis Community College

Library

5801 Wilson Avenue
St. Louis, Missouri 63110

The Man Who Wrote
Dracula

The Man Who Wrote

Dracula

A biography of Bram Stoker

Daniel Farson

London
Michael Joseph

First published in Great Britain by Michael Joseph Ltd
52 Bedford Square, London, W.C.1
1975

ISBN 0 7181 1098 6

Set and printed in Great Britain by
Tonbridge Printers Ltd, Peach Hall Works, Tonbridge, Kent
in Plantin eleven on twelve point on paper supplied by
P. F. Bingham Ltd, and bound by James Burn
at Esher, Surrey

For Ann MacCaw, Bram's granddaughter, in appreciation of her help; also for my friends in Romania with gratitude for their welcome on both my visits to their country; and not forgetting my fellow members of the Dracula Society, in particular Bruce Wightman and Bernard Davies.

ACKNOWLEDGEMENTS

I am happy to express my gratitude to the following:

G. W. Nash and Jennifer Aylmer, respectively of the Theatre Section and Theatre Museum at the Victoria and Albert Museum.

The staff of the Library at the Shakespeare Centre, Stratford on Avon; for their efforts in tracing documents and having them copied.

David Farmer, of the Humanities Research Centre, University of Texas.

My relatives Ann MacCaw and Noel Dobbs; and my colleagues in the Dracula Society, Bruce Wightman and Bernard Davies.

To Laurence Irving for his kind advice and the valuable information to be found in his life of Irving, his grandfather.

Of the many books I have read on the subject, often credited in context, I am indebted, above all, to Harry Ludlam's *A Biography of Dracula*.

My thanks to Professor Leonard Wolf of the San Francisco State College, for his entertaining correspondence and his book: *Dream of Dracula*.

To Dr R. C. MacGillivray, of the University of Waterloo, Ontario; and Dr Seymour Shuster, for sending me their papers on *Dracula*, and to Dr Joseph S. Bierman for his paper, also, and for taking the trouble to visit me in North Devon.

To the City of Lincoln Library, for allowing me to quote the letter which is in the Tennyson Research Centre, Lincoln, and is published by kind permission of Lord Tennyson and the Director of the Lincoln City Library.

My personal thanks to Mrs Kyrle Fletcher; Miss Cruickshank; and Christopher Lee.

To my friends in Romania, especially Georges Ionel.

And to Peter Bradshaw who gave me the idea of writing this book in the first place.

Contents

Introduction

When I was a child I was told of the eccentric behaviour of my great-uncle, Bram Stoker. Only when I started to write this book did I realise not only how strange he was, but also how under-estimated. Until recently, his name has seldom figured in national biographies or encyclopaedias.

He was a man who was taken for granted in his lifetime. As the acting manager of the Lyceum, he applauded from the wings while Henry Irving took the stage. Inevitably, this is partly the story of his friendship with Irving, for the great actor consumed Bram's energy with a voraciousness worthy of Count Dracula himself.

Stoker received no honours in his lifetime but at least, and at last, he is gaining recognition now. The Dracula Society, founded a few years ago, is not the sensational venture people might expect, but a serious literary undertaking. Encouraged by their applications and my own, it is probable that in 1976 the Greater London Council will honour Stoker's memory with a commemorative plaque to mark the house where he lived.

The time is ripe, for Bram Stoker has long remained one of the least known authors of one of the best known books ever written.

North Devon 1975

Illustrations

Illustrations

Part One

CHAPTER ONE

𝔇ublin, and the 𝔠hild who was 𝔖ickly

Bram Stoker was born in Dublin, at 15 The Crescent, Clontarf, on 8 November 1847. The place is shabbier now, yet still imposing with a small, fenced-in private park in front, a gracious anachronism that seems to have been left high and dry in the surrounding swamp of suburbia.

Once there was a clear view to Dublin Bay and the sea beyond, a view that must have been all-important to Bram as a child. For the first eight years of his life he struggled to survive, so sickly that he hardly left his room. There has been no explanation for this illness but it may have been psychological, an ailment which is not all that uncommon and which would account for his sudden physical recovery.

ᴠBram was named after his father, Abraham, a civil servant in Dublin Castle. His mother, Charlotte, may have been twenty years younger than her husband but was the more formidable personality with a vaulting ambition for her five sons, though little time for her two daughters. Her father was Lieut. Thomas Thornley (1796–1850) of the 43rd Reg and married her mother, Matilda Blake, in 1817. Bram's elder brother, William, became known as W. Thornley Stoker. Tom, my grandfather, was two years younger.

My grandmother Enid married Tom when she was little more than a girl, in 1891. She was not a fanciful woman and she told me that the family were in awe of Charlotte if not actually afraid of her. When one of the boys failed to come first in an examination, Charlotte did not conceal her resentment, even though he came second out of a thousand. There is one story which was passed on to me and may have kindled Bram's interest in the macabre if he, too, heard it as a child. It took place in the cholera epidemic which swept through Western Europe

13

and across Ireland in 1832. Charlotte was twenty-four years old, living with her parents in the town of Sligo in the West, and her written account is quoted at length by Harry Ludlam in *A Biography of Dracula:*

> One action I vividly remember. A poor traveller was taken ill on the roadside some miles from the town, and how did those samaritans tend him? They dug a pit and with long poles pushed him living into it, and covered him up quick, alive. Severely, like Sodom, did our city pay for such crimes.
>
> Trenches were now cut across the roads in the direction in which the cholera was said to come, concisely for the purpose of stopping all intercourse with the infected districts. No use, no use!
>
> One evening we heard that a Mrs Feeny, a very fat woman who was a music teacher, had died suddenly and, by the doctor's orders, had been buried an hour after. With blanched faces men looked at each other and whispered 'Cholera!'; but the whispers next day deepened to a roar, and in many houses lay one, nay two or three dead. One house would be attacked and the next spared. There was no telling who would go next, and when one said goodbye to a friend he said it as if for ever.
>
> In a very few days the town became a place of the dead. No vehicles moved except the cholera carts or doctors' carriages. Many people fled, and many of these were overtaken by the plague and died by the way.

Charlotte's family stayed inside their house, with the safety of fumigation, as their neighbours were carried away. On the ninth day, four corpses were taken from the house opposite and the families on both sides died, except for a little girl who was left alone. Hearing her cries, Charlotte begged her mother to allow her to help and Mary died in her arms an hour later. 'I returned home and being well fumigated, was not affected.'

A coffin-maker used to knock at their doors, touting for custom.

This was a climax hard to bear. Few nerves could stand it, and we asked Young to desist. But still he would come, and one day I told him that if he came again I would throw water on him. Next day he knocked as usual – and out went the full [contents] of a big jug on his head. The fellow shook himself, looked up at me with a diabolical grin, shook his fist and said, 'If you die in an hour you shall not have a coffin.'

'Thank you,' said I. 'In that case I shan't care.' He came no more.

The story I heard from my grandmother was not recorded. Though I was unaware of the document written by Charlotte, I remember my grandmother's description of a great plague, so devastating that the family were finally besieged in their home. I remember that coffin-makers knocked repeatedly on the door, just as Charlotte reported, and a specific mention of the looters who robbed the deserted houses. But my grandmother had a startling addition to the tale: that on one of the last, desperate days, Charlotte saw a hand reaching through the skylight. Seizing an axe, she cut it off with one tremendous blow.

Could this story be true? If so, it is understandable that Charlotte excluded it in retrospect. Even if it is not true, it shows the nature of the woman that it should have become a family legend.

When she told Bram her experiences of the epidemic, it is probable that she included stories of people who had been buried alive. This must have been an early influence. And if they seem strange bedtime tales for a sick child, Bram's own collection of children's stories *Under the Sunset,* published in London in 1882, is equally bizarre. It is dedicated to his baby son Noel – 'whose Angel Doth Behold the Face of the King' – but a more unsuitable book for children can hardly be imagined.

It contains one story which has particular, and reminiscent power, 'The Invisible Giant,' about an orphan girl who tries to warn the people of impending plague:

Presently she looked up from her work and gazed across the city. There she saw a terrible thing – something so terrible that she gave a low cry of fear and wonder, and leaned out of the window, shading her eyes with her hand to see more clearly.

In the sky beyond the city she saw a vast shadowy Form with its arms raised. It was shrouded in a great misty robe that covered it, fading away into air so that she could only see the face and the grim, spectral hands. The Form was so mighty that the city below it seemed like a child's toy. It was still far off from the city.

The people laugh and ignore the 'pure-hearted child', until the plague reaches them:

The hand of one who was a ringleader was already out-stretched, when he gave a low cry, and pressed his hand to his side; and, whilst the others turned to look at him in wonder, he cried out in great pain, and screamed horribly. Even whilst the people looked, his face grew blacker and blacker, and he fell down before them, and writhed a while in pain, and then died.

All the people screamed out in terror, and ran away, cry-ing aloud, 'The Giant! The Giant! he is indeed amongst us!' They feared all the more that they could not see him. But before they could leave the market-place, in the centre of which was the fountain, many fell dead, and their corpses lay. There in the centre knelt the old man and the little maid, praying; and the birds sat perched around the fountain, mute and still, and there was no sound heard save the cries of the people far off. Then their wailing sounded louder and louder, for the Giant – Plague – was amongst and around them, and there was no escaping, for it was now too late to fly.

The population is decimated, including the good old man, though Zaya, the pure-hearted girl, asks to be taken instead. 'Then Zaya knelt to the Giant, and said: "Spare him! oh! spare him and take me! but spare him! spare him!"' The old man dies, but the Giant moves away.

The Giant turned as he passed on, and Zaya saw that his blind eyes looked towards her as though he was trying to see. He raised the great shadowy arms, draped still in his shroud of mist, as though blessing her; and she thought that the wind that came by her moaning bore the echo of the words:

Innocence and devotion save the land.

Presently she saw far off the great shadowy Giant Plague moving away to the border of the Land, and passing between the Guardian Spirits out through the Portal into the deserts and beyond – for ever.

There is an echo of the closing words of his mother's manuscript when the plague abated and she was able to return to Sligo: 'There we found the streets grass grown and five-eighths of the population dead. We had great reason to thank God who had spared us.'

CHAPTER TWO

𝕿𝖍𝖊 𝕽𝖊𝖉-𝖍𝖆𝖎𝖗𝖊𝖉 𝕲𝖎𝖆𝖓𝖙

Bram's recovery from his childhood sickness was absolute. He regained – or rather gained – his strength swiftly, as if he was compensating for the wasted years. His exceptional intelligence is less surprising for he had plenty of time to study and was helped by his sister Matilda, who was a year older, his younger brother Tom, and of course Charlotte. In particular, he had the skilled tutorship of the Reverend Williams Woods who kept a private day-school in Dublin and has been described as a man of 'limitless patience'.

It was Bram's physical excellence that is so remarkable. When he entered Trinity College he was a red-haired giant, though barely seventeen. Possibly a need to eradicate the feebleness of the boy explains a contradiction in the man. He hurled himself into university life. Overcoming his early shyness, he joined the Philosophical Society and became its President: his first address was entitled 'Sensationalism in Fiction and Society'. Later, he became the 'auditor' of the Historical Society, a post that is equivalent to our President of the Union. As well as this academic distinction, he won his cap as footballer, was unbeaten in his walking marathons, and after two years became the athletics champion of Trinity.

His granddaughter has shown me the silver goblets he received. One is from the Dublin University Gymnasium in 1870, 1st Weights, won by Abraham Stoker as he was known then. The others are for walking: Dublin University Foot Races, 31 May 1866, and 1st prize for the Seven Mile Walking Race. This was repeated in 1868; also in that year came the most revealing and prophetic inscription of all, from the CSAS: '30 May 1868, 5 miles walking, Presented to A. Stoker in appreciation of his *gallant struggle* in the above race'.

Outwardly, Bram had become what he was to remain: a hearty, stalwart figure, a loyal friend, chivalrous towards the 'gentler sex', a 'man's man'. But beneath the bluff façade lay another, sensitive personality. The more I learn of Bram the more schizophrenic he appears.

Prepared to use his fists, he 'knocked down two ruffians and dragged them to the nearest police station', when they tried to rob him as he returned to his hotel after a lecture to Edinburgh University; ready to risk his life, he jumped into the Thames from a passing boat when he saw a man drowning; but he was no less afraid to champion Walt Whitman when his *Selected Poems* were published by William Michael Rossetti in 1868 and were attacked as morally offensive.

Whitman was a controversial and frequently reviled figure, as Horace Traubel recalled in his introduction to the Everyman Edition of *Leaves of Grass* in 1912:

When I first met him I was a small boy in Camden. Then nearly everyone discredited him. Everybody found some reason – it was not always the same reason – for dissent. They went to my mother and protested against my association with 'the lecherous old man'. They wondered if it was safe to invite him into their houses. I grew up in that atmosphere of suspicion. I got accustomed to thinking of him as an outlaw. But I had no doubts of him. He would talk to me about his supporters. 'They are very few,' he would say: 'but they are devoted.' He one day gave me a bunch of letters to take to the post-office. They were all to Englishmen. I remember that one was to Symonds, that one was to William Michael Rossetti, that one was to Dowden, and that one was to Tennyson.

Traubel added that it was true that, both in England and America, Whitman did not impress the critics or the second-rate but that 'first-rate men deferred to him at once'.

The Dowden referred to was Edward Dowden, Professor of English Literature at Trinity. Bram wrote that Dowden took 'the large and liberal view of *Leaves of Grass*' and together they fought on Whitman's behalf. When Dowden addressed the Philosophical Society in 1871 on 'Walt Whitman and the

Poetry of Democracy', Bram had 'the honour of opening the debate'.

Bram was twenty-one when he read the poems for the first time.

In my own University, [he wrote years later] the book was received with homeric laughter, and more than a few of the students sent over to Trubners for copies of the complete *Leaves of Grass* – that being the only place where they could then be had. Needless to say that amongst young men the objectionable passages were searched for and more noxious ones expected. For days we all talked of Walt Whitman and the new poetry with scorn – especially those of us who had not seen the book. One day I met a man in the Quad who had a copy, and I asked him to let me look at it. He acquiesced readily:

'Take the damn thing,' he said; 'I've had enough of it! '

I took the book with me into the Park and in the shade of an elm tree began to read it. Very shortly my own opinion began to form; it was diametrically opposed to that which I had been hearing. From that hour I became a lover of Walt Whitman.

Bram sent Whitman several letters but received no answer. The attacks on Whitman continued, reaching a climax one 'militant evening' at the Fortnightly Club, a group of Dublin men who met for free discussions. The paper was given by a scholar who was respected, judging by Bram's comments, but it was 'a violent, incisive attack on Walt Whitman; had we not been accustomed to such for years it would have seemed outrageous.' At one point, the man did go too far – 'In challenging the existence in the whole collection of poems for mention of one decent woman – which is in itself ridiculous, for Walt Whitman honoured women – he drew an impassioned speech from Edward Dowden . . .' Bram wrote emotionally to Whitman after midnight: 'This letter was one in which I poured out my heart. I had long wished to do so but was, somehow ashamed or diffident – the qualities are much alike. That night I spoke out; the stress of the evening had given me courage.' This time he received an answer, from Camden in New Jersey.

'Bram Stoker – My dear young man, – Your letters have been most welcome to me – welcome to me as a Person and then as Author – I don't know which most. You did well to write to me so unconventionally, so fresh, so manly, and so affectionately too. I, too, hope (though it is not probable) that we shall one day personally meet each other.'

By this time, Whitman had suffered from the stroke which he refers to at the close of his letter: 'My physique is entirely shatter'd – doubtless permanently – from paralysis and other ailments. But I am up and dress'd, and get out every day a little, live here quite lonesome, but hearty, and good spirits. – Write to me again. Walt Whitman.'

The meeting, which seemed improbable, did take place, in 1884. They met in Philadelphia, with Henry Irving, and Bram knew Whitman at once. 'On the opposite side of the room sat an old man of leonine appearance. He was burly, with a large head and high forehead slightly bald. Great shaggy masses of grey-white hair fell over his collar. His moustache was large and thick and fell over his mouth so as to mingle with the top of the mass of the bushy flowing beard.' When it was Bram's turn to be introduced, Whitman leant forward eagerly as he heard the name: 'Bram Stoker – Abraham Stoker, is it?'

Bram was to rhapsodize, 'I found him all that I had ever dreamed of, or wished for in him: large-minded, broad-viewed, tolerant to the last degree; incarnate sympathy; understanding with an insight that seemed more than human ... No wonder that men opened their hearts to him – told him their secrets, their woes and hopes and griefs and loves! A man amongst men!' When he forgot his adulation, Bram could bring personality to life so vividly that he should have devoted a book to the famous men he met. On his second visit, two years later, he described Whitman in a big rocking-chair

specially made for him, as he was a man of over six feet high and very thick-set. He was dressed all in grey, the trousers cut straight and wide, and the coat loose. All the cloth was a sort of thick smooth frieze. His shirt was of rather coarse cotton, unstarched, with a very wide full collar open low – very low in the neck and fastened with a big white stud. The old lady who cared for him and nursed him had for him a manifest admiration. She evidently liked to add on her own account some little adornment; she had fastened a bit of cheap narrow lace on his wide soft shirt-cuffs and at the neck of his collar. It was clumsily sewn on and was pathetic to see, for it marked a limited but devoted intelligence used for his care.

After Bram left, a mutual friend recorded the meeting and Whitman's reaction: ' "Well, well; what a broth of a boy he is! My gracious, he knows enough for four or five ordinary men; and what tact! Henry Irving knows a good thing when he sees it, eh? Stoker is an adroit lad, and many think that he made Mr Irving's path, in a business way, a smooth one, over here."
' "Indeed," replied the mutual friend.
' "I should say so!" Whitman continued. "See that he comes over again to see me before he leaves the country. He's like a breath of good, healthy, breezy sea air." '
There was a third visit a year later. 'His hair was more snowy white than ever and more picturesque. He looked like King Lear in Ford Maddox Brown's picture. He seemed very glad to see me and greeted me quite affectionately.' This was the final visit – 'the last time I ever saw the man who for nearly twenty years I had held in my heart as a dear friend'.

These extracts reveal Stoker as much as Whitman. A man of acute observation, a man who laughed loudly but had little sense of humour, a man of unusual openness, and a man who was devoid of guile. I doubt if Bram realised the homosexual implications of Whitman's concept of idyllic boy-love; I doubt if he recognised the lesbianism in *Carmilla,* the novel that was to influence him so deeply; and I am sure he was unaware of the sexuality inherent in *Dracula.*

CHAPTER THREE

The Fateful Meeting

There are always striking contrasts in Stoker's life. While he was absorbed in the vampirism of *Carmilla,* published two years after he left Trinity, and written by his fellow Dubliner Sheridan Le Fanu, Bram was also immersed in a tome of his own: *Duties of Clerks of Petty Sessions in Ireland.* Few titles in the history of literature have sounded so deadly, but this was part of his job in the Civil Service. It was published in Dublin in 1879.

Bram had graduated from Trinity in 1870, with honours in science, and returned in due course to collect his MA. According to the *Irish Times,* he was the most popular man in the Trinity of the '70s. Proud of his association with the university, he kept in touch faithfully but was never rewarded with the recognition he would have valued so highly.

Now he exchanged the élitist freedom of university life for the slavish whispers of an office in Dublin Castle, where he worked as a clerk. Bram intended this to be his career, though it cannot have been an encouragement to know that his father had retired in debt after fifty years' service. Abraham received a full pension, equal to his salary, of £650 a year, but he had been unable to manage for some time, largely owing to the fees of William at medical college, Bram, joined by Tom, at Trinity, and the schooling of the two younger boys and two younger girls. At least he was solvent enough to be able to continue in debt and to pay for Bram to take a week's holiday in London. But after Bram left Trinity the debts became so critical that Abraham and Charlotte sold the house and all their furniture and moved to France, far cheaper then, with their daughters. By now the education of the boys was nearly complete: William was about to set up his own medical practice; Tom, my grandfather, was ready to join the Indian Civil Service; Dick and

23

George were finishing at medical school. Bram was entrusted with forwarding his father's monthly pension and paying off whatever debts he could manage. Plainly he made his own contribution, for Abraham wrote from abroad, 'Having to take your pittance breaks my heart. But the time must come when we will have the means of repaying you the *money*, which is the least part of all we owe you.' As with the majority of such promises, the time never came.

Meanwhile, Bram escaped from the monotony of his office work into the more creative worlds of his own writing and the Dublin theatre. Fortunately, the two combined.

Bram was stage-struck from the age of nineteen, when he saw Henry Irving for the first time, as Captain Absolute in *The Rivals*. The actor was ten years older and Bram was impressed, like a young girl meeting her hero:

> What I saw, to my amazement and delight, was a patrician figure as real as the person of one's dreams, and endowed with the same poetic grace. A young soldier, handsome, distinguished, self-dependent; compact of grace and slumbrous energy. A man of quality who stood out from his surroundings on the stage as a being of another social world. A figure full of dash and fine irony, and whose ridicule seemed to *bite*; buoyant with the joy of life; self-conscious; an inoffensive egoist even in his love-making; of supreme and unsurpassable insolence, veiled and shrouded in his fine quality of manner.

Bram was writing of the actor as well as the character. He resented Dublin's indifference, especially the critic who damned him as 'stiff and constrained'.

Three years later, Irving returned with the comedy *Two Roses*. His characterisation of the eccentric Digby Grant 'stood out star-like', according to Bram. 'An inimitable character which Irving impersonated in a manner so complete that . . . I have been unable to get it out of my mind as a reality.' Again, there was no appreciation in the Press: 'There was not a word in any of the papers of the acting of any of the accomplished players who took part in it; not even the mention of their names.' This prompted Bram to visit Dr Henry Maunsell, the proprietor of the *Dublin Mail*, and offer himself as dramatic critic. 'He told me frankly that the paper could not afford to pay for such special work, as it was, in accordance with the local custom of the time, done by the regular staff who wrote on all subjects as required. I replied that I would gladly do it without fee or reward. This he allowed me to carry out.'

It was a turning-point. 'From my beginning the work in November 1871 I had an absolutely free hand.' With a typical mixture of immodest modesty, he accepted his unpaid job as one of real responsibility: 'as I have always held that in matters critical the critic's personal honour is involved in every word he writes I could always feel that the duty I had undertaken was a grave one.' He added, 'I did not shirk work in any way.' This was an understatement. Bram's capacity for work was abnormal: throughout his life he ran two careers simultaneously, wrote scores of letters in his own hand, at one time several hundred a week, and enjoyed that Victorian ability to maintain friendship which we seem to have lost. And even then, as if he had a surplus of energy, he set out on marathon walking tours.

Slaving over his legal tome in Dublin Castle, writing dramatic criticism for the *Dublin Mail*, he became an editor three years later of *The Halfpenny Press*. This venture was not successful, and he resigned after four months. His next contribution was to *Shamrock*, a magazine that published a four-part serial *The Chain of Destiny*, by 'A. Stoker, Esq'. This was Bram's first exploration into horror, with a character called 'the phantom of the fiend'.

Bram's passion for the theatre continued with youthful enthusiasm: 'Mr Barry Jackson is at present acknowledged to be the leading legitimate actor of our stage,' a verdict he was soon to change.

In the summer, helped by his fee from *Shamrock*, he visited his parents in their small hotel at Zermatt, Switzerland. He lacked the nerve to tell his father of his latest obsession, an actress with the curious name of 'Miss Henry', whom he had met in Paris where he broke his journey. Eager to write a play for her, anxious to escape from the routine of Dublin Castle, he confided his intention to throw up his job and go to London to make his living as an author. Abraham Stoker was aghast, as Harry Ludlam relates, sending a fatherly letter of caution:

I know your present income is not by any means a liberal one, but still it is an increasing one, and your prospect of succeeding to a better class is not by any means hopeless. I was eighteen years in the civil service before I had as good a salary as you have now. You must know that there are few men of your standing now in the castle who have a larger income – and you can also guess how many competitors there would be if a vacancy took place tomorrow in your office.

As for 'Miss Henry', Abraham was plainly distressed by the association with an actress:

I am sure you will not think that I want to dictate to you as to the class of acquaintances which you ought to make, but I may offer you some experience of my own early life, which was very varied, and during which I was acquainted with both actors and actresses. Although I am ready to admit that in many instances their society was very agreeable, still I don't think they are altogether desirable acquaintances to those not connected with their own profession (if I may call it,) because it may involve expense and other matters which are not at all times advantageous. Under all the circumstances I believe such acquaintanceship is better avoided.

This letter might have impressed Bram but it is more likely that his infatuation cooled: he remained in the Civil Service. But restlessness had taken root and he wrote to his father that he had applied for the post of Dublin city treasurer. Abraham replied scathingly, 'Any trouble you may take in looking for the vacancy will only be lost time. An outsider has no chance, particularly when there is a member of their own body looking for it, and even if there were not, I should say that none but an advanced Liberal or a Roman Catholic would be elected.' So ended the paternal advice, and at least Bram could console himself that he had followed it obediently when he learnt of Abraham's death in Naples at the age of seventy-seven. Bram and William left for Italy, to settle business for Charlotte and the two girls, who wished to remain there, and then Bram returned to Dublin.

By the time Henry Irving returned to Dublin in 1876, Stoker has been writing as a dramatic critic for five years. This time he was able to express his feelings in print: 'In his fits of passion (as Hamlet) there is a realism that no one but a genius can ever effect.' Pleased by the review, which he read on Tuesday morning, Irving asked the manager of the Theatre Royal to introduce him to Bram and invited him to his hotel for supper after the play. Bram was so impressed that he saw *Hamlet* three times, and wrote a second criticism which appeared on Saturday. When they met again, for dinner on Sunday, Irving was 'full of it'. As Bram wrote, many years later, in his *Personal Reminiscences of Henry Irving*, 'then began the close friendship between us which only terminated with his life – if indeed friendship, like any other form of love, can ever terminate.' *'Love'* is not too strong a word for the relationship that developed.

Discussing the production, and Bram's criticisms, the two men began to realise how much they had in common. 'Thus it was that on this particular night my host's heart was from the beginning something toward me, as mine had been toward him. He had learned that I could appreciate high effort; and with the instinct of his craft liked, I suppose, to prove himself again to his new, sympathetic and understanding friend. And so after dinner he said he would like to recite for me Thomas Hood's poem *The Dream of Eugene Aram*.'

Then there followed an extraordinary scene.

The narrative ballad, based on a true incident of the period, verges on the melodramatic today. Even then, Irving must have brought an extra dimension to his recital to have had such an effect. It starts with deceptive gentleness:

> 'Twas in the prime of summer time,
> An evening calm and cool
> And four and twenty happy boys
> Came bounding out of school
> There were some that ran and some that leapt
> Like troutlets in a pool.

Eugene Aram grows more fevered as he describes 'a murder in a dream':

> One that had never done me wrong
> A feeble man and old
> I led him to a lonely field
> The moon shone clear and cold:
> Now here, said I, this man shall die
> And I will have his gold!

Stoker sat there 'outwardly of stone', but inwardly he was 'shattered' as the recital continued:

Here in a hotel drawing-room, amid a dozen friends, a man in evening dress stood up to recite a poem with which we had all been familiar from our schooldays . . .

But such was Irving's commanding force, so great was the magnetism of his genius, so profound was the sense of his dominance that I sat spellbound . . . The whole thing was new, re-created by a force of passion which was like a new power . . . Here was incarnate power, incarnate passion, so close that one could meet it eye to eye, within touch of one's outstretched hand. The surroundings became non-existent; the dress ceased to be noticeable; recurring thoughts of self-existence were not at all. Here was indeed Eugene Aram as he was face to face with his Lord; his very soul aflame in the light of his abiding horror.

That experience I shall never – can never – forget. The recitation was different, both in kind and degree, from anything I had ever heard; and in those days there were some noble experiences of moving speech.

> Nothing but lifeless flesh and bone
> That could not do me ill
> And yet I fear'd him all the more
> For lying there so still
> There was a manhood in his look
> That murder could not kill.

> And, lo, the universal air
> Seem'd lit with ghastly flame
> Ten thousand thousand dreadful eyes

Were looking down in blame
I took the dead man by his hand
And call'd upon his name.

Oh God it made me quake to see
Such sense within the slain
But when I touch'd the lifeless clay
The blood gushed out amain
For every clot, a burning spot,
Was scorching in my brain.

It was the perfect choice with which to impress Irving's new friend. Bram noted 'How a change of tone and time denoted the personality of the "Blood-avenging Sprite" – and how the nervous, eloquent hands slowly moving, outspread fanlike, round the fixed face – set as doom, with eyes as inflexible as Fate – emphasised it till one instinctively quivered with pity.'

Oh God! that horrid, horrid dream
Besets me now awake
Again – again with dizzy brain
The human life I take
And my red right hand grows raging hot
Like Cranmer's at the stake.

And still no peace for the restless clay
Will wave or mould allow
The horrid thing pursues my soul
It stands before me now.'
The fearful boy looked up and saw
Huge drops upon his brow.

There are several more verses before the poem reaches its climax. Stoker described the effect on Irving: 'The awful horror on the murderer's face as the ghost in his brain seemed to take external shape before his eyes, and enforced on him that from his sin there was no refuge.

'After the climax of horror the Actor was able by art and habit to control himself to the narrative mood whilst he spoke the few concluding lines of the poem':

> That very night, while gentle sleep
> The urchin eyelids kiss'd
> Two stern faced men set out from Lynn
> Through the cold and heavy mist
> And Eugene Aram walked between
> With gyves upon his wrist.

After this dying fall, Henry Irving collapsed.

Bram Stoker sat motionless for a few seconds of silence, then he burst into something approaching hysterics:

> I was no hysterical subject. I was no green youth; no weak individual, yielding to a superior emotional force. I was as men go a strong man ... I was a very strong man. It is true I had known weakness. In my babyhood I used, I understand, to be often at the point of death. Certainly till I was about seven years old I never knew what it was to stand upright ...
>
> When, therefore, after his recitation I became hysterical, it was distinctly a surprise to my friends; for myself surprise had no part in my then state of mind.

He stressed his physical strength, not in his vindication but in praise of Irving's 'splendid power' which had moved him so greatly. There must have been a magic in the hotel room that night.

There are great moments even to the great.

That night Irving was inspired. Many times since then I saw and heard him – for such an effort eyes as well as ears are required – recite that poem and hold audiences, big or little, spellbound till the moment came for the thunderous outlet of their pent-up feelings; but that particular vein I never met again. Art can do much; but in all things even in art there is a summit somewhere. That night for a brief time in which the rest of the world seemed to sit still, Irving's genius floated in blazing triumph above the summit of art. There is something in the soul which lifts it above all that has its base in material things. If once only in a lifetime the soul of man can take wings and sweep for an instant into mortal gaze, then that 'once' for Irving was on that, to me, ever memorable occasion.

Equally disturbed, Irving fell into his bedroom and emerged a few minutes later with a photograph of himself, the inscription still wet:

MY DEAR FRIEND STOKER. GOD BLESS YOU! GOD BLESS YOU! HENRY IRVING. DUBLIN, DECEMBER 3, 1876.

'In those moments of our mutual emotion,' wrote Bram, 'he too had found a friend and knew it. Soul had looked into soul! From that hour began a friendship as profound, as close, as lasting as can be between two men.'

A turning-point, in any man's life, is seldom as irrevocable as it was that night for Bram.

A few days later, on 11 December, Irving received two honours from Trinity College. The first was an Address presented in the dining hall by graduates and undergraduates, drafted by Bram Stoker: 'It is something more than gratitude for personal pleasure or improvement that moves us to offer this public homage to your genius. Acting such as yours ennobles and elevates the stage, and serves to restore it to its true function as a potent instrument for intellectual and moral culture.'

Irving accepted with a graciousness that gives an indication of the quality of the man:

Such honour as you have now bestowed enters not into the actor's dreams of success. Our hopes, it is true, are dazzling! We seek our reward in the approval of audiences, and in the tribute of their tears and smiles; but the calm honour of academic distinction is and must be to us, as actors, the Unattainable, and therefore the more dear when given unsought.

For my Profession, I tender you gratitude; for my Art I honour you; for myself, I would that I could speak all that is in my soul.

But I cannot; and so falteringly tender you my most grateful thanks.

That evening there was even greater excitement. Trinity had bought all the seats for the 'University Night' and crowds assembled outside the doors. Just before seven, heralded by bugles and horns, five hundred students flooded into the pit of the theatre. Bram described the scene in the *Dublin Mail*: '. . . the boxes began to fill, and as each Fellow and Professor and well-known University character made his appearance, he was cheered according to the measure of his popularity.'

When Irving made his entrance 'he was received with a cheer which somewhat resembled a May shower, for it was sudden, fierce and short, as the burst of welcome was not allowed to interrupt the play.' The play was *Hamlet* and, even allowing for Bram's idolatry, Irving rose above the occasion:

> In the scene with Ophelia he acted as though inspired, for there was a depth of passionate emotion evident which even a great actor can but seldom feel; and in the play he stirred the house to such a state of feeling that there was a roar of applause. During the performance he was called before the drop-scene several times; but it was not till the green curtain fell that the pent-up enthusiasm burst forth. There was tremendous applause, and when the actor came forward the whole house rose simultaneously to their feet, and there was a shout that made the walls ring again. Hats and handkerchiefs were waved, and cheer upon cheer swelled louder and louder as the player stood proudly before his audience, with a light upon his face such as never shone from the floats. It was a pleasant sight to behold – the sea of upturned faces in the pit, clear, strong, young faces, with broad foreheads and bright eyes – the glimpse of colour as the crimson rosettes which the students wore flashed with their every movement – the gleaming jewels of the ladies in their boxes – the moving mass of hats and handkerchiefs, and above all the unanimity with which everything was done. It was, indeed, a tribute of which any human being might be proud.

No stage actor today would receive such a combination of rapture and respect. Later, Irving was heaped with honours unparalleled in his profession, but on this night in Dublin he was at the threshold. Plainly, his star was rising and the students recognised it. Now, our idols are instantly accessible, on the screen, but Irving arrived in cities as a comparative stranger, yet became immediately tangible – and glamorous – when seen on stage. The veneration of the students was sincere, not fabricated into mob hysteria by any advance posse of publicity men. If Stoker was to attach himself to the promise of another, he chose the best in Irving: an autocrat, a complex character, and in many ways a selfish man, but infinitely rewarding through his work.

This 'University Night' must have been bitter-sweet satisfaction for Irving, in a way the students could not have realised. His first appearance in Dublin, at the Queen's Theatre, had occurred when he was barely twenty-one. He arrived full of anticipation, having accepted the engagement at short notice, unaware that he was replacing a popular local favourite who had been sacked. His entrance was greeted with a storm of stamping, cat-calls and hisses. Irving described his reaction in an interview thirty years later:

'There was I standing aghast, ignorant of having given any cause of offence, and in front of me a raging Irish audience, shouting, gesticulating, swearing probably, and in various forms indicating their disapproval of my appearance. I was simply thunderstruck at the warmth of my reception .. I simply went through my part amid a continual uproar – groans, hoots, hisses, catcalls, and all the appliances of concerted opposition. It was a roguish experience, that!'

'Surely it did not last long?' asked the journalist.

'That depends,' said Irving gravely, 'on what you call long. It lasted six weeks.'

This humiliation was stamped on his memory and may have accounted for the future stiffness of his bow before the curtain as if he tolerated the applause. He knew how treacherous it could be. But on the occasion of the University Night his reply was phrased meticulously.

Honest and steadfast work in any path of life is almost sure to bring rewards and honours; but they are rewards and honours so unexpected and so unprecedented that they may well give the recipient a new zest for existence.

Such honours you have heaped upon me ... Accept the
truest, warmest, and most earnest thanks that an overflowing heart tries to utter, and you cannot think it strange
that every fibre of my soul throbs and my eyes are dim
with emotion as I look upon your faces and know that I
must say 'goodbye'. Your brilliant attendance on this, my
parting performance, sheds a lustre upon my life. I only
hope that I have your 'God's blessing' as you have mine.

Outside the stage-door, more than a thousand students
gathered and waited. When he emerged, two hundred of these
harnessed themselves to his carriage instead of the horses and
drew it along Grafton Street to the Shelbourne Hotel in St
Stephen's Green. Bram sat proudly beside him – on 'that exciting progress through a solid moving mass and wild uproar'.
When they reached the Shelbourne the cheering moved Irving
so profoundly that he asked Bram if it was possible to ask all
his friends to join him at supper. A mere wave from Bram
towards the vast crowd proved the impossibility of such a
gesture, and, at last, they forced their way inside.

CHAPTER FOUR

Oscar Wilde Rejected

Irving returned six months later for a brief visit, fulfilling his promise of a reading to Trinity College of extracts from *Richard III* and *Othello*; Copperfield and the waiter; and *The Dream of Eugene Aram*. He was accompanied by his new stage-manager, Harry Loveday.

A fortnight later, Bram went to London for his own summer holiday and closer acquaintance with Irving, who was playing at the Lyceum in *The Lyons Mail*.

They met again in the autumn when Irving returned for another season in Dublin, and Bram was impressed by the growth of his performance: '*Hamlet*, as Mr Irving now acts it, is the wild, fitful, irresolute, mystic melancholy prince that we know in the play; but given with a sad, picturesque gracefulness which is the actor's special gift.' But it is fair to say that, so far as Irving was concerned, Bram's reviews could no longer be described as 'criticism'. His loyalty became so fierce that he could not bear to hear a word against his friend, let alone utter one himself.

A chance comment reveals the growing affection between the two men: 'A small party of us, *of whom Irving and I were always two,* very often had supper in those restaurants which were a famous feature of men's social life in Dublin.' A favourite was Corless's, famous for hot lobster.

One Sunday afternoon, the two friends drove out to Phoenix Park and stopped their carriage when they noticed a small crowd encircling two wrestlers. They mingled, unrecognised – 'but they saw we were gentlemen', Bram recalled complacently, 'strangers to themselves, and with the universal courtesy of their race put us in the front when the ring had been formed.' It was a scene to delight Irving's sense of theatre and Bram's respect for fair play. No police, no ropes, not a word of encouragement or cheer in case this gave one of the men an unfair advantage. The style of wrestling was traditional, with defeat the moment that both shoulders touched the ground at once. A single bout could last as long as fifteen minutes. It was a scene that should have been recorded on canvas – the two combatants, with their traditional stance; the circle of Irishmen in their simple clothes, contrasting with the elegance of the two visitors – set in the open field, the carriage waiting in the background. The ring was formed in a startling fashion: 'A powerful fellow was given a drayman's heavy whip. Then one of those with him took off his cap and put it before the face of the armed man. Another guided him from behind in the required direction. Warning was called out lustily, and any one not getting at once out of the way had to take the consequence of that fiercely falling whip. It was wonderful how soon and how excellently that ring was formed.' The protagonists were 'two splendid young men . . . Rafferty of Dublin and Finlay of Drogheda – as hard as nails and full of pluck.' When the bout was over, Irving asked permission to present a prize to be divided equally between the two contestants. He gave so generously that there was difficulty in 'breaking' the bank-note, and when Bram proudly revealed the identity of his companion everyone gave a mighty cheer.

Such shared experiences must have been deeply satisfying. Best of all was the evening when Irving came to Bram's new rooms in Harcourt Street, an elegant row of houses which can still be seen, and they discussed the future: Irving was in partnership with a Mrs Bateman, but anxious to break free. He returned to a suggestion, hinted at earlier, that Bram might share his fortunes. The effect on Bram can be imagined: if he was restless over 'Miss Henry', he was more so now. The same name, shared by the actress and the actor, is a pleasing coincidence. Bram wrote gleefully in his diary that night – 22 November 1877 – 'London in view!'

A practice-run occurred, in June of the following year, when Bram crossed to London to attend the first night of *Vanderdecken*, a new version of *The Flying Dutchman* at the Lyceum. Inevitably, it was the actor, rather than the production, which attracted him: 'I think his first appearance was the most striking and startling thing I ever saw on the stage . . . There was no appearance anywhere of a man or anything else alive. But suddenly there stood a mariner in old-time dress of picturesque cut and faded colour of brown and peacock blue with a touch of red. On his head was a sable cap. He stood there, silent, still and fixed, more like a vision made solid than a living man.' Despite this personal enthusiasm, Bram's critical faculty knew that something was basically wrong with the play, and the two men worked through the night in Irving's rooms in Grafton Street, cutting and shaping. When Bram saw the play again he noticed an improvement.

Two months later, Irving returned to Ireland for a 'working holiday' and was met by Bram at Kingstown. He stayed with William Stoker who was already on the climb to the social success for which he cared so much. After several days of re-laxation, largely spent in driving to the countryside, Bram accom-panied Irving to Ulster for a reading attended by 3,000 people. Afterwards they started a practice that became a habit, talking together until the chimes of the clock and the light through the curtains told them that the night was over.

I well understood even then, though I understand it better now, that after a hard and exciting day or night – or both – the person most concerned does not want to go to bed. He feels that sleep is at arm's length until it is summoned. Irving knew that the next day he would have to start at three o'clock on a continuous journey to London, which would occupy some fifteen hours; but I did not like to thwart him when he felt that a friendly chat of no matter how exaggerated dimensions would rest him better than some sleepless hours in bed.

At the end of the year – in September 1878 – Irving returned to Dublin for another season. They saw each other constantly and Bram lived happily in anticipation: 'It was a sort of gala time to us all, and through every phrase of it – and through the working time as well – our friendship grew and grew.

'We had now been close friends for over two years. We under-stood each other's nature, needs and ambitions, and had a mutual confidence, each towards the other in his own way, rare amongst men.'

It was no surprise, six weeks later, when he received a telegram from Irving summoning him immediately to Glasgow to discuss 'important business'. The following evening, Irving told him the news: he had taken on the Lyceum and wanted Bram to join him as acting manager. Bram accepted without hesitation. The next morning he sent in his resignation, discarding his career in the Civil Service after thirteen years and forfeiting his chance of a pension. His colleagues presented him with a handsome silver wine-ewer, inscribed 'To Bram Stoker MA from the Members of his office.' And in the middle of all this activity, ending one career to start another, he acquired a wife. The marriage was hurried forward but it is likely that Bram had known Florence Anne Lemon Balcombe for many years, first when she lived at 1 Marino Crescent near his old home in Clontarf, later as a neighbour when she moved into the heart of Dublin, to Harcourt Street. She was the third of five daughters of Lieutenant-Colonel James Balcombe, who served in India and the Crimea, but apparently she was named not after Miss Nightingale, but after the Italian town. Her looks were exceptional – George du Maurier considered her one of the three most beautiful women he had ever seen – but the most startling thing about her was the name of her former suitor: Oscar Wilde. This might surprise some people, and indeed Oscar's protestations of his love for her were sometimes over-dramatic: 'She thinks I never loved her, thinks I forget. My God how could I!' But anyone who has studied the case of Mrs Oscar Wilde, the woman who was virtually forgotten in the scandal, can believe that his love for Constance Lloyd who became his wife, and for Florence Balcombe who did not, was genuine. Outwardly he was flippant about Constance: when asked why he married her, he replied, 'She never speaks and I am always wondering what her thoughts are like'; yet he crossed to Dublin between lectures just to be with her for a few hours. 'We telegraph to each other twice a day . . . and do all the foolish things that wise lovers do.'

Prophetically, he wrote these verses for his wife:

> For if of these fallen petals
> One to you seems fair,
> Love will waft it till it settles

On your hair.
And when the wind and winter harden
All the loveless land
It will whisper of the garden
You will understand.

After Wilde married, when he was lecturing in Edinburgh on 16 December 1884, he wrote this letter to Constance, the only one to escape obliteration by her family:

Dear and Beloved, Here am I, and you at the Antipodes. O execrable facts, that keep our lips from kissing, though our souls are one. What can I tell you by letter? Alas! nothing that I would tell you. The messages of the gods to each other travel not by pen and ink and indeed your bodily presence here would not make you more real: for I feel your fingers in my hair, and your cheek brushing mine. The air is full of the music of your voice, my soul and body seem no longer mine, but mingled in some exquisite ecstasy with yours. I feel incomplete without you. Ever and ever yours. Oscar.

Bram could not have written such a letter. In spite of their mutual interests, the two men could hardly have been more different – Oscar's cynicism, at the very least, would have outraged Bram's sense of morality. Doubtless they knew each other, for Bram was a regular visitor to Wilde's home in Merrion Square, and a favourite of Sir William and Lady Wilde. Sir William's accounts of his archaeological explorations in Egypt encouraged Bram's own interest in this subject which led to the publication of *The Jewel of Seven Stars* in 1903. Lady Wilde, who wrote poems under the name of 'Speranza', welcomed Bram to their artistic circle, for they were among the leaders of Dublin society in spite of the notoriety of Sir William's misconduct with women which landed him in court. The robust atmosphere that surrounded them must have been to Bram's liking, more than the behaviour of their son.

If the two men were so contrasted, why did Florence exchange Oscar for Bram? For one thing, she was not so naive as Constance Lloyd, who was prepared to forget and forgive Oscar's 'past misdemeanours' and the fact that he was 'decidedly extra affected'. Writing to her brother about O.W., Constance referred to a threat to 'duck him'. Florence would not have tolerated gossip: equally, if she had married Oscar she would have revelled in the role of society hostess and might have brought him to heel, avoiding the public scandal. Would she have proved a match for Bosie? An intriguing speculation!

In 1878, Florence was twenty years old, Oscar twenty-four, and Bram thirty-one. Perhaps she preferred the safety of the older man, whose future promised excitement.

The extent of her feelings for Oscar Wilde, and her reactions on learning of his downfall, can only be guessed, But the early drawing he made of her reveals a tenderness that shows another aspect of his nature, as well as his talent. In the summer of 1876, two years earlier, Oscar had written to Reginald Harding, 'I am just going out to bring an *exquisitely pretty girl* to afternoon service in the Cathedral. She is just seventeen with the *most perfectly beautiful face I ever saw and not a sixpence of money.*' Rupert Hart-Davis, in *The Letters of Oscar Wilde*, is certain that this refers to Florence Balcombe. The following spring, in another letter to Harding, Oscar refers to her again: 'The weather is charming, Florrie more lovely than ever.'

When I was a boy, collecting autographs, Noel Stoker – the only child of Bram and Florence – gave me a small sack of letters which he thought might be of interest to me. I shiver now when I think of the treasures I failed to appreciate. Many were disposed of, some were lost! I can only be thankful that the rest are safe in various museums. This innocent-looking bag contained recriminating letters from Wilde to Florence when he learnt of her engagement. But an earlier letter – 'to wish you a pleasant Easter' – could hardly be described as passionate. 'I have been greatly disappointed in not being able to come over, but I could only spare four days and as I was not feeling well came down here (Bournemouth) to try and get some ozone. The weather is delightful and if I had not a good memory of the past I would be very happy.'

The tone of the three letters, undated but obviously written in quick succession, which I found in Noel Stoker's sack (Florence was shrewd enough to keep them, *after* the scandal) suggests that Oscar's pride was hurt more than his heart. The first letter was signed, 'Adieu and God bless you. Oscar.' The second, 'Very truly yours Oscar Wilde'. The third, 'Goodbye, and believe me yours very truly Oscar Wilde'. His growing petulance concerned a small golden cross he had given to Florence one Christmas, and her reluctance to return it. In his first letter he explains that he would like to take it back with him to England:

> I need hardly say that I would not ask it from you if it was anything you valued, but worthless though the trinket be, it serves as a memory of two sweet years – the sweetest of all the years of my youth – and I should like to have it always with me. If you would care to give it to me yourself I could meet you any time on Wednesday, or you might hand it to Phil, [her sister] whom I am going to meet that afternoon.
>
> Though you have not thought it worth while to let me know of your marriage, still I cannot leave Ireland without sending you my wishes that you may be happy; I at least cannot be indifferent to your welfare: the currents of our lives flowed too long beside one another for that.
>
> We stand apart now, but the little cross will serve to remind me of the bygone days, and though we shall never meet again, after I leave Ireland, still I shall always remember you at prayer.

This gives a suitable impression of Oscar wiping away a forlorn tear as he sealed the envelope, but Florence was unimpressed. She suggested a meeting at Harcourt Street, but Oscar replied this would be too painful and suggested they see each other for the last time at 'the Crescent on Friday at two o'clock'. He promised to return her letters when he reached Oxford, and enclosed a scrap of paper 'I used to carry with me: it was written eighteen months ago: how strange and out of tune it all reads now.'

Her reply must have seemed a rebuke, for he wrote back coldly:

> Dear Florence [no longer 'Florrie'], As you expressed a wish to see me I thought that *your mother's house* would

be the only suitable place and that we should part where we first met. As for my calling at Harcourt Street, you know, my dear Florence, that such a thing is quite out of the question: it would have been unfair to you, and me, and to the man you are going to marry, had we met anywhere else but under your mother's roof, and with your mother's sanction. I am sure that you will see this yourself on reflection; as a man of honour I could not have met you except with the full sanction of your parents and in their house.

As regards the cross, there is nothing 'exceptional' in the trinket except the fact of my name being on it, which of course would have prevented you from wearing it ever, and I am not foolish enough to imagine that you care now for any memento of me. It would have been impossible for you to keep it.

I am sorry that you should appear to think, from your postscript, that I desired any clandestine 'meeting': after all, I find you know me very little.

Bram and Florence were married at St Anne's Church in Dublin on 4 December 1878. There was no time for a proper honeymoon. Five days later they joined Henry Irving in Birmingham.

Charlotte was not amused by this irrevocable break in her son's career. Contemptuously, she referred to his new appointment as that of 'Manager to a strolling player'.

CHAPTER FIVE

First Night at the Lyceum

To be involved from the beginning with a new venture, be it a magazine or corner-shop, is one of the most exhilarating moments of life. Bram had a double excitement: for the first time he was closely concerned with the production of a play with all the dramas inside the drama culminating in the first night, and he also supervised the birth of one of the greatest theatrical managements in history. He was equally involved with and equally important in both the artistic and administrative sides of the Lyceum. For Henry Irving, he became the indispensable buffer, leaving the actor free to concentrate on the largesse of the productions and his own performance.

Bram was thrown in at the deep end, immersed instantly in business. Though most were cursory acknowledgements, it was seldom that he wrote less than fifty letters on a working day. The rest of the company had gone to Bristol, on Sunday 15 December, but he travelled to London to find the Lyceum in confusion:

> The builders who were making certain structural alterations had not got through their work; plasterers, paperhangers, painters, upholsterers were tumbling over each other. The outside of the building was covered with men and scaffolding. The whole of the auditorium was a mass of poles and platforms. On the stage and in the paint room and the property rooms, the gas-rooms and carpenter's shop and wardrobe-room, the new production of *Hamlet*... was being hurried on under high pressure.

No wonder if Bram was alarmed – *Hamlet* was due to open on the 30th, a mere fortnight later. The Lyceum was like a vast liner preparing for her maiden voyage, and Bram was the captain who had never been to sea.

Financially, he was shocked to discover Irving's recklessness. The Lyceum had been taken over, after a series of flops, with no real capital and a personal overdraft of £12,000 of which £10,000 had already been spent in improvements. Irving wanted everything to be new. Debts were being incurred daily and Bram soon realised the expense of keeping a large theatre idle. Everything depended on the success of *Hamlet*: if it failed they were finished. The challenge must have been all the more exciting because it was such a gamble.

Bram worked with Irving and Harry Loveday the stage manager, in the same room. This allowed immediate communication between them. In view of the shortage of money, Bram quickly evolved a stern system of his own with the simple aim of preventing anyone else from knowing what he was doing. He called this 'reticence'. He kept all the books, playing one department against the other, so that each might have a glimmering in part but none would know the whole. These books were kept in a large safe in the office and Bram possessed the key. No one else, apart from the accountants and Irving himself, had an accurate knowledge of Irving's affairs. It is to the credit of both men that Irving trusted Bram completely. Bram's success can be judged later, but his responsibility for the administration was only exceeded by the need for Irving to provide the ultimate magic.

Then Irving was regarded as an innovator, frequently accused of being too 'modern', but today it is hard to realise his magic, except that he possessed it in abundance. People say he would seem artificial now – if so, what will future generations make of Olivier's *Othello*, recorded on film and already greeted with laughter in the cinema? If Olivier is a chameleon of versatility, while showing the actor beneath the skin, I suspect that Irving always played Irving. He was an autocrat of the theatre, egotistical, cultivating eccentricities of enunciation – like 'gud' instead of 'god'. He cultivated his appearance too, with long hair under a 'wide-awake' hat, fur-collared overcoat, black cane – all ebony and eyebrow. In retrospect, he seems to have been physically gigantic – but in some photographs he looks quite slight.

He never saw his rivals. He employed inferior actors so that he would shine himself. He ignored the critics, particularly George Bernard Shaw, who was critical of 'that strange Lyceum intensity which comes from the perpetual struggle between Sir Henry Irving and Shakespeare'. That was written years later, in 1897, but the critics had never been generous. One devastating review mocked Irving's rendering of words: 'He delivers long speeches in a curious monotone as to pitch; he cuts up sentences into disjointed bits with apparently little reference to meaning, taking breath, as one would say of a singer, in most adventurous places.'

But long before the Lyceum's re-opening in 1878, Irving had been the popular idol of the audience – a 'draw'. Referring to his *Hamlet* in 1874, Dutton Cook mentioned the 'large audience' and recorded that 'Mr Irving was applauded as though he were another Garrick'. Cook referred again to that singular delivery: 'His voice seems sometimes artificially treble in quality and to be jerked out with effort.' Two years later, reviewing *Othello*, he spoke of 'what are known as Mr Irving's "mannerisms" . . . he became curiously effeminate in the presence of his bride'.

However, in the last two years, Irving had taken gigantic steps forward, not only in controlling his mannerisms but also in stagecraft as a whole. He was a genius with lighting. He was a perfectionist, and Bram was witness to this during rehearsals: when Hamlet seized the poisoned cup and threw it aside,

the cup, flung down desperately, rolled away for some distance then following the shape of the stage rolled down to the footlights. There is a sort of fascination in the uncertain movement of an inanimate object and such an occurrence during the play would infallibly distract the attention of the audience. Irving at once ordered that the massive metal goblet used should have some bosses fixed below the rim so that it could not roll. At a previous rehearsal he had ordered that as the wine from the cup splashed the stage, coloured sawdust should be used – which it did to exactly the same artistic effect.

Bram added that Irving's 'natural kindness' created 'a sweet little episode' in this same scene, which was kept in: 'When he said to the pretty little cup-bearer who offered him the poisoned goblet, "Set it by awhile!" he smiled at the child and passed his hand caressingly over the golden hair.'

Later, an unhappier occasion revealed Irving's concept of loyalty to the Company as a whole. He was standing beside Bram in the wings at the beginning of the third scene in the first act when Polonius makes his entrance to give the celebrated advice to his children. The moment his voice was heard, Irving swung round instinctively and, after a quick glance, signalled to the prompter to drop the curtain. Bram recalled, 'I was standing beside him at the time and was struck by the marvellous rapidity of thought and action of the decision which seemed almost automatic.' Irving stepped in front of the curtain and addressed the audience: 'Ladies and gentlemen, I regret I have to tell you that something has happened which I should not like to tell you; and will ask you to bear in patience a minute. We shall, with your permission, go on from the beginning with third scene of Act One.' Taking their 'instantaneous and sympathetic applause' as their permission, he withdrew, and the play started up again after eight minutes with a new Polonius. Plainly, the first Polonius was drunk.

The next afternoon, with Bram and Loveday beside him, Irving addressed the entire company with the exception of the first Polonius, who had received 'a kindly intimation that he need not attend' (and, presumably, his dismissal at the same time). Irving made a short speech referring to the loyalty they owed to each other:

By that want of loyalty in any of the forms, you have helped to ruin your comrade. Some of you *must* have noticed; at least those who dressed in the room with him or saw him in the Green Room. Had I been told – had the stage-manager had a single hint from any one, we could, and would, have saved him. The lesson would perhaps have been to him a bitter one, but it would have saved him from disaster. As it is, no other course was open to me to save him from public shame. As it is, the disaster of last night may injure him for life. And it is *you* who have done this. Now, my dear friends and comrades, let this be a lesson to us all. We must be loyal to each other. That is to be helpful, and it is to the honour of our art and calling.

The cast left in silence.

As he elevated his company so he enjoyed a remarkable rapport with his audience, 'who took his success as much to heart as though it had been their own; whose cheers and applause – whose very presence, was a stimulant and a help to artistic effort.' Bram had noticed this at once. 'I myself, as a neophyte, was in full sympathy with them. With such an audience an artist can go far.' For Irving it was essential: he told Bram the story of another actor who came down to the footlights during a 'poor' house and addressed the audience, 'Ladies and gentlemen, if you don't applaud I can't act!'

The audience did not fail him on the night of 30 December, 'that wonderful opening night when the great audience all aflame with generous welcome and exalted by ready sympathy lifted us to unwonted heights'. This was how Bram remembered it. For the audience it was the first time they were greeted at the head of the vast staircase by the tall red-bearded Stoker in evening dress, a first-night tradition that was to continue.

Reginald Auberon describes the scene in *The Nineteen Hundreds*:

To see Stoker in his element was to see him standing at the top of the theatre's stairs, surveying a 'first-night' crowd trooping up them. There was no mistake about it – a Lyceum *première* did draw an audience that really was representative of the best of that period in the realms of art, literature, and society.

Admittance was a very jealously guarded privilege. Stoker, indeed, looked upon the stalls, dress circle, and boxes as if they were annexes to the Royal Enclosure at Ascot, and one almost had to be proposed and seconded before the coveted ticket would be issued.

Braziers outside threw light on the crowds, lines of carriages, drawn by the finest horses, brought the élite of London society, while the pit and the gallery filled rapidly with enthusiasts of the theatre. 'We ascend the steps,' wrote J. B. Booth, 'and enter the heavily carpeted vestibule from which an immensely wide staircase, covered with thick, soft carpets, leads to the back of the circles, and on each side of this staircase stand the programme attendants – small boys in Eton suits, for the programme girl is not yet. At the top ... a tall reddish-bearded man in evening dress greets us. It is Bram Stoker, Irving's faithful friend and manager. To Bram his chief is as a god who can do no wrong.'

Irving triumphed. The gamble had succeeded. Even Dutton Cook had few reservations now:

Mr Irving's managerial career has commenced most auspiciously. The opening representation was, indeed, from first to last simply triumphant. A distinguished audience filled to overflowing the redecorated Lyceum Theatre and the new impresario was received with unbounded enthusiasm. These gratifying evidences of goodwill were scarcely required, however, to convince Mr Irving that his enterprise carried with it very general sympathy. His proved devotion to his art, his determination to uphold the national drama to his utmost, have secured for him the suffrages of all classes of society. And it is recognised that he has become a manager, not to enhance his position as an actor – for already he stands in the front rank of his profession – but the better to promote the interests of the whole stage, and to serve more fully, to gratify more absolutely, the public his patrons.

When the cheering finished and the curtain fell, the scenery was replaced by long trestle tables stacked with food and drink. Then the curtain rose again, revealing the supper to which several hundred special guests had been invited verbally by Bram. At the same time, he had been considerate enough to supply free first-night refreshments, of tea, bread and butter, for the queues who had lined up for the pit – a detail of management that created immediate good-will for the theatre.

There was one person conspicuously absent from the celebration, the young girl who played Ophelia, whose fortunes became linked with those of Irving, Bram and the Lyceum: Miss Ellen Terry.

CHAPTER SIX

Bram's 'Dutiful Daughter'

Bram saw Ellen Terry for the first time a week before the opening. He wrote, 'I think that Ellen Terry fascinated every one who ever met her – men, women and children.' He was no exception. He saw her in a dark passage under the staircase leading to the star dressing-rooms. 'But not even the darkness of that December day could shut out the radiant beauty of the woman to whom Irving, who was walking with her, introduced me. Her face was full of colour and animation, either of which would have made her beautiful. In addition was the fine form, the easy rhythmic swing, the large graceful, goddess-like way in which she moved.'

Irving was a magician: she had the gift of captivating with her contrasting qualities of warmth and openness. Irving's handwriting was thin; hers was round and expansive, heavily underlined, and punctuated with exclamation marks that seemed to rise with good humour. 'No sooner had she come to the Lyceum than all in the place were her devoted servants,' but though she did it with a smile she used Bram as ceaselessly as did Irving. From now on she bombarded him with little notes, usually sent round by hand: 'Please give two *lovely* seats to charming bearer!' or 'Please put my friends into a box and pilot them round to me after the play – your dutiful daughter.' Such nicknames were characteristic: for a time, Bram was her big brother – 'Brother Bram', but more often he was her 'Mama' and she his 'daughter'. A photograph signed ten years later, showing her with Drummie and Fussie, had the inscription: 'To my Ma! I am her dutiful child.' Drummie was her dog, Fussie became Irving's.

When told of some dreary official function she ought to attend, she made a 'wry face' and asked – 'Bram, is this earnest?'

'Yes. Honest injun.'

'All right, Mama.' And then Bram knew that 'she was going to play the part as nicely as it could be played by any human being. Indeed it was hardly "playing a part" for she was genuinely glad to meet cordiality with equal feeling. It was only the beginning and the publicity that she disliked.'

At their first meeting she promised to come to Bram for *everything*! She asked a special favour. 'When I come on in the fourth act holding that great bunch – that armful of flowers – could they be real? I absolutely *hate* artificial flowers, it's one of my quirks.' Bram promised he would choose them himself.

He had known her husband, Charles Kelly, and felt they met as friends. They remained so throughout. She was not a woman to quarrel with or to take offence, she was too *gay* for that. This did not prevent her from being astute, nor did her affection blind her to Irving's nature. She dared to tease him, in a way that was beyond Bram, recognising that the 'Guv'nor' was something of a blood-sucker, even if she was prepared to accept it: 'Were I to be run over by a steam-roller tomorrow Henry would be deeply grieved, would say quietly "what a pity!" and would add after two moments' reflection: "Who is there . . . er . . . to go on for her tonight?" '

On his part, with a premonition of their compatibility on stage, Irving was enchanted. When he took Bram and Florence to supper, he exclaimed, 'How Shakespeare must have dreamed when he was able to write a part like Ophelia, knowing that it would have to be played by a boy! Conceive his delight and gratitude if he could but have seen Ellen Terry in it!'

Bram regarded them both as revolutionary actors: 'She belongs to the age of investigation. She is one of those who have brought in the new school of acting. Not only has she a divine instinct for the truth, in stage-art, but she is a conscious artist to her finger-tips. No one on the stage in our time has seen more clearly the direct force of sympathy and understanding between the actor and audience.' Bram was enslaved, but he had exceptional masters.

Ellen Terry was instantly popular with the Company. She was devoid of envy – a rarity in such a profession – and eager to encourage players who were younger and less experienced. She was a generous artist and, to make it perfect, she did not share the high opinion in which she was held by everyone else.

Her aim was not to excel but to be useful – exactly what Irving
wanted. Everyone loved her, even the critics. Dutton Cook
wrote of her Ophelia, in that first production,

> so tender, so graceful, so picturesque, and so pathetic ...
> Miss Terry is now without a rival, is indeed unapproached
> by any other actress upon our stage. Her personal graces
> and endowments, her elocutionary skill, her musical speech,
> and above all her singular powers of depicting intensity of
> feeling, are most happily combined, as the audience were
> quick to discover and applaud in this very exquisite present-
> ment of Ophelia.

Yet she thought she had failed. She was so uncertain that
she ran from the theatre after her final scene. There was good
reason for her agitation for, in spite of all the compliments and
praise, Irving had treated her with professional indifference.
His first communication had arrived on 20 June: 'Dear Miss
Terry, – I look forward to the pleasure of calling upon you on
Tuesday next at two o'clock. With every good wish, believe
me, Yours sincerely, Henry Irving.' She joined his Company at
a weekly salary of £40. A mutual friend had impressed on him
that all London was talking in praise of her Olivia, and Irving
took this on trust. Never once did he visit the Court Theatre
to see her performance in the adaptation of *The Vicar of
Wakefield*. It is possible that he was too busy, but as she wrote
later: 'It was never any pleasure to him to see the acting of
other actors and actresses.' Characteristically, he invited her to
see him act in *Hamlet* in Birmingham in mid-December.

> He knew I was there. He played – I say it without vanity
> – for me. We players are not above that weakness, if it be
> weakness. If ever anything inspires us to do our best it is
> the presence in the audience of some fellow-artist who must
> in the nature of things know more completely than any one
> what we intend, what we do, what we feel. The response
> from such a member of the audience flies across the foot-
> lights to us like a flame.

If she believed she failed on that first night, it was not due
to any lack of preparation on her part. She went to an asylum

to study the patients, hoping for material to use in the portrayal of Ophelia. At first she was disappointed: 'There was no beauty, no nature, no pity in most of the lunatics. Strange as it may sound, they were too theatrical.' As she was leaving she noticed a young girl gazing at the wall, and walked in between. The girl's face was vacant, but the body conveyed that she was waiting, until suddenly she threw up her hands and sped across the room. 'I never forgot it. She was very thin, very pathetic, very young, and the movement was as poignant as it was beautiful.' She saw another woman laugh – without a gleam of mirth – and used that laugh to full effect on stage.

At the first rehearsal, wearing cloak and rapier, Irving read through *every* part except Ophelia's. With ten days to go, her scenes were still unrehearsed. To add to her nervousness, she committed a bad indiscretion regarding her costumes, which she organised well in advance.

'Finished?' exclaimed Irving when she told him. 'That's very interesting.' He listened attentively, too much so, when she described the last scene and 'a transparent black dress'. 'I see,' he said ominously, 'In mourning for her father?' It was explained to her later, that no one wears black on the stage of *Hamlet* apart from the Prince. 'I did feel a fool,' she wrote later. 'What a blithering donkey I had been not to see it before. I was very thrifty in those days and the thought of having been the cause of needless expense worried me.' The lack of rehearsal was far more worrying. 'I grew very anxious and miserable. I was still a stranger in the theatre and in awe of H.I. personally.' Finally she plucked up the courage to ask him outright if they could rehearse their scenes.

'We shall be all right,' he answered, but ultimately he betrayed her and she knew it. He failed to give the support she had been hoping for.

Perhaps because I was nervous and irritable about my own part from insufficient rehearsal, perhaps because his responsibility as lessee weighed upon him, Henry Irving's Hamlet on the first night of the Lyceum seemed to me less wonderful than it had at Birmingham. At rehearsals he had been the perfection of grace. On the night itself, he dragged his leg and seemed stiff from self-consciousness.

Perhaps, also, he realised his neglect too late, and sensed her misery at last. 'The only person who did not profit by Henry's ceaseless labours was poor Ophelia. When the first night came I did not play the part well, although the critics and the public were pleased. To myself I *failed*.'

'I have failed, I have failed,' she cried out, hurrying from the theatre before the fifth act, driving up and down the Embankment before she decided to return home. When Irving heard of her departure, his concern turned to alarm when the Embankment was mentioned, but he was assured that she was being looked after. Later that night, according to Marguerite Steen, he knocked at her door at Longridge Road to tell her that her 'failure' was in fact a triumph.

Were they lovers in private, as well as on stage? It is claimed that this midnight meeting was the start of a long 'attachment'. Their respective marriages were unsuccessful. Irving's, to Florence O'Callaghan, had ended in a startling manner after his first success in *The Bells*. When the cheers and congratulations were over he had driven home in a hired brougham, presumably in a condition of blissful euphoria. He laid his hand gently on her arm. 'Now we too shall soon have our own carriage and pair,' he told his wife.

This reference to his personal triumph inflamed her jealousy and she turned on him with the astonishing question, 'Are you going to make a fool of yourself like this all your life?' Irving stopped the brougham and stepped out. He walked into the darkness of Hyde Park and never spoke to her again, though he sent her a letter offering her £8 out of his weekly salary of £15. The emotional strain drained him, and the Batemans had difficulty with his heavy drinking after his performances on stage in the evening.

Two children were born: Henry Brodribb (Irving's real name) in 1870 and Laurence in 1871. Irving did not attend the christening of his second child and it became Bram's early duty, among so many others, to look after the welfare of the boys and visit them at school. Surprisingly, Irving continued the formality of sending his wife reservations for a box for every first night and, just as surprisingly, she accepted, which cannot have helped his first-night nerves.

Estranged from his wife, Irving conducted his private affairs with superb discretion. Scandal never damaged him seriously, not even on the American tours, when his relationship with Ellen Terry was watched closely for any sign of a romance. Wisely, they stayed in separate hotels and their behaviour in public was impeccable, but Ellen Terry's private life was so unusual that her acceptance by society seems surprising. In Noel Stoker's bag I found her account of a visit to Windsor with her third husband, James Carew: 'The Queen was so sweet and gracious. When she saw me she *ran* across to me and asked me to introduce my husband, which I did and she shook hands with us and was full of kind congratulations to both of us.' No mention that Carew was young enough to be Ellen's son! At the end of her life in 1925, she was created a Dame. Presumably her acceptance was part of the Victorian genius of drawing the curtain at the convenient moment!

Ellen Terry was married to the artist George Watts in 1864, when she was sixteen and he was three days short of forty-seven. There is doubt if the marriage was consummated, and they parted ten months later. Soon afterwards she resumed a friendship with the architect Edward Godwin and in 1868 she left the theatre, her family and friends to live with him in the country. It was a blissful, domestic love-affair to begin with and she bore him two illegitimate children – Edy and Ted, who were known later as Edith and Gordon Craig. It was lack of money which forced her back to the stage after threats from the bailiffs to remove the furniture. But she returned with a wider knowledge of life and was now a more mature actress. Her new stage success was the end of the affair and she and Godwin parted in November 1875: 'E.T. worked on,' wrote her son. 'Brave. Strange to realise now that she did not kill herself.' Godwin married a twenty-one-year-old girl the following January, but apparently went off on his own to have dinner at his club after the wedding. He died in 1886 and his widow married his close friend, Whistler.

It was a mixture of loneliness and a need to have a father for the children that encouraged Ellen to marry an actor called Charles Kelly. They moved into 33 Longridge Road in Earls Court and soon she became the favourite of London with her personal success as Olivia which had brought her to Irving's attention.

There is some doubt if any of her legal marriages were consummated. She was not 'marriageable', as Gordon Craig remarked later, and he made the penetrating observation that
she was one of those women who like to think of themselves as
'wretchedly weak' but are really stronger than the men they
marry. Kelly seems to have lost his role as 'leading man' in
every way, apart from a tour with Ellen Terry in the provinces
which she performed dutifully. There was a legal separation in
1881, but they parted before that.

A neighbour in Longridge Road, who seems to have spent
much of his time by the window, noticed that Ellen was never
short of callers. The 'bulldog sort of man' (Kelly) was replaced
by another 'spare and grim and jaunty' with a tilted wide-awake
hat (Irving), and Gordon Craig remembered his mother's good
humour on Sundays as she drove off to the country with Irving,
'waving her lily white hand'.

Neither Ellen Terry nor Irving were the marrying kind.
'Attachment', as she described their relationship many years
later to Marguerite Steen, was the perfect word. Their partnership lasted for twenty years and they acted together in twenty-
seven productions.

Bram expressed his admiration in an article for the American
Cosmopolitan in 1901, stressing the value of Ellen's early experience with Mrs Charles Kean, when she was only a child,
and the technical training this gave her. He returned to his
constant theme that 'Art is not to *be* real, it is to *seem* real',
and gave voice projection as an example: 'Mere volume of
voice is not sufficient; nor does it suffice that the method of
speaking be cultured and natural. Both are necessary, if the
deadening effect of a couple of thousand persons breathing in
an opposite direction to the speaker is to be overcome.' He
added that he did not know a better lesson for any young artist
than to study Ellen Terry's delivery – in such a speech as
Portia's 'Quality of mercy' – in which 'every condition of truth
and finesse is observed as perfectly as though speaker and
auditor were alone in a drawing-room'.

The article is ponderous, as Bram was prone to be, but it
does illustrate her unique sense of joy, which made invididuals
of the audience feel as if she was relating to each person directly,
especially in *Madame Sans-Gêne* in which she played a

'Pygmalion' part, a washerwoman turned duchess, decidedly clumsy in her attempts at dancing. Ellen Terry was 'delightfully awkward, with an assumption of ungainliness which to a naturally graceful woman must mean study and intention of no small degree'. There was elaborate 'business' with a long court-dress train which keeps getting in the way while she is learning her steps. Finally she tucks it under her arm, but it keeps slipping off, to everyone's amusement. This scene worked well in London, without any change until they went on tour and she played it with exceptional verve in a northern industrial town. Bram claims that 'she was lost in the assumed character so thoroughly that it was real to her, and the ex-washerwoman, with her mind harassed and worried by the trying conditions of her artificial court-life, instinctively returned to the habits of her youth. In a moment of abstraction, finding the fat coil of stuff across her arm, she instinctively began to *wring it out*.' The audience reacted with an immediate roar of recognition and applause – 'half the women in the audience did their own washing and half the men knew the action' – and the business was kept in from then on.

Bram called her the greatest actress of her time – 'loved by everyone who knew her. Her presence is a charm, her friendship a delight.'

As she said to Don Pedro, in the role of Beatrice in *Much Ado*, 'I was born in a merry hour!'

Alternating with popular 'draws', like *The Corsican Brothers*, the Lyceum excelled with the Shakespearian productions that followed that first season of *Hamlet*, which played for ninety-eight nights. Irving was delighted with the box-office receipts of £36,000 after the first seven months, and left on a Mediterranean cruise on board the *Walrus*, the private yacht of the Baroness Burdett-Coutts. His visit to Venice encouraged him to withdraw another play on his return and instead to present *The Merchant of Venice* after only three weeks of rehearsal and production. This opened on 1 November 1880 and played for 250 nights. *Othello* opened on 2 May 1881, and a lavish production of *Romeo and Juliet* on 8 May 1882 was followed by *Much Ado about Nothing* which ran for 212 nights. Irving's reputation soared. They could do nothing wrong.

These first years were the most absorbing and enjoyable in Bram's life. Without previous experience, he fitted the role of acting manager superbly, controlling his staff of 128 like a regiment, with inspections on every first night before the doors of the Lyceum were flung open. He indulged in occasional bursts of temperament, but these were strictly in the cause of professionalism or in the face of cowardice. Actors soon learnt to respect him, like the young Frank Benson who received a tongue-lashing after his first appearance on stage. They had met before when Benson came up from Oxford as a student and had been placed in Bram's care. He was an arrogant boy with strong theories of his own about the lack of realism in the theatre. Bram tried to put him right:

Surely we have to concede that acting is different from everyday life. You have to use art convention. You have to enlarge. You're right when you say there is a great deal of unnatural acting, but you're wrong about it being easy to be natural on the stage. I've won many a bet from actors that they could not go out of the room, return, and say in a natural voice, 'Good evening. Very fine today, is it not?' Not one in a hundred can do it. It needs self-control, humour, and acquired self-consciousness – in a word technique. And there is only one way to get that – work, work, work.

Benson was unimpressed. Bram got his revenge when the actor appeared in *Romeo and Juliet* without stage make-up.

'Mrs Kendal thinks that making-up hides the expression,' he explained to the others.

'Yes, but Mrs Kendal, after all, is Mrs Kendal,' William Terris warned him. 'You can make up as you think best, but if the Gov'nor or Loveday catches you, or, most of all, that devil Bram Stoker in the front – he can see through a brick wall – God help you!'

Bram pounced as predicted. 'Good God, Benson, you have got a dirty face. It shows from the front. It's a hot night, you're nervous and sweating like a pig in a blue funk.'

'I have this theory . . .'

'Theory be damned! You can't go on to the stage of this

theatre with a dirty face. Here –' and he turned to an assistant – 'get him some greasepaint and show him how to do it.' Benson had the humour to admit that it did improve his appearance.

Bram's harsh treatment seems to have been part of a policy, or even plot, to put the young man in his place and teach him that a university education was no substitute for hard experience on the boards. Laurence Irving wrote that Benson was 'stripped of every shred of his self-esteem as an actor' during the rehearsals. When the day came to practise the duel between Romeo and Paris, he showed his pride in his swordsmanship, which he had studied at university and fell instantly into the correct stance, confident that at last his quality would be recognised.

Taking in the situation with a glance, Irving adjusted the tiny rimless glasses that he wore on stage, and fell suddenly on the astonished Benson, seized his foil, hit him over the knuckles with his sword, prodded him in the stomach and clashed swords once for effect. Then he elbowed and kneed him into the tomb muttering, 'Die – me boy – die – down – down.' Laurence commented, 'The polite posturing . . . had succumbed to the furious onslaught.'

Benson persevered, but he made one fatal mistake. He persuaded Ellen Terry to intercede with Irving and grant him the privilege of sitting in the prompt corner of the wings where he could make notes. Once he approached Irving who was resting in his chair between scenes. This in itself was a bad breach of etiquette, but his idiotic remark was asking for trouble.

'A very beautiful part, that of Romeo,' he said to Irving.

'Yes,' snapped the actor. 'And the odd thing about it is that every damn young fool who's been on stage for two minutes thinks he can play it.'

Before long, Benson's engagement was terminated.

There was always the threat of fire and one evening this was realised when a lighted torch set fire to a drapery. A stage-hand trampled out the flames but one unfortunate young man in the audience rose in panic and started to dash up the aisle. Bram seized him by the throat and flung him to the floor. 'Go back to your seat sir!' he thundered as he dragged the man to his feet. 'It is cowards like you who cause death to helpless women.'

Always that strong sense of chivalry towards 'the gentler sex'!

Every production involved large numbers of extras, or supers, frequently soldiers from the Brigade of Guards who were glad to make the extra few pennies on their nights off duty. While most managers gave them sixpence, Irving gave them a shilling and raised this to eighteen pence and later to two shillings. Justifying the customary smallness of their pay, Bram stressed that supers were not supposed to exist on it but to regard it simply as a bonus to their day-time job. He added, cruelly, that if someone depended on his super's pay, 'we took it for granted that he was in reality a loafer, and did not keep him.' He commented that the soldiers liked the work – 'for it provided easy beer-money, and the officers like them to have the opportunity as it kept them out of mischief.' A sergeant of the Guards was kept permanently on the Lyceum's staff to supply the men and keep them in order.

The guardsmen were vital to the production of *The Lady of Lyons* which started in April 1879. 'As Irving stage-managed it the (French) army, already on its way, was tramping along the road outside. Through window and open door the endless columns were seen, officers and men in due order and the flags in proper place. It seemed as if the line would stretch out till the crack of doom!' The guardsmen marched four abreast and the moment they disappeared out of sight they doubled back and fell into line again. This gave the impression of the endless procession: even so, as many as a hundred and fifty guardsmen were employed. 'That marching army never stopped. No matter how often the curtain went up on the scene – and sometimes there were seven or eight calls, for the scene was one especially exciting to the more demonstrative parts of the house – it always rose on that martial array, always moving on with the resistless time and energy of an overwhelming force.' Spectacle, in the century before cinema or Cinerama, was one of the attractions of the Lyceum.

Bram became involved as a super in *The Corsican Brothers*, which started in September 1880 and ran for 190 performances, sometimes following Tennyson's verse play *The Cup*. The spectacle in this production was a vast masked ball in 'the opera house at Fontainebleau', contrived in such a way that the Lyceum audience felt they were looking into a gigantic mirror.

So many supers were needed that a rack was kept in the office with dominoes, masks and slouch hats so that any visitor could take part if the idea amused him. When Bram went on stage, soon after the opening night, he was seized by the eight clowns – who performed a special dance and ran in and out of the boxes – and was spun round like a ball, thrown from one side to the other. 'Sometimes they would rush me right down to the footlights and then whirl me back again breathless. But all the time they never let me fall or gave me away. I could not but admire their physical power as well as their agility and dexterity in their own craft.' The next time, Bram stayed safely at the back, but this produced an explosive guffaw from Irving as he made his exit up stage. Bram had forgotten that the scene was arranged carefully to give a false sense of perspective, with the smallest supers, then boys and girls, and finally children – all in adult evening dress – placed respectively towards the back, Bram, secure among the children, six feet two, with a great feathered hat, seemed fifty feet tall, as Irving explained when Bram followed him anxiously into the wings to ask what was the matter.

Irving received heads of state as if he himself was royalty. The Chinese ambassador, the Marquis Tseng, in vivid robes of mandarin yellow, unattended for a moment backstage, was caught by Bram just before he wandered into the limelight. For a second Bram relished the publicity this would have caused, but realised it would have wrecked Ellen Terry's mad scene as Ophelia. Edward VII, as the Prince of Wales, also came backstage during *The Corsican Brothers,* and subsequently presented Bram with a gold pen, the Prince of Wales Feathers engraved in enamel. Mr Gladstone attended the first night of *The Cup.* He was placed secretly in one of the imitation boxes in the masked scene which followed, and at one point became so excited that he leant forward and was recognised instantly by the audience, which broke into 'a quick and sudden roar that seemed to shake the building'. There was another super, special to Bram in that first production of *The Cup* – Florence who took part as a vestal virgin with a hundred other young women. The first night was 3 January 1881 and she received a crown of flowers passed on to her by Ellen Terry. These came secretly from Oscar Wilde, who wrote to the actress:

My dear Nellie, I write to wish you *every success* tonight. *You* could not do anything that would not be a mirror of the highest artistic beauty, and I am so glad to hear you have an opportunity of showing us that passionate power which *I know you have*. You will have a great success – perhaps one of your greatest.

I send you some flowers – two crowns. Will you accept one of them, whichever you think will suit you best. The other – don't think me treacherous, Nellie – but the other please give to Florrie *from yourself*. I should like to think that she was wearing something of mine the first night she comes on the stage, that anything of mine should touch her. Of course if you think – but you won't think she will suspect? How could she?

She thinks I never loved her, thinks I forget. My God how could I?

When I first saw this letter, in Noel Stoker's bag, it was placed in an envelope with a covering letter from Ellen Terry to Florence. This was written towards the end of her life; the handwriting was shaky, and there was a trembling note of sadness in contrast to those early underlinings and exclamation marks. She explained she had been tearing up old letters all that evening and thought that 'by rights this belongs to you. I think your Noel had just come into the world.' The letter finished pathetically, 'Forget me not, forget me not, Yours Nell.' Her memory was faulty, at this long distance. Noel, Bram's only child, had been born on 29 December 1879.

I remember Noel, from my own childhood, as sympathetic though exceptionally withdrawn – in marked contrast to the volatility of his wife Neelie. When he was a boy he spent much of his time with my grandmother, who told me that Florence was not particularly fond of him. I would not suggest that Florence found him a handicap to her vaulting social ambition, but her attitude was one of lack of interest rather than maternal warmth.

Florence's social life with Bram must have exceeded expectation: even if she had married Oscar Wilde, she would not have encountered so many 'lions'. With their fortunes apparently secure, the Stokers had moved at once into 27 Cheyne Walk, the fashionable line of private houses alongside the river at Chelsea. According to the ritual of the time, Florence was 'at home' every Sunday, the only day that Bram was certain to be free. Wilde had recovered sufficiently from his broken heart to be a regular visitor to her salon, which makes the secrecy of the 'crown of flowers' rather exaggerated. They remained friends and, as late as 1893, two years before his downfall, he sent her a copy of *Salome* 'with kind regards to Bram', and signed himself 'Your sincere friend'.

Another guest was J. McNeill Whistler, a nearby neighbour in Cheyne Walk. His fortunes fluctuated, usually disastrously, and at one point he became so impressed with Bram's acumen that he asked him to look after his business affairs: 'I can't do it myself; and I really think it would be worth a good man's while – some man like yourself. I would give half of all I earned to such a man, and would be grateful to him also for a life without care.' Curiously, Bram refused. Presumably he felt that Irving needed his exclusive services. Yet he could see the wisdom of Whistler's suggestion:

> He was before his time – long before it. He did fine work and created a new public taste ... and he became bankrupt. His house and all he had were sold; and the whole sum he owed would, I think, have been covered by the proper sale of a few of the pictures which were bought almost *en bloc* by a picture-dealer who sold them for almost any price offered. He had a mass of them in his gallery several feet thick as they were piled against the wall. One of them he sold to Irving for either £20 or £40, I forget which.

This was the picture of Irving as King Philip in Tennyson's drama *Queen Mary*. It was sold at Christie's amongst Irving's other effects after his death and fetched over five thousand pounds. Bram's refusal to help was not only curious but also astonishingly ill-judged from his own point of view.

Bram had contact with most of the leading artists of the day. He was a constant visitor to the splendid house of Sir Laurence Alma-Tadema, the Victorian artist, to discuss his proposed sets for *Coriolanus*. Sir Edward Burne-Jones undertook the designs for *King Arthur*. In those days, portrait painters were abundant, and Bram was bombarded with requests for sittings with Irving – a familiar pattern of praise for their own work and false assurance that money did not matter. Ellen Terry was painted by Sargent; Irving by J. B. Yeats, James Pryde, Whistler, and frequently by Bernard Partridge. Edwin Ward painted an informal portrait of Irving at home, with one of his dogs. His request was characteristic:

I wonder if Mr Irving could grant me an interview about the sittings for his picture – I feel sure I could arrange to proceed with the work at very small inconvenience to him if we could have a few minutes' talk. [And later] I wanted Mr Irving to sit to me in order that I might exhibit the portrait and possibly publish it in the form of an etching afterwards – I take it as a very great compliment that Mr Irving feels inclined to give me a commission – but under the circumstances I would rather give him a perfectly free hand in the matter – the portrait will be of the greatest possible service to *me* but should Mr Irving think sufficiently well of it as to wish to possess it I should be the last person in the world to decline such an honour and I'm sure we shouldn't quarrel about the price.

This varied between 75 and 100 guineas, and perhaps there was a quarrel after all, for the picture went to the collection of a wealthy MP called Sir Henry Lucy.

Bram commissioned an artist called Walter Osborne to paint a portrait of Florence. As Osborne painted Mrs Thornley Stoker, and his mother Charlotte, he was evidently a family favourite. His letters reveal that the hanging of the portrait in the Royal Academy was just as important as the likeness:

Dear Mrs Stoker, I am sure you would like to know how the portrait has progressed ... I have asked many of your friends here to come and see your portrait and I am glad to think they were unanimous in approval ... It leaves here Wednesday morning and I do trust it may meet with a merciful judgement from the Hanging Committee ...
Dear Mrs Stoker, I am glad I have been able to offer

you and Mr Stoker a picture which has met with such favourable criticism. [And finally] My Dear Stoker, I must endeavour to thank you fully for your most kind letter and your generosity in sending me a cheque for seventy-five pounds for Mrs Stoker's portrait. I am but expressing feelings which I have held since the picture was painted, when I tell you that it is a matter of regret to me that my artistic equipment hindered me from doing anything approaching an adequate picture of her.

His self-praise had been so rampant that it is hard to tell if this is false modesty or not. The portrait was accepted by the Royal Academy, though Florence became ill and was unable to attend the private view, and a reproduction indicates that his regrets may have been justified. The magazine describes it as 'refined and graceful', and perhaps the first word is apt. The result is stiff. Florence has a cool, almost disdainful expression, her hair is scraped back severely, she has vast leg-of-mutton sleeves, and her hand rests on a dead animal – presumably a fox fur. It is hardly flattering for someone who is supposed to have been such a celebrated beauty, though Osborne did point out at the time that the reproductions did neither of them justice. Charlotte Stoker had no doubts about her portrait, as Osborne confided in a letter to Florence: 'Dr (George) Stoker has been most kind concerning Mrs Stoker's portrait, but she has said one or two bitter things though to me alas. I feel bound to offer to paint her again at some future time. I would that no such obligation occurred.' The implied criticism of her mother-in-law suggests there might have been a coolness between the two women for Osborne to have written so candidly.

Inevitably, after the portrait had been accepted, Osborne wrote to Bram, 'I need hardly tell you it would not only be an honour, but a real pleasure to me to try and paint Irving for you.' But the Stokers appear to have lost their enthusiasm.

If Bram and Florence were 'celebrity snobs', which they were, they had an abundance of names to choose from. One of the great literary lions of the day was Mark Twain, who was highly irritated when one of my great-aunts crept up behind him and cut off one of his locks of hair with a pair of scissors. According to my grandmother, Florence decided to go one better than the

other hostesses by inviting him to tea on his own. Giving her
maid instructions to admit no one else, she waited – and waited.
At last she rang down and asked the maid if there had been
any word for her.

'Oh no, Mum,' said the maid.

'I thought I heard the doorbell.'

'Yes, it was a Mr Clemens but I told him you weren't at
home.'

Of course S. L. Clemens was Twain's real name. The story
seems uneasily familiar, but it was a family legend.

Bram and Florence had their separate friendships. His closest
friend was Hall Caine, while Florence enjoyed an amiable flirta-
tion with W. S. Gilbert over many years. He wrote to her archly
about one of his productions: 'I have had rather a bad time of
it, but now that the baby is born I shall soon recover. I'm not
at all a proud mother and I never want to see the ugly misshapen
little brat again,' and sent her dramatic accounts of his adventures with his new locomobile, including the time when a lunatic
tried to commit suicide by throwing himself in front of it. The
car moved far too slowly to do any harm and his chauffeur –
'fortunately a gentleman' – stepped out and took the wretched
man in charge. 'This is a lovely day for a motor-ride – can I
tempt you for one?' The novelty of his American steam-car
which he acquired in 1902, and later his Rolls-Royce, delighted
Gilbert in spite and perhaps because of the break-downs: 'The
real charm of a car is that it affords one such a lot of walking
exercise,' he wrote to her proudly.

It seems that it was Gilbert who presented Florence with a
curious companion, delivered with detailed instructions from
Nancy McIntosh, one of the leading singers in his operas and
his close personal friend. The first part of her letter in my
possession is missing, so that her instructions seem bizarre—

. . . the slapping that he knows always follows. Please slap
him when he does do wrong or he might get into bad habits.
He likes best to sit in his little chair but will not sit in it
unless it is somewhere near the fire, and we keep always
a bit of flannel inside the fender for him to sit upon when
he wishes to toast himself. Warmth and being petted are
what he most wants and his greatest joy is having his head

rubbed. If you are sitting near him and he comes to you
and takes your hand in both of his and pulls it to his head
you will know that he is wanting his head rubbed. His only
language is a funny little cooing when he is uncomfortable,
or discontented about not receiving enough attention, and
sometimes, only once in a long while, he treats one to a very
strange cry that we do not quite understand but it is accompanied by a very determined upsetting of everything within
his reach unless he is very much petted.

He has hay on the bottom of his cage and a rug thrown
all over it when the weather is cold. He is perfectly quiet
and good at night and would never disturb anyone. Once in
a way we allow him to run about the room for a few minutes
but it does not seem to be necessary for his health. What a
lot to write about so small a person . . . Mr Gilbert is feeling
very stiff from the damp but is otherwise very much the
same. We are glad to leave this weather. With love from
Mrs Gilbert and mine also if I may send it.

What could this 'small person' have been! 'Cooing' suggests
a bird, though this is contradicted by his 'little chair' and the
running. Perhaps a marmoset?

Bram and Florence were frequent guests at Gilbert's home,
Grim's Dyke, at Harrow. His affection for Florence is understandable – she was an attractive young woman – but his liking
for Bram, and Bram's for him, is surprising in view of Gilbert's
outspoken criticism of Irving. He was one of the few contemporaries who was unimpressed. When asked if he had seen
Irving in some Lyceum production, he replied, 'Madam, I go
to the pantomime only at Christmas.'

Yet he was able to treat Bram as a confidant. Once there was
an almighty row when Gilbert gave a tactless interview to the
Edinburgh Dispatch on the subject of blank verse in modern
plays, and why this was at such a discount at that time that 'I
will write no more plays.' Perhaps the failure of his own verse
plays accounted for a certain bitterness:

I attributed it to the prevailing fashion among modern
actors of speaking blank verse in a monotone – raising or
sinking the voice at the end of a sentence, according as it

was a question or a statement. Asked whether any of my remarks applied to Irving, Tree and Alexander – I replied that I could think of no leading actor who did not follow the fashion in this respect – that the effect of it was to render a 30 line speech so difficult to follow that it became tedious and the listener's attention wandered.

This is my opinion . . . [he continued in a letter to Bram (27/10/97)] which is entertained by many besides myself.

Irving retaliated after a performance of *Madame Sans-Gêne* at Sheffield, when members of his Company, including his son Laurence, Bram and Loveday, were entertained to supper by the Sheffield and District Press Club. Irving was a brilliant after-dinner speaker; his gift must have been natural or the strain after a long performance would have been unendurable. He contributed all the required light and shade – the compliments, the emotion and humour. He had a teasing sense of wit which belies the apparent severity of the man. On this night he started by praising Sheffield as one of 'our great and noble cities', adding his memory of a former visit when some grouse were thrown from the gallery 'which I appreciated very much'.

Then he indulged his sense of humour at Gilbert's expense.

Thanking the press for their constant generosity and goodwill, he referred to a 'trifling reason' why he felt bound up with them that night.

This time it is not a matter of principle, but of accident, since I have been in a way arraigned as a fellow-criminal with you in the melancholy charges made by a gentleman who possesses, and has a very just and enviable reputation as a comic opera librettist. The gentleman seems to see – from a recent interview that he had in a newspaper – nothing but unworthiness in all or in any – press, managers, actors and public – all except the dramatist, who, laying aside his lyre – and I may say I mean no disrespect to my friend – has chosen again to dare the heights of serious drama, and with what success I fear is greatly shown by his very childish statements and his very jaundiced behaviour.

He seems to me to be in the unfortunate position of the

proverbial bull, but, instead of going into a china shop, has got into some ironmongery establishment, and has hurt nothing but himself.

Irving finished his speech with the promise that he would continue even if he was unable to 'speak successfully thirty lines of verse'. Bram then delivered the toast to the Press Club in a humorous speech of his own.

Like many critics, Gilbert resented criticism and used Bram as a go-between saying that he was unable to write to Irving personally, as he had done to Tree and Alexander, because of the speech at Sheffield which was 'unworthy of himself and of me'. But he added that Bram was free to show Irving the letter if he saw fit. His excuses were familiar: that the 'interviewer did as interviewers do – he boiled down a mumble of questions and answers into one unvarnished statement . . . as to make me appear to blurt out an uncalled for and unmannerly piece of criticism [which] . . . has had the effect of placing me in an entirely false light.'

Bram was a fellow-sufferer from gout and perhaps he understood Gilbert's show of truculence. Somehow he forgave such volleys against his 'chief' which he would not have tolerated from anyone else. For everything stemmed from Irving and enabled Bram to become a social 'lion' in his own right. His power as acting manager of the Lyceum, coupled with his natural charm and intelligence, earned him more respect than any aide-de-camp or equerry who might meet everyone yet know nobody. It was not just the quantity but the variety of 'names' that made his world so interesting: heads of state; Chirgwin 'the white-eyed Kaffir', asking for seats; the young Ethel Barrymore asking for an audition; Barrie; Pinero; Arthur Conan Doyle, complaining that the author's name has been omitted from the advertisement of *Waterloo* in *The Times*' theatre column: 'As you know it brought me very little pecuniarily, considering its success, but of that I make no grievance. I do feel however that I should be hardly used if I lose my authorship also.'

Bram became a personal friend of Lord Tennyson from the time of his visit to *Hamlet* in 1879, when Bram spoke to him afterwards. Tennyson mentioned that he was seventy, yet did not feel old – 'I wonder how it is!' – and Bram quoted back his own words:

> Unto him that works, and feels he works,
> The same grand year is ever at the doors.

After this meeting, Bram and Florence lunched with the poet and Lady Tennyson on the latter's visits to London and entertained their sons, Hallam and Lionel, on their Sunday evenings in Cheyne Walk.

Ironically, it was an act of heroism on Bram's part that soured Florence's enjoyment of this house and the parties they gave there. Travelling down the Thames by steamboat from Chelsea on Thursday 14 September 1882 (presumably on his way to Charing Cross and the Lyceum, since it was 6 p.m.), Bram saw a man jump overboard and characteristically, threw off his coat and dived in after him. The man was doing his utmost to commit suicide and 'persistently kept his face under the water' in spite of Bram's efforts to bring it to the surface. They struggled for nearly five minutes, until they were hauled back on board the *Twilight*. As the man was insensible, Bram carried the body to 27 Cheyne Walk where his brother Dr George Stoker tried to revive him, but his efforts failed to bring the man to life. No one identified him at the inquest; he was described as a soldier, on the grounds that he was tattooed with a 'D', and his age was estimated at between sixty and seventy. The man had lost a finger and was bald.

For Florence, the house was never the same after she discovered a dripping corpse in the dining-room, but Bram was the hero of the hour. He received a telegram from the actor J. L. Toole – 'Bravo Bram, splendid, shall drink to your health tonight' – a letter from Pinero – 'How proud I am to count myself amongst those who have the privilege of your acquaintance' – and even a scribbled note from Irving – 'Look out to-morrow morning! You'll find yourself immortalised in the *Telegraph* or I'm a Dutchman!' The newspapers did in fact record that it was the wish of the jury 'to publicly recognise the gallant conduct of Mr Stoker in attempting to save life. A juryman remarked that to jump from the boat when the tide was strong was a very brave act. The Coroner said it was undoubtedly an act of heroism.' Eventually Bram received the Bronze Medal of the Royal Humane Society.

Three years later, he and Florence left their first and most distinguished home in London. Florence's reaction against the house was over-fastidious. It is possible, also, that she was genuinely depressed by Bram's allegiance to Irving and the Lyceum which frequently prevented him from returning home until dawn. It would be fascinating to know if she ever discussed Bram's absences at night with Constance Wilde, who suffered from the same deprivation for very different reasons. Oscar had started accepting invitations without his wife, which closed the grander doors to him.

On one occasion he wrote: 'My dear Bram – my wife is not very well and has gone to Brighton for ten days rest, but I will be very happy to come to supper on the 26th myself. Sincerely yours, Oscar Wilde.' This indicates that the two men were now on friendly terms.

At least Florence was able to share the excitement of the lavish social events inside the Lyceum, such as the banquet for 350 guests on 14 February 1880 to celebrate the 100th night of *The Merchant of Venice*. On 25 March 1882, ninety-two guests sat down to celebrate the 100th night of *Romeo and Juliet,* and a year later the Prince of Wales came to dinner in a party of fifty, with a table on stage and a bouquet of yellow flowers in the middle measuring thirty feet across and nine inches high.

On Christmas Eve, 1882, Irving gave a small dinner-party for twenty close friends, including Ellen Terry's family and Bram's, with spiced beef, roast beef, turkey, plum pudding, and a roulette wheel on the table when these had been cleared.

Irving had panache, for at that moment a canvas bag of silver, in different denominations amounting to five pounds, was placed in front of every guest so that they could play with a clear conscience. Panache and superb consideration: that evening every member of the staff, even the supers, was presented with a Christmas hamper containing a goose and all the trimmings, and a bottle of gin. The children had the goose, but a cake instead of the gin. Some four or five hundred baskets were handed out and as the staff left the theatre, Bram recalled that he 'could trace them through distant streets by their scent'. Meanwhile, in the Green Room there was a punch-bowl for the company, re-filled as often as required from a five-gallon keg of old whisky.

The bond between the players and the audience at the Lyceum was unique. This loyalty was proved on the last night of the season in 1883, on the eve of Irving's first visit to America, a journey that was an adventure at that time. The occasion sparked off the sort of emotional good-will that cheered Charles Dickens on his way when he left for his lecture tours. Bram recalled that night with pride, when 'the house was jammed to suffocation and seemingly not one present but was a friend'. When the curtain fell the hand-clapping and feet-stamping were lost in the general uproar for

the audience were shouting with that detonating effect which is only to be found from a multitude animated with a common feeling. The sight and sound were moving. Wherever one looked were tears; and not from women or the young alone.

At the last, after a pause a little longer than usual – from which the audience evidently took it that the dramatic moment had arrived – came a marvellous silence.

The curtain went up, showing on the stage the entire *personnel* of the company and staff.

Then that audience simply went crazy. All the cheers that had been for the play seemed merely a preparation for those of the parting. The air wherever one looked was a mass of waving hands and handkerchiefs, through which came wave after wave of that wild, heart-stirring detonating sound. All were overcome, before and behind the floats alike. When the curtain fell, it did so on two thousand people swept with emotion.

No wonder that Bram idolised the man who made this possible. Now, Florence had to bear a longer absence as Bram left England to pave the way for Irving's reception in America.

CHAPTER SEVEN

Hero and Valet

'Four Americans of varying degrees of ugliness who arrived yesterday morning and make the salon ring with their nasal twangs (and) make me ashamed of my language.' So wrote my grandfather Tom Stoker to my grandmother during their engagement, from a sanatorium in France. Such insularity was all too common, but Bram had no such prejudice. He did not share the general belief in the infallibility of the British. At the start of his shilling booklet, *A Glimpse of America*, published at the end of 1885, he wrote, 'We Londoners have opportunities of witnessing, in our daily life, the whole scheme of human existence. We have points of contact with as high a civilisation as the earth affords; and also, I fear, with here and there, as complete a system of savagery as distinguished those aborigines who won a place in history by resting on the outside of Captain Cook.'

If most Londoners were badly informed about conditions in their own city – unaware of the festering sores that made up the East End – they had no concept at all of America. Arriving as an ambassador of good-will, Bram condemned the ignorance and plain lack of interest he had left behind:

It is to me, having once visited America, deplorable that we can be left so ignorant of a nation, not merely like ourselves – the same in blood, religion, and social ideas, with an almost identical common law, and with whom our manifold interests are not only vast, but almost vital. I really doubt if the average educated Briton could tell how many States or Territories are in the American Union, the extent of the population, or of the space they spread over, or of the practical conditions under which they live.

72

Bram reached New York in October 1883. There was no
need for him to whip up enthusiasm: the cheers of the Lyceum
had crossed the Atlantic. This was the first time an entire
theatrical management, with all its equipment, had been brought
to America, and the excitement grew as the first riches of the
Lyceum were unloaded – the painted scenery, the props, the
calcium lights, the splendid costumes – followed a week later
by an entourage of forty players and staff, led by Bram. Forty-
eight hours after that, travelling on another ship, came Ellen
Terry and the visiting conqueror. Far from having to manu-
facture publicity, Bram had to hold the reporters back, for
Irving could not possibly accede to all the interviews requested.
Bram came to respect the American newspapermen totally. In
all the hundreds of interviews he gave on Irving's behalf 'I
never once found one that went back on me. I could always
speak quite openly to them individually on a subject which we
wished for the present to keep dark, simply telling him or them
that the matter was not for present publication.' Irving insisted
that when he did grant an interview all proofs should be submitted before publication for his signature if he approved. Not
one newspaper failed to honour this agreement. Irving was
equally cautious with his speeches, too widely reported for him
to be able to afford mistakes or omissions, and even those that
seemed impromptu were carefully learnt by heart or read from
large headlines on the table in front of him, which his acting
skill disguised.

With public interest at the desired peak, the curtain rose on
the night of 29 October. Irving chose *The Bells*, which he had
made into his own personal triumph. 'There was the hush of
expectation,' wrote Bram, 'prolonged till the moment when the
door of the inn parlour was thrown open and Irving seemed
swept in by the rushing snowstorm.' The cheering lasted for
six or seven minutes – a staggering length of time, if one takes
Bram's figures literally.

That welcome lasted for twenty years. A return tour was
agreed on immediately and America was visited, almost yearly,
until Irving made his farewell on 25 March 1904 at the Harlem
Opera House: 'I go with only one feeling on my lips and one
thought in my heart – God Bless America! '

During that first tour they played in Boston, Baltimore,

Chicago, Washington, St Louis, Cincinatti, and New Orleans, where Bram gleaned material for his story 'Snowbound', about a touring theatrical company. They played *The Merchant of Venice* before the West Point Military Academy, and during the inevitable speech afterwards Irving remarked, 'I believe joy bells are ringing in London tonight because for the first time the British have captured West Point.' He addressed Harvard University on 'The Art of Acting'.

They were fêted like royalty for, as Bram observed, 'As Americans have no princes of their own, they make princes of whom they love,' even though this was a period when actors were not regarded as socially acceptable.

Friendships were formed and perpetuated, such as that with Walt Whitman, and another with Mark Twain, which ended less happily when he persuaded Bram and Irving to invest in stock:

My Dear Stoker, [he wrote ebulliently at an early stage], *Now* it's all fixed. If you want some type-setter stock at 50 cents which must go to par in six months in *my* opinion, speak up and tell me how much you want. In three years I judge that this stock will bring fabulous prices.

It is the strongest company that – well, there couldn't be a stronger company, I guess. It has the best business man among the millionaires of America at its back and he has chosen its President, its board of directors, its executive committee and the Chief Engineer of the factory himself. Work was resumed on the machines last Monday and ten of them will be pushed to completion with all dispatch, without wasting energy on the forty unfinished ones.

Sincerely yours, S. L. Clemens.

It is a letter that reeks with false confidence, and was followed by another:

My Dear Stoker, I am not dating this because it is not to be mailed at present. When it reaches you it will mean that there is a hitch in my machine enterprise – a hitch so serious as to make it take to itself the aspect of a dissolved dream. This letter, then, will contain a cheque for the hundred dollars which you have paid. And will you tell

Irving for me – I can't get up courage enough to talk
about this misfortune myself, except to you, whom by good
luck I haven't damaged yet – that when the wreckage
presently floats ashore he will get a good deal of his five
hundred dollars back; and a dab at a time I will make up
to him the rest.

I'm not feeling as fine as I was when I saw you there
in your home. Please remember me kindly to Mrs Stoker.
I gave up that London lecture project entirely. Had to –
there's never been a chance since to find the time.

Sincerely yours, S. L. Clemens.

His type-setting venture proved too complicated and it closed
with the *Times Herald* at the end of 1894.

What is the counterpart of 'Anglophile'? Or is it characteristic that we have such a word about ourselves but not for
America? Whatever the name, Bram was wide-eyed with admiration over everything he saw. In *A Glimpse of America* he
described the cool verandahs in summertime and 'generously-
opened doorways where the burning sunshine cannot penetrate,
even by reflection'. He relished the lack of class-consciousness:
'With us persons of a certain class think it *infra dignate* to ride
in tramcars, as also to wear overshoes, or to wrap up against
the weather; in all these things Americans are quite free, and do
not hesitate to do as they think best.' And he was impressed
by the standard of life: 'I may here remark that all through
America men and women of the working classes are much better
dressed than at home.'

He made a startling exception of tramps:

A traveller, going through the country in the ordinary way,
by railways, steamboats, stages and road-cars, could not
possibly distinguish classes as at home, except when they
are of very marked difference, or, of course, in the case of
tramps, and other *excretions* of civilisation [My italics].

The tramp is, in America, a class by himself, tolerated
simply for the time. In the vast population of the country
there is of course, a percentage of incurable drones; their
number is not many, but they form a dangerous element,
since they have no home, and are without the responsi-

bilities which regulate in some degree to their fellows; consequently, they are at times treated with ruthless severity,
when, for instance, some outrage has been committed, particularly when a woman has been the victim. In the latter
instance, when a negro has been the delinquent, he is
almost *invariably lynched.* [My startled italics again].

Bram fitted easily into club life:

Every city has several. They are, as a rule, large, handsome,
and excellently appointed. Their hospitality is unbounded,
and the stranger who is properly introduced is made a
member for the necessary time with a facility and rapidity
which is impossible amongst our denser population. The
club in America, is indeed, to the masculine wayfarer the
shadow of a great rock in a lone and thirsty land. I often
felt chagrin at the thought that we English can never repay
in any similar way this expression of American hospitality.

He was surprised by the cheapness of property:

Nearly every one of moderate means has some country or
seaside residence. It may be small, but it is the absolute
possession of the owner, and is at present easily obtainable.
I have known a player in the orchestra of a theatre who had
his cottage in the country, bought with and supported by
his own savings. This possession of real estate is in every
way fostered and encouraged by the policy of the United
States. Land is supposed to be held for useful purposes,
and its transfer is exceedingly cheap and simple. A few
hours and a few dollars can transfer a whole estate.

Another page in the booklet is entitled 'Chivalry towards
Women', a subject dear to him.

One of the most marked characteristics of American life
is the high regard in which woman is held. It seems, now
and then, as if a page of an old book of chivalry had been
taken as the text of a social law. Everywhere there is the
greatest deference, everywhere a protective spirit. Such a

thing as a woman suffering molestation or affront, save at the hands of the criminal classes – which are the same all the world over – is almost unknown, and would be promptly resented by the first man coming along. I think I may fairly say, that from the Canadian lakes to the Gulf of Mexico, or from Sandy Hook to the Golden Gate, a woman can walk abroad as safely as she can remain at home.

Still on the subject of gallantry towards the gentler sex, Bram was even in favour of the courtesy which allowed them to jump queues: 'Every man, of course, takes his place in turn and waits; but when a woman comes she at once heads the rank, instead of taking her place in it. A half-grown girl, or servant-maid will thus keep waiting, in the busiest hour of the day, men whose minutes are golden.' Perhaps Bram had underlings to stand in line for him, to avoid such an infuriating native custom. He conceded that this 'freedom' could have a reverse effect. 'I was much struck with this point in relation to suicides. There is not, that I know, any means of forming an exact estimate, but it seemed to me that of the suicides reported in the papers the vast majority were women, mostly young, and with, in every case, a sad, old story behind.'

With his legal background, Bram was impressed by the state of American justice, unlike a previous visitor who asked his host 'Why is it that you prefer to elect your officials from the criminal classes?' Bram's own experience was high-lighted in Cincinnati by a warning from a leading lawyer: 'Something will occur here before long, for the administration of justice is at present a farce. There are at present eight murderers in the gaol await-ing trial. They were nearly every one caught red-handed, but I will venture to say that not one of them will be hanged.' Bram reported that a month later the people of the town rose up and burned down the Courthouse and the prison, the guilty officials fleeing for their lives. 'Ever since, I understand, the administration of justice in Cincinnati has been unattended with complaint.'

On his first visit to New York he was the guest of the police, who took him on an exploration of the seedier parts of town. Bram was shocked. 'I there saw vice in an open form which amazed me, even when I remembered Paris fifteen years ago.'

In Chicago, 'the manner and quantity of gambling, which was openly allowed, was terrible to think of. The gambling saloons were in leading streets, and were open all night long. I have never seen anything more pitiful than the workmen's gambling saloons, where every vice that cupidity can suggest was given in *duodecimo*.' But on his next visit Bram noticed the great change for the better in New York, and in Chicago, where the gambling system had been destroyed, 'the last I heard was that the gamblers were looking for the hulk of a vessel, which they might moor in the lake, and form a saloon outside the city bounds.'

He concluded his glimpse of America with affection:

We have not, all the world through, so strong an ally, so close a friend. America has got over her childhood.

There is every reason we can think of why the English on both sides of the Atlantic should hold together as one. Our history is their history – our fame is their pride – their progress is our glory. They are bound to us, and we to them, by every tie of love and sympathy . . .

We are bound each to each by the instinct of a common race, which makes brotherhood and the love of brothers a natural law.

We have not advanced far since these fulsome words, in our appreciation or understanding.

The booklet was something of a rarity then, the converse of so many accounts by American visitors to England. It was one of the few books taken by Henry Morton Stanley on his exploration of Africa, and it gave him more information about America 'than any other book that had ever been written'. Over a private dinner in Manchester on 4 June 1890, Stanley told Irving that Bram had mistaken his vocation: 'He should be a literary man.' It is touching that Bram should have welcomed such back-handed approval: 'Of course such praise from such a man gave me great pleasure.' Seldom was Bram honoured in his literary right, yet he never kicked against the role of minion and became positively jealous when it was usurped.

There were revealing incidents on the tours of America. The first concerned a journalist stowaway on the night train from

Chicago to Detroit, who was discovered shortly before departure. Bram explained that they never travelled with strangers, that the Company was divided into family groups and they would not feel comfortable. The reporter announced his intention of writing a story about 'the incidents of the night', which produced the reasonable reaction from Bram – 'I did not know what kind of incidents he expected! However, I was firm and would not let him come.' When the train drew into Detroit the next morning, a messenger came on board with a special letter addressed to Bram. This contained the reporter's revenge: a colourful report of the company, glimpsed on board the train *en deshabille*. Explaining that he had been forbidden to accompany them, the reporter referred to 'an individual who *called himself* Bram Stoker ... who seems to occupy some anomalous position between secretary and valet. Whose manifest duties are to see that there is mustard in the sandwiches and to take the dogs out for a run; and who unites in his own person every vulgarity of the English speaking race.' Bram's response was good-humoured: 'I forgave him on the spot for the whole thing on account of that last sub-sentence.'

There is some hurt in the accusation of 'valet'. In fact, Irving was served faithfully by a valet of his own, Walter Collinson, who acted also as his dresser and wig-maker, having worked previously at Clarkson's. Laurence Irving, the actor's grandson, describes his value:

When on his master's business, he exercised a certain brusque authority which was respected by everybody in the theatre. He accepted Irving's occasional paroxysms of cold rage with equanimity and carried out his varied duties with quiet dexterity and affectionate zeal. Alone of all men he held the key to Irving's lonely inner life with which he became intimately acquainted and with it he locked within himself the confidences entrusted to him. He had no life outside the situation of his master. He became Irving's fifth limb and his loss at any time would have been crippling. He was a bantam-weight Sancho Panza to his dolorous and much-loved knight.

Ellen Terry, who said that Collinson resembled Shakespeare's bust in Stratford church, quoted his reply when Irving asked him which part was his best. For a long time Collinson would not be 'drawn', but finally he said, 'Macbeth,' which pleased the actor greatly as he thought so himself.

'It is generally conceded to be Hamlet,' said Henry.

'Oh no sir,' said Walter. 'Macbeth. You sweat twice as much in that.'

The third member of the palace guard was Harry Loveday, the stage-manager, 'as absolutely devoted to Henry as any one except his fox-terrier Fussy. Loveday's loyalty made him agree with everything that Henry said, however preposterous, and didn't Henry trade on it sometimes!'

Ellen Terry recalled an evening when Irving was making-up, and absent-mindedly removed a white lily from a bowl and started to stripe and dot it with the grease-stick in his hand. When he stopped, he looked at the object and tore off some of the petals.

> Pretty flower, isn't it?
> Oh, don't be ridiculous, Henry! Ellen Terry replied.
> You wait, he said. We'll show it to Loveday. The manager was called to the dressing-room on some pretext and Irving held out the flower, remarking carelessly,
> Pretty, isn't it?
> Very, said Loveday. I always like those lilies. A friend of mine has his garden full of them, and he says they're not so difficult to grow if only you give 'em enough water.

Irving's delight was so childish that Loveday may well have seen through the game and fell loyally into the trap. Such was his devotion.

The triumvirate of Collinson, Loveday and Stoker worked together amicably. So it is not surprising that they were upset by the arrival of a brash new confidant, Louis Frederick Austin, who had been an unofficial secretary to the Baroness Burdett-Coutts and now joined Irving in the same capacity. His presence was bitter to Bram, for Austin was a lively personality, born in Brooklyn of Irish parents, with a natural flair for writing and a reputation as a popular after-dinner speaker. Later he returned to journalism and wrote the literary page in the *Illustrated News* until he was succeeded by G. K. Chesterton. He admired Irving, but was no sycophant. Unlike the others, he expressed his doubts openly. In return, Irving gave him his confidence.

On that first American tour Austin was left behind to look after the Lyceum. At times he was desperate in their absence, with sole responsibility for paying the few remaining salaries, including his own. As soon as they arrived in New York he sent 'numbered bills' to Stoker, 'which Mr Irving said were to be forwarded', a total of £81. He added that he hoped they had had a pleasant voyage.

In November, he wrote: 'Dear Stoker, I have been expecting money from you every day but in vain,' and in December: 'Your very welcome letter came in the nick of time. We were destitute all round and I was on the point of telegraphing. The £100 is most useful, but I am sorry to say it does not meet the case!'.

While on 10 January 1884, he telegraphed a terse message to Bram at Haverleys Theatre in Chicago – 'CHEQUE SHORT SEND SIXTY POUNDS. AUSTIN.' The triumvirate had all the fun and glory – the company travelling like a vast family, with pet dogs and parrots, talking, arguing, cooking, playing cards and practical jokes. Irving received devotion from men and gave it to his dog Fussie, who belonged originally to Ellen Terry until he won him over with a course of 'chops, tomatoes, strawberries, asparagus, biscuits soaked in champagne, and a beautiful fur rug of his very own presented by the Baroness Burdett-Coutts'. It sounds a diet that, apart from the chops, would have alienated most dogs, but Ellen Terry described their devotion: 'I have caught them often sitting opposite each other at Grafton Street, just adoring each other! Occasionally Fussie would thump his tail on the ground to express his pleasure.' When Charlie, the other terrier, was alive, she found them curled up on the two chairs in the dressing-room while Irving stood by the table rather than disturb them.

Apart from one long, painful separation, Fussie (or Fussy) was Irving's constant companion on the tours of America, even in the theatre. Stage-trained at the Lyceum, he was both a delight and a disgrace in America, barred from some hotels (whereupon Irving would walk straight out and find another). Sometimes Fussie made a personal appearance on stage. This happened at a charity performance after Irving had 'done his bit', as Ellen Terry related, and put on his coat and hat to leave. Fussie assumed that the play was over and bounded on to the stage, where John Drew and Maude Adams were playing *A Pair of Lunatics*. The actress was gazing into the stage-fire and was astonished to hear Drew departing from the text, so crazily that for a moment she wondered if he really had gone mad:

> Is this a dog I see before me
> His tail towards my hand?
> Come, let me clutch thee . . .

as Fussie ran across to the stage-door.

On that first tour, Irving missed his secretary's help with the inevitable speeches that had to be written and delivered in every town they played. When they set out again in 1884, Austin went with them. The power of the triumvirate was broken. To make his presence even more bitter, Austin's bonhomie earned him instant popularity with the rest of the Company.

The tour started cheerfully enough. Writing to his wife on their arrival in Quebec on 30 September, Austin exclaimed:

> No wonder that all the miseries of the sea voyage were soon forgotten or that everybody skipped about in the highest spirits. Henry was in the highest good humour and Ellen seemed to lose the terrible weariness which had nearly quenched the light in her eyes. On Sunday night I dined with Henry, Ellen, Loveday and his wife, and Stoker, and a pleasanter party could not have been gathered. I've settled down into an understanding with Stoker and he has become remarkably genial and obliging.

At this stage every makeshift condition was a delightful novelty:

> Tonight we give our first performance and then leave by special train to Montreal where we shall arrive at eight or nine in the morning . . . the theatre here would make you

shriek. It is a cross between a chapel and a very small concert room and the stage is about half the size of that of St George's Hall! The entrance is being washed now but no amount of soap and water will repair the broken windows. The kind of people who play here as a rule are of the least intellectual order – we found two members of the preceding troupe on the stage – they were two hens!!

The truce with Stoker was short-lived and was not redeemed by seasonal good will. In Pittsburgh – 'hell with the lid off' – the Company subscribed to a silver tea-service as a Christmas present for Ellen Terry, and asked Austin to write a 'Lyceum Christmas Play' in which every actor recited a verse about himself. Ellen Terry and Irving were kept in the dark until the celebration dinner on Christmas Eve. The meal itself was disastrous, according to Austin, who wrote to his wife the next day: 'There's so little civilisation in this town even in the kitchen of the best hotel that the staff was perfectly paralysed by a banquet for 76 people. The intervals between the courses were so long and the food so indifferent that the whole affair would have been a failure but for the simply perfect way in which H.I. played host.'

Ellen Terry described the dinner as 'Burned Hare Soup', but it ended with a Christmas pudding sent over by her mother. 'Very odd,' said Irving, 'I think this is a camphor pudding.' When Ellen tasted it, she realised it had been packed with her furs surrounded by moth-balls. Irving saved the occasion with his wit and quantities of his own wine brought over from England: 'It seems to me that we aren't going to get anything to eat, but we'll make up for it by drinking.'

The Company helped themselves lavishly and were more cheerful when the 'event of the night' was introduced by Loveday, who recited the first verse, about himself, and was followed by the others.

'It was a tremendous hit,' wrote Austin to his wife. 'Every allusion told and when Stoker began: 'I'm in a mortal hurry' – there was a yell of laughter that lasted several moments. The phrase described Stoker to a hair.'

When the play was complete, one of the younger girls made the presentation:

To offer you this little gift,
Dear Portia, now we crave your leave,
And let it have the grace to lift
Our hearts to you this Christmas Eve.

And so we pray that you may live
Thro' many, many happy years,
And feel what you so often give—
The joy that is akin to tears!

She spoke her lines with such sweetness that Ellen Terry was overcome, according to Austin: 'The surprise, the pleasure, and the choking emotion made her such a picture as she has never looked on the stage. Then she stood up, with great tears rolling down her cheeks – while Henry tried to conceal his behind his glasses – and said a few broken words more eloquent than any speech.' Writing about the incident later, Ellen Terry was less lyrical: 'It more than compensated for the mortification of the camphor pudding.'

It was a happy occasion for the Company, with one exception. Austin continued, 'I was delighted by the readiness with which everybody – Stoker excepted – consented to read a little satire on himself. Stoker, of course, resented every joke of mine on *his* personality and was in a rage of jealousy because I had done something so successful. You would be amused by the petty jealousies of this expedition. This contemptible littleness seems to be fostered by the theatrical atmosphere.'

Laurence Irving sympathised. 'Poor strenuous Stoker must have suffered torments of jealousy.' To make his anguish worse, 'Irving, who enjoyed pulling the legs of his lieutenants and testing the extremes to which their eager assertions would carry them, got a good deal of sardonic fun out of their rivalries.' 'Sardonic' is an apt word.

The tour continued with Austin, as the life and soul of the party, killing it for Bram. When the train stopped for twenty minutes to let the Company dine, Ellen left the train to play in the snow with her twelve-year-old son Teddy (Edward Gordon Craig). He had a small sledge which Austin carried outside and, after giving the child a ride, he sat on it himself while Ellen Terry acted as the horse. 'I wonder what the Lyceum stalls would have thought if they could have seen the sight. We couldn't persuade Henry to compromise his dignity by taking a ride. He stood on the steps of the car and gazed at us with a tragic air . . .' If Irving looked tragic – Bram's gaze must have been cast in granite.

The 'simmering quarrel', as Laurence Irving called it, boiled over in March, when Austin prepared Irving's address to Harvard University and then his speech to the farewell banquet in New York. Irving was delighted with the result, as Austin related in another gleeful letter:

I actually made him tearful when I read that speech to him yesterday. I am conceited enough to think that it will make a small sensation – provided he doesn't spoil it. We are always wrangling over little words concerning the meaning and importance of which he has eccentric and not altogether literary ideas. I am chiefly delighted about this business because that idiot Stoker wrote a speech for the same occasion and I was disgusted to find it on the Governor's table. When I read mine to Henry, he said: 'Poor old Bram has been trying *his* hand but there isn't an idea in the whole thing.'

'I should be very much surprised if there was,' said Austin, treacherously.

Poor old Bram, indeed! Yet Austin claimed that he was not vindictive and was driven to such savagery by Bram's 'colossal humbug'. 'The fact is Stoker tells everybody that he writes Henry's speeches and articles, and he wants to have some real basis for this lie. This is why he worried H.I. into putting his name to an article which appeared in the *Fortnightly Review,* a fearful piece of twaddle about American audiences that B.S. was three months in writing.'

Evidently Austin thought it his duty to inform the Governor that Bram's 'ghosted' articles demeaned his signature. But another comment suggests that he *was* vindictive, in a devious way: 'The misfortune is that my position as a *very* private secretary compels me to keep in the background. I cannot tell the truth about my own work for that would not be right. Luckily I have a faithful friend and ally in Alexander, who

knows everybody in London worth knowing and will prick
Stoker's bubble effectively.'

Jealousy for Irving's attention spoilt the tour for the two
rivals. Writing wearily to his wife from New York on 17 March
1885, Austin referred to their imminent departure for home:

.... three weeks today Henry will sail in the *Arizona*
and still I don't know whether I shall go with him or not!
Stoker goes with the company in the *City of Chicago*
on the 9th April two days later. The Lovedays sail with
H.I. and Ellen and if they could possible prevent me from
going with them they would move heaven and earth to do it.
Yet we are good friends and don't quarrel; but their morbid
jealousy of everybody else near H.I. is such that they are
constantly making themselves ridiculous. You don't know
how weary I am of the childish pettiness of the whole
atmosphere. Stoker does nothing but scheme and manoeuvre
to ingratiate himself in good society and to keep me in
the background. The Alexanders checkmate this to a great
extent and so he hates them. He and I had a furious
quarrel lately about some lie of his and he apologised to
me afterwards to prevent me from appealing to Irving. If I
could do the mean contemptible things he does such as
lavishly giving tickets to people who can perfectly well
afford to pay I might push myself more than I do. But I
would rather live in a garret than fawn upon people as
Stoker does for the sake of sticking my legs under their
mahogany. To associate with people who are always striving
to take advantage of one another in a stupidly small way is
most unpleasant and so I keep away from the theatre as
much as possible now.

Austin's final word from America conveyed total disillusionment: he was thankful, he wrote, that this would be his last
letter from the expedition he had looked forward to so eagerly.

And Bram? His disillusionment must surely have been even
greater. Suddenly there is a new twist to his image – the vul-
nerability behind that bluff façade is revealed. Irving's preference
for Austin as his literary adviser must have shaken any belief
Bram had that he was indispensable. If he suffered, as I believe,

from some deep insecurity, this tour must have confirmed it. Austin did not conceal his contempt for Bram as a writer:

> ... he will go about London next season blarneying of his literary labours for Irving! Moreover he had written a book about America, save the mark, and this will appear shortly I suppose. His first effort in literature that marvellous book neither you nor I nor anybody else could understand, cost him seven hundred pounds, for which he has never had and never will have the smallest return.

That 'marvellous book' must have been either *The Duties of Clerks of Petty Sessions in Ireland* (which is most unlikely) or the collection of stories for children, *Under the Sunset*. Austin's comment is a savage condemnation of such a harmless book, but at the same time provides a surprising revelation. Seven hundred pounds was, after all, a considerable sum in those days. The fact that Stoker was prepared to invest such a sum in his book shows his new prosperity with the Lyceum, but also, and more significantly, it indicates how much faith he, at least, had in his own talent.

And so the second tour of America ended in discord, with only one person remaining immune from the quarrels, of which he himself was the cause. Irving was delightfully aloof.

'To what do you attribute your success, Mr Irving?' asked an eager American reporter.

'To my acting,' came the sardonic reply.

CHAPTER EIGHT

𝔄 𝔏iterary 𝔐an on ℌoliday

With a stamina that seems colossal today, Bram Stoker managed the business affairs of the Lyceum, advised Irving on the productions, arranged the tours of America, and accompanied the actor on his journeys throughout Britain. It seems incredible that he could raise the energy and time to concentrate on anything else. Yet, during this period, he resumed his legal studies and succeeded in passing his examinations. He was called to the bar in 1890, which at least saved him the time-consuming chore of jury duty.

And he wrote books! By the time he quoted Stanley's 'compliment', '*He should be a literary man!*', Bram had already published eleven books including *Dracula*.

In addition to all these activities, he cultivated friendships and somehow managed to escape on holidays of his own. Of necessity, these were not idle affairs: with his photographic memory he transformed the places he visited into locations for future stories.

Like Charles Dickens, he strode cheerfully through the countryside on long walking-tours, and in 1892, spending his Easter Holiday in Cornwall, he came across the small fishing village of Boscastle on the west coast, which he 'hit upon by accident'. My grandmother told me that Bram was responsible for making the place fashionable by describing it so glowingly to his friends. Irving stayed there later for two holidays. Today it is a tourist attraction in the height of summer, though still comparatively unspoilt apart from the inevitable car-park and souvenir-shop and, more surprisingly, a witches' museum.

The incoming tide squeezes through the rocks at the narrow opening, almost shouldering its way in as it fills the harbour. The swell resounds deeply in the caves, and it was probably this sense of power that appealed to Stoker in the first place, together with the discovery that ships had to be hauled by cables into the safety of the cove. Boscastle became 'Pencastle' in his short story 'The Coming of Abel Behenna', which tells of jealousy between two fishermen in love with the same girl, and a corpse washed up in a wild storm on the hour of the wedding. This was a favourite theme.

'Behenna' was the maiden name of Sarah Penberthy, Irving's aged aunt who had looked after him as a child and doted on him still though now it was Bram's task to keep in touch with her. It has been suggested that she told Bram about Boscastle on one of his early visits to her home in St Ives further down the coast. Bram performed such duties honourably and formed a genuine friendship with the old lady.

As far back as Christmas 1883, Sarah Penberthy wrote lovingly to her nephew, who was then touring America. The envelope was addressed simply: Henry Irving Esq, Philadelphia. U.S.A.

My Dearest Johnnie,

I think that you will be glad of a few lines from your aged aunt as I should be to receive a few lines from your own hand. I am pleased to hear of your and Miss Terry's success in America. Indeed you seem to be blazing over the wide world like a comet. My daily prayer is that the blessing of God may attend you and that the blessings of God may attend you in all your undertakings and that in due time you may return to England a happier, a better and a richer man.

... My kind regards to Mr and Mrs Stoker, it was very kind of you to send them down to see. Thank you for the two £5 that he gave me, I have one of them still unchanged. Thank the Lord my health is still good but my sight is very dim. I am just entered my eighty fourth year. I can still walk about a little and help myself in everything which is a great mercy. A few a line [sic] would be thankful received. With love to Miss Terry.

And Dearest love to yourself, I remain,

Your affectionate Aunt Sarah Penberthy.

Bram scribbled in the margin of the letter £20, and the date 25/1/84.

The following month Sarah Penberthy wrote directly to Bram, referring to their last meeting which had made such an impression on her:

> Dear Sir,
>
> I often speak of you, but oftener think of you since your visit to Cornwall.
>
> I can sympathise with you in your separation from your wife and child, though only for a short time – it is – that a good wife is from the Lord, and I think you fortunate in your choice, and I pray that God may grant you long life, and that you may have a blessing in each other and that you may train your child for the Lord.
>
> I heartily endorse all that is said about my dear nephew, and I pray that after all the scenes and actings of the Theatre are over that he may decide for the Lord, and spend his last days in peace.
>
> If spared until another summer I shall be very pleased to see you and your dear wife in Cornwall. With kindest love to yourself and Mrs Stoker, I remain, Yours sincerely, S. Penberthy.
>
> P.S. You will be sorry to hear that my sight is almost gone.

But a holiday for Bram was a luxury that Henry Irving could ill afford. On Good Friday Bram was recalled suddenly from Boscastle. 'I felt so in love with the place,' he wrote afterwards, but it was a short romance. He travelled through the night in a snowstorm to find Irving waiting for him impatiently at the Lyceum in the afternoon. After the Saturday performance, they dined with Loveday in the Beefsteak Rooms; cigars were produced, and Irving opened the manuscript of *Becket* that he had been adapting ('I think I have got it at last!') and read it to them.

'There was no doubting how the part of Becket appealed to him. He was greatly moved at some of the passages . . .'

Though they finished at four on the Sunday morning, Bram lost no time in writing to Lord Tennyson's son, dating his letter Saturday, 16 April 1892:

'My dear Mr Hallam Tennyson,

Mr Irving asks me to say that he has spent his holiday over Becket and has it now in the form that he thinks is best and would like to have it submitted. He thinks it would be best as you and your father and he are so distant from each other if I were to run down and take the altered work with me and explain his views in case there may be anything to talk over. If this will suit you I can come down any day next week – as the sooner the better all round. You might let me have a line by return. With kind regards to Lord and Lady and Mrs Tennyson

Believe me Yours very sincerely Bram Stoker

The reply arrived on Monday; Bram took the 10.30 train from Victoria on Tuesday morning and was with Hallam Tennyson on the Isle of Wight by four o'clock. It says much for the efficiency of Stoker and the speed of the Victorian postal service.

After discussing such business as copyright and royalties with Hallam, Bram was taken to Alfred Lord Tennyson to discuss the alterations. Fretful at first with a bad cold – he was then eighty-three – he proved surprisingly co-operative until the need for a new dramatic speech was mentioned.

'But where am I to get such a speech?' he asked. Bram pointed out of the window across the water to the English Downs:

'There it is! In the roar of the sea!'

Tennyson was pleased and the new material, full of the requisite surge and splendour, was sent a few days later.

This began a short friendship with the old man. Bram paid him several subsequent visits, including one in September, when he and Florence spent the day with Lord and Lady Tennyson – 'perhaps the most sweet and saintly woman I have ever met.' But Tennyson was feeble and in pain. 'Gout was flying through his knees and jaws' when Bram went to his bedroom.

'Don't let them know how ill I am, or they'll have me buried before twenty-four hours.' When he moaned that he wished he had never written a line, Bram consoled him with genuine dismay: 'Ah, don't say that! Don't think of it! You have given delight to too many millions, and your words have done too much good for you to wish to take them back.'

'Outside our tears fell. We knew that we should see him no more; we had said goodbye for ever.' Tennyson died eleven days later.

Meeting, and *knowing*, such idols was part of the thrill of living with Irving. Always surprising, always constructive, Bram's was the least routine of jobs. There were odd, unexpected bonuses, such as the splendid silver-topped cane of black zebra wood, now in my possession, inscribed:

> Presented to Bram Stoker Esq
> By the crew of U.S. Chicago 1894.

This was given to Bram after he paid a courtesy visit with Irving to the *U.S. Chicago,* moored at Gravesend. On board was Admiral Erben, a man who was regarded as a hero since he went to the help of a flotilla of British ships stranded on some Chinese mud-flats. The crew of the ostensibly neutral American warship pulled the British sailors to safety while their officers turned a blind eye. When the Chinese protested, Admiral Erben replied *'Blood is Thicker than Water',* a phrase which delighted the hearts of Englishmen and was later displayed in gigantic letters at a banquet given in his honour. Irving was ill, but sent Stoker to represent him, since 'he felt that all that could possibly be done to cement the good feeling between Great Britain and America was the duty of every Englishman'. After his recovery Irving invited the officers to the Beefsteak Rooms, and the crew to the theatre – 'a fine and hearty body of men', recorded Stoker characteristically. Hence the return visit. At lunch, Stoker was offered wine but refused it 'because of his gout', asking for whisky and soda instead. As the embarrassed officer beside him explained that U.S. Navy ships are 'dry', another officer exclaimed in alarm, 'What's wrong with you? You're quite pale!' In spite of Stoker's baffled protestations, the doctor was called, noticed the untouched wine, and wrote a rapid prescription. This must have been a familiar ploy for when the medicine arrived, it tasted 'exceedingly like whisky and soda'.

Bram was delighted, and moved, by the farewell cheer at their departure.

It pealed over the water that still Sabbath afternoon and startled the quiet folk on the frontages at Gravesend. Cheer after cheer came ringing and resonant with a heartiness that made one's blood leap. For there is no such sound in the world as that full throated Anglo Saxon cheer which begins at the heart – that inspiring, resolute, intentional cheer which has through the memory of ten thousand victories and endless moments of stress and daring become the heritage of the race.

Always stirred by the applause of the crowd, Bram enjoyed more than his share in his association with Irving. Equally, his keen sense of patriotism – so alien today – was gratified by the first of several Royal 'Commands' at Windsor, which he was responsible for organising. With the special telegraph office in the castle at his disposal, he reported the private performance of *Becket* to the world press, with the confirmation from Queen Victoria that 'Mr Bram Stoker may write whatever he pleases about the event'. And she paid for the telegrams.

In 1902, he raced the Company from Belfast to Sandringham for a special performance before Edward VII and the Kaiser. Such dallying with royalty must have satisfied his ego enormously. In America, he became friends with Theodore Roosevelt, when he was the Police Commissioner of New York, and continued to see him when he was President. He was accepted everywhere.

More significant than the brief time spent in Boscastle was Bram's discovery of Cruden Bay in Scotland the following year. Surprisingly he was on his own, without Irving and without Florence, as he set out from Peterhead one August day along the east coast of Aberdeenshire. After walking south for eight miles, he happened on Cruden, also known as Port Erroll, a fishing village that depended on the local herring industry. Bram was enchanted: 'When I first saw the place I fell in love with it. Had it been possible I should have spent my summer there in a house of my own, but the want of any place to live in forbade such an opportunity. So I stayed in the little hotel, the Kilmarnock Arms. The next year I came again, and the next, and the next . . .' This is how the narrator remembers the place in *The Mystery of the Sea*, 1902, but plainly they are Bram's thoughts as well.

There seemed little difference in Cruden when I went there

in 1970, though the scene may be changing drastically with the
discovery of off-shore oil. This is landed by pipe-line at the
'scaurs' of Cruden at the south end of the bay. The new
proprietor of the Kilmarnock Arms has done his best to retain
the 'Victorian character' of the hotel, but its tranquillity will
soon be lost if he is correct in his estimate that the population
of the village will increase from the present figure of six hundred
to two thousand.

On my visit, Cruden was immensely peaceful with an atmosphere of space and timelessness and air. Telegraph lines were
the only disfigurement. The cottages of the fishermen were
low-lying and simple, with tarred roofs; their boats were outside, upside down, painted in layers of red, white and blue, and
their nets were stretched high on poles, suggesting the black
tents of some exotic desert caravan.

The small harbour and the sands were less active than before;
indeed, the main change was retrograde, as with Slains Castle
on the top of the cliff. The castle was formerly the home of
the Earls of Erroll, who owned the estate since the thirteen
century and ran it on strictly temperance lines. Samuel Johnson
described it as the noblest castle, though in the print that was
shown to me it looks indifferent. It is a ruin now, and it is
possible to look through the open windows and fallen archways
on to the surf lashing the rocks below. Paradoxically, it is far
more Stokerish than it could have been in Bram's own
day.

Bram used Cruden as the setting for his story *The Watter's
Mou* (1895). He was always fascinated by storms, and his opening was typical: 'It threatened to be a wild night. All day banks
of sea-fog had come and gone, sweeping on shore with the south-
east wind, which is so fatal at Cruden Bay . . .' It is a romantic,
indeed over-romantic, tale of a young coastguard in love with
the daughter of a fisherman whose debts have forced him into
the smuggling racket which was rife along the coast at that time,
with 'stuff' being landed from Germany and Holland. The coastguard, William Barrow, known as 'Sailor Willy', is so manly
that he is mawkish: 'The manhood in him rose to the occasion
– Willy Barrow was of the stuff of which heroes are made . . .'
and 'Willy was something frightened, for a woman's distress
touches a strong man in direct ratio to his manliness.' And

again, the girl's brother 'grasped Willy's hand in his own strong one, and the hearts of both men, the gentle and the simple, went out each to the other, and became bound together as men's hearts do when touched with flame of any kind.'

Some critics have found Bram's use of dialect delightful; I find it ludicrous. Usually it was the Irish accent that suffered, as in this extract from his story of *The Gombeen Man,* taken from the novel *The Snake's Pass,* 1890. ' "Musha!" said old Dan Moriarty, sotto voce. "An' is that the way of it! An' is he too in the clutches iv that wolf? Him that we all thought was so warrum. Glory be to God! but it's a quare wurrld it is; an' it's few there is in it that is what they seems. Me poor frind! is there any way I can help ye? I have a bit iv money by me that yer wilkim to the lend iv av ye want it?" '

Now it was the turn of the Scots: ' "Our coo died, and the shed was blawn doon, and then the blight touched the potatoes in our field. Father could dae naething, and had to borrow money on the boat to go on with his wark; and the debt grew ..." ' This was the daughter, explaining the family misfortune. Later, fearing her father's impending arrest, she urges Sailor Willy to stay with her: ' "O Willy, Willy! dinna turn frae me this nicht! My heart is sae fu' o' trouble that I am nigh mad! I dinna ken what to dae nor where to look for help! I think, and think, and think, and everywhere there is nought but dark before me, just as there is blackness oot ower the sea, when I look for my father. And noo when I want ye to help me – ye that are all I hae, and the only ane on earth that I can look tae in my wae and trouble – I can dae nae mair than turn ye frae me! Ye that I love! oh, love more than my life or soul! I must dishonour and mak ye hate me! Oh, what shall I dae? What shall I dae? What shall I dae?" '

The sincerity of the writing barely saves the story, though Maggie's desperate voyage into the storm, to warn her father that the coastguards and customs men are waiting for him, is moving. As she leaves the water's mouth she notices the castle as it would have been then: 'As she passed the cleft, driven somewhere more out into the middle of the channel, she caught, in a pause between the rush of the waves, a glimpse of the lighted windows of the castle on the cliff. The sight for an instant unnerved her, for it brought into opposition her own dreadful situation, mental and physical, with the happy faces of those clustered round the comforting light.'

Maggie reaches her father's fishing smack and he throws the contraband overboard after her warning, but when he turns to haul her aboard she has vanished. Sailor Willy waits for her ashore, distraught:

> As one of these great waves rushed in, Willy's heart beat loudly, and for a second he looked around as though for some voice, from whence he knew not, which was calling to him. Then he looked down and saw, far below him, tossed high upon the summit of the wave, a mass that in the gloom of the evening and the storm looked like a tangle of wreckage – spar and sail and rope – twirling in the rushing water round a dead woman, whose white face was set in an aureole of floating hair. Without a word, but with the bound of a panther, Willy Barrow sprang out on the projecting point of rock, and plunged down into the rushing wave whence he could meet that precious wreckage and grasp it tight.

Again the theme that appealed to Bram so much: a corpse washed ashore – this time, two:

> There on the very spot whence the boat had set sail on its warning errand, lay its wreckage, and tangled in it the body of the noble girl who had steered it – her brown hair floating wide and twined round the neck of Sailor Willy, who held her tight in his dead arms.
>
> The requiem of the twain was the roar of the breaking waves and the scream of the white birds that circled round the Watter's Mou.

Anyone visiting Cruden should read the story; conversely, anyone reading *The Watter's Mou* will find it far more convincing if he does so at Cruden.

Crooken Sands, which is also set in Cruden, is a Stoker story with a pleasing difference – a humorous account of a cockney determined to impress the natives with his Scottishness, hideous new tartan and all. Far from impressing anyone, his appearance

Signed portrait of Bram Stoker as a young man

His wife Florence and Noel

Tom Stoker, Bram's brother
and the author's
grandfather

Florence drawn by Oscar Wilde

Florence by Edward Burne-Jones

Sir Henry Irving

Ellen Terry with her dogs
in 1888

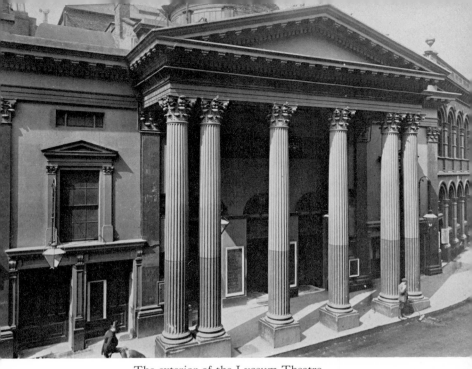

The exterior of the Lyceum Theatre

Sir Henry Irving and Bram Stoker leaving the Lyceum Theatre

The castle at Cruden Bay where Bram Stoker wrote *Dracula*

The snowbound graveyard at Whitby as Bram would have known it

Portrait of Vlad Dracula, allegedly the inspiration for Bram Stoker's book

Dracula on film, one of the many portrayals by Christopher Lee, who kindly supplied this still. For once, the concept is close to Stoker's original, complete with white moustache

Bran Castle in Romania, where Vlad Dracula stayed and which has now become a part of the 'Dracula Tour'

in highland costume reduces his own family to hysterics of laughter and stuns the Scots: 'Man! but he's forgotten the pipes!'

Again there is a detailed description of Crooken, or rather Cruden:

At either end of the bay is a rocky promontory, and when the dawn or sunset falls on the rocks of red syenite the effect is very lovely. The bay itself is floored with level sand and the tide runs far out, leaving a smooth waste of hard sand on which are dotted here and there the stake nets and bag nets of the salmon fishers. At one end of the bay there is a little group or cluster of rocks whose heads are raised something above high water, except when in rough weather the waves come over them green. At low tide, they are exposed to sand level; and here is perhaps the only little bit of dangerous sand on this part of the eastern coast. Between the rocks, which are apart some fifty feet, is a small quicksand, which, like the Goodwins, is dangerous only with the incoming tide.

This quicksand, of Bram's imagination, is the mainspring of the plot and the pleasing twist at the end.

He wrote many short stories. Most of them have been forgotten like the majority of his novels, and are indeed forgettable, with such descriptions as this one of the heroine of 'A Star Trap':

She was more than flesh and blood could stand. She had come into the panto. the season before as a high-kicker – and she could! She could kick higher than girls that was more than a foot taller than her; for she was a wee bit of a thing and as pretty as pie; a gold-haired, blue-eyed slim thing with much the figure of a boy, except for . . . and they saved her from any mistaken idea of that kind. Jack Haliday went crazy over her.

But Bram was a writer of extremes: he could wallow in the depths of sentimentality yet write two classic stories of the macabre. Both concerned rats. 'The Judge's House' tells of a

D

scholar, Malcom Malcomson, who is anxious to prepare for his examinations in an atmosphere of solitude, and rents a desolate house on the outskirts of a market town. The landlady of the local inn, where he is staying, is aghast:

'Not in the Judge's House!' she said, and grew pale as she spoke. He explained the locality of the house, saying that he did not know its name. When he had finished she answered: 'Aye, sure enough – sure enough the very place . . .'

Warned against staying there on his own, Malcom replies rather pompously, as Stoker's male characters tend to do:

'But, my dear Mrs Witham, indeed you need not be concerned about me! A man who is reading for the Mathematical Tripos has too much to think of to be disturbed by any of these mysterious "somethings".'

His charwoman, also, is unafraid:

'I'll tell you what it is, sir,' she said; 'bogies is all kinds and sorts of things – except bogies! Rats and mice, and beetles; and creaky doors, and loose slates, and broken panes, and stiff drawer handles, that stay out when you pull them and then fall down in the middle of the night. Look at the wainscot of the room! It is old – hundreds of years old! Do you think there's no rats and beetles there! And do you imagine, sir, that you won't see none of them? Rats is bogies, I tell you, and bogies is rats; and don't you get to think anything else!'

(Bram's use of exclamation marks was prolific.)
After his supper in the great old room, he notices the noise the rats are making:

'Surely,' he thought, 'they cannot have been at it all the time I was reading. Had they been, I must have noticed it!' Presently, when the noise increased, he satisfied himself that it was really new. It was evident that at first the rats had been frightened at the presence of a stranger, and the light of fire and lamp; but that as the time went on they had grown bolder and were now disporting themselves as was their wont.

He worked until dawn. Then he looked up suddenly – and with greater alarm this time, for the rats were silent:

It was the sudden cessation which had disturbed him. The fire had fallen low, but still it threw out a deep red glow. As he looked he started in spite of his sang froid.

There on the great high-backed carved oak chair by the right side of the fireplace sat an enormous rat steadily glaring at him with baleful eyes. He made a motion to it as though to hunt it away, but it did not stir. Then he made the motion of throwing something. Still it did not stir, but showed its great white teeth angrily, and its cruel eyes shone in the lamplight with an added vindictiveness.

Malcomson felt amazed, and seizing the poker from the hearth ran at it to kill it. Before, however, he could strike it, the rat, with a squeak that sounded like the concentration of hate, jumped upon the floor, and, running up the rope of the alarm bell, disappeared in the darkness beyond the range of the green-shaded lamp. Instantly, strange to say, the noisy scampering of the rats in the wainscoat began again.

The story is too good to disclose in further condensation for it has a dimension all its own. Like the greatest of horror stories, it is rendered straight, like the report of an accident or the committal to paper of a nightmare while it is still livid in the mind. His use of rats to enhance the reader's fear is brilliant – creatures we know to be real and commonplace, but strangely sinister. The setting of the lonely house is of no importance here; it is a product of Bram's imagination, but 'The Burial of the Rats', equally uncanny, was inspired by his early visits to Paris. It is set among the endless dust-heaps that lie outside the town at Montrouge: 'In this year I was very much in love with a young lady who, though she returned my passion, so far yielded to the wishes of her parents that she had promised not to see me or correspond with me for a year.' Could this be an oblique reference to 'Miss Henry'?

Bram writing in the first person, loses his way until he finds a dilapidated shanty occupied by an old woman, and asks the direction:

> The place was full of all sorts of curious objects of lumber, and of many things that I wished far away. In one corner was a heap of rags which seemed to move from the number of vermin it contained, and in the other a heap of bones whose odour was something shocking. Every now and then, glancing at the heaps, I could see the gleaming eyes of some of the rats which infested the place. These loathsome objects were bad enough, but what looked even more dreadful was an old butcher's axe with an iron handle stained with clots of blood leaning up against the wall on the right side. Still, these things did not give me much concern. The talk of the two old people was so fascinating that I stayed on and on, till the evening came and the dust heaps threw dark shadows over the vales between them.

The narrator conveys his terror to the reader. He continues:

> After a time I began to grow uneasy. I could not tell how or why, but somehow I did not feel satisfied. Uneasiness is an instinct and means warning. The psychic faculties are often the sentries of the intellect, and when they sound alarm the reason begins to act, although perhaps not consciously.
>
> This was so with me. I began to bethink me where I was and by what surrounded, and to wonder how I should fare in case I should be attacked; and then the thought suddenly burst upon me, although without any overt cause, that I was in danger.

'Uneasiness is an instinct and means warning': Bram Stoker was a master of *unease*.

'The Secret of the Growing Gold', in which the hair of a murdered woman continues to grow until it finally traps the murderer, her husband, is no more far-fetched than 'The Judge's

House' but infinitely less compelling. A third story succeeds: 'The Squaw', a straightforward horrific narrative, set in Nuremberg Castle. A young couple, who could be Bram and Florence, are joined by an American with the unlikely name of Elias P. Hutcheson, from Isthmian City, Bleeding Gulch, Maple Tree Country, Neb.

Looking down from a high parapet, he sees a cat playing with her kitten in the old moat sixty feet below and decides to give them a surprise by dropping a pebble beside them. The woman protests: 'You might hit the dear little thing!' 'Not me, ma'am' said Elias P. 'Why, I'm as tender as a Maine cherry-tree. Lord, bless ye – I wouldn't hurt the poor pooty little critter more'n I'd scalp a baby. An' you may bet your variegated socks on that!' It is the American dialect that takes the punishment this time.

Inevitable the joke misfires and the stone plumps on the kitten's head, shattering its brains on the ground:

The black cat cast a swift upward glance, and we saw her eyes like green fire fixed an instant on Elias P. Hutcheson; and then her attention was given to the kitten, which lay still with just a quiver of her tiny limbs, whilst a thin red stream trickled from a gaping wound. With a muffled cry, such as a human being might give, she bent over the kitten licking its wounds and moaning. Suddenly she seemed to realise that it was dead, and again threw her eyes up at us. I shall never forget the sight, for she looked the perfect incarnation of hate. Her green eyes blazed with lurid fire, and the white, sharp teeth seemed to almost shine through the blood which dabbled her mouth and whiskers. She gnashed her teeth, and her claws stood out stark and at full length on every paw. Then she made a wild rush up the wall as if to reach us, but when the momentum ended fell back, and further added to her horrible appearance for she fell on the kitten, and rose with her black fur smeared with its brains and blood.

They go inside the castle to the ancient torture chamber where the American is particularly intrigued by the 'Iron Virgin', and insists on standing inside it so that he can imagine the victim's anguish as the other half closes slowly, with the lethal spikes that will puncture his body.

The custodian must have had in him some of the blood of his predecessors in that ghastly tower, for he worked the engine with a deliberate and excruciating slowness which after five minutes, in which the outer edge of the door had not moved half as many inches, began to overcome Amelia [the English woman]. I saw her lips whiten, and felt her hold upon my arm relax. I looked around an instant for a place whereon to lay her, and when I looked at her again found that her eye had become fixed on the side of the Virgin. Following its direction I saw the black cat crouching out of sight. Her green eyes shone like danger lamps in the gloom of the place, and their colour was heightened by the blood which still smeared her coat and reddened her mouth. I cried out:

'The cat! look out for the cat!' for even then she sprang out before the engine. At this moment she looked like a triumphant demon. Her eyes blazed with ferocity, her hair bristled out till she seemed twice her normal size and her tail lashed about as does a tiger's when the quarry is before it. Elias P. Hutcheson when he saw her was amused, and his eyes positively sparkled with fun.

Amelia faints and the narrator clutches hold of her. He sees the black cat crouching, ready to spring, and jumps up to turn the animal out:

But at that instant, with a sort of hellish scream, she hurled herself, not as we expected at Hutcheson, but straight at the face of the custodian. Her claws seemed to be tearing wildly as one sees in the Chinese drawings of the dragon rampant, and as I looked I saw one of them light on the poor man's eye, and actually tear through it and down his cheek, leaving a wide band of red where the blood seemed to spurt from every vein.

With a yell of sheer terror which came quicker than even his sense of pain, the man leaped back, dropping as he did so the rope which held the iron door. I jumped for it, but was too late, for the cord ran like lightning through the pulley-block, and the heavy mass fell forward from its own weight.

As the door closed I caught a glimpse of our poor companion's face. He seemed frozen with terror. His eyes stared with a horrible anguish as if dazed, and no sound came from his lips.

And then the spikes did their work.

The story ends with the cat sitting on the American's head, purring as she licks the blood which trickles from the sockets of his eyes.

'I think no one will call me cruel,' says the narrator, 'because I seized one of the executioner's old swords and shore her in two as she sat.'

But the cat retains the reader's sympathy, or mine at least.

'The Squaw' was inspired by a visit that Bram made to Nuremberg in 1885 with Henry Irving and Ellen Terry, to gather atmosphere for the production of *Faust* which opened at the Lyceum on 19 December, where it proved one of the theatre's triumphs, with a total of 577 performances. In October 1886, Bram sailed for New York to arrange for the American tour of *Faust* and when this opened he was joined by Florence, who had been hysterical throughout the voyage, largely owing to a previous experience when she had been shipwrecked with Noel crossing the channel from Newhaven to Dieppe. They spent twelve hours in a ship's boat, then in a lifeboat, and finally in a trawler from Fécamp where they were at last landed safely. Her telegram to London was mislaid and for two days Bram was uncertain if his wife and child had drowned. After this, the Atlantic was too great an ordeal for her. But Cruden Bay was now the tranquil holiday home to which they returned year after year, Florence playing golf on the spacious course, while Bram paced the sands and plotted his novels.

He completed *The Watter's Mou* in the summer of 1894, writing in the Kilmarnock visitors' book, 'Second visit – delighted with everything and everybody and hope to come again.' It was published in 1895, as a companion volume to Conan Doyle's *The Parasite*, and received faint praise from the *Athenaeum*: 'The chief defect of the book, inevitable perhaps from the author's associations, is a tendency to melodramatic and stagey writing in some of the speeches and situations.'

The Shoulder of Shasta, also published that year, was dismissed with contempt: 'This story will not increase his literary reputation nor appeal to many readers . . . This want of maturity and a sense of humour may be due to haste, for the book bears the stamp of being roughly and carelessly put together. Mr Stoker can probably do much better than this.'

Bram returned to Cruden Bay. And wrote *Dracula*.

Part Two

CHAPTER NINE

They Believed in Vampires

Why should anyone believe in such a weird superstition as vampirism? Why should anyone believe that corpses rise from their coffins at night to suck the blood of the living? Yet they did. And have done so from the beginning of time all over the world. Legends reach back to Assyria and Babylonia. In China, the family guarded the corpse at night in case a dog or a cat jumped over it, which would transform the body into a vampire. In Greece, where vampirism was prevalent, they had a word for it: *Vrukalakos,* a vampire who resuscitates the dead and sends them out to feast on the living. Anyone with red hair was suspect. In 1717, the French botanist Joseph de Tournefort stated: 'Throughout the whole Archipelago there is no Orthodox Greek who does not firmly believe that the devil is able to re-energise and re-vitalise dead bodies.'

'The blood is the life' wrote Bram Stoker in *Dracula,* and vampirism is linked inextricably with the drinking of blood. In Mexico, Aztecs poured the blood of their victims into the mouths of their idols; in India, Rajahs drank the blood from severed heads. In Africa, blood has been a constant feature in tribal rites up to and including Mau Mau. I do not refer to the Masai who insert a tube in the neck of a living animal and drink its warm blood, enabling it to keep on living; that is a separate way of life. But the Leopard Men of the Belgian Congo come closer to the legend. My father described a conversation with the Governor of Stanleyville in *Behind God's Back*:

The Governor put his hands on either side of his throat, and gave a jerk.

'Like that!' he said. 'You find the woman with these five cuts across her throat; it is the mark of the Leopard Men.

Her jugular has been severed. Her breasts have always been cut off; the Leopard Men eat them.'

'Oh, impossible!'

The Governor pointed towards the reports on his desk: 'In 1938, 400 native women were killed around Wamba. One Leopard Man, caught, took the white police to 38 dead bodies, all with their breasts cut off, and their hearts cut out. The Leopard Men had eaten them. *Who* knows *what* goes on: the district is full of dead bodies!'

Primitive beliefs were carried straight across the Atlantic, with the slave trade from French Africa, to the island of Haiti. By 1750, 30,000 slaves were landed every year and a strange blend of primitive religion evolved, echoing the past. Folk memory and tribal rite, and even, despite the fear and hatred of their French Colonial masters, the influence of Catholicism, came together in Voodoo, a religion redolent of superstition, including vampires and werewolves, and their own 'living dead' – the Zombie.

But vampirism is not peculiar to the remoter parts of Europe or distant, darker landscapes. In America, as late as 1874, a Mr Rose of Rhode Island dug up his daughter and burnt her heart because he was convinced she was draining the life blood from the rest of the family. Closer to home, there have been reports of vampires in England, Ireland and Scotland. These are usually apocryphal, passed off by imaginative writers as fact. The Scottish peasant Sawney Bean existed, and was executed in 1435, but he was a cannibal rather than a vampire.

The most famous case in England is that of the Croglin Grange vampire, told by a Captain Fisher to Augustus Hare, who included the account in *Story of My Life*. There is no such place as Croglin Grange, but there *is* a farmhouse called Croglin Low Hall, a mile from the churchyard, which gives the legend some credence. It concerns an intruder, a creature who came scratching at the window of the young girl who, with her two brothers, had become the new tenant of the Grange. The glass was broken, a long bony finger turned the handle, more bony fingers dragged her head over the bed and she was bitten in the throat. Her screams brought her brothers but the 'thing' escaped. When she had recovered from the shock, after convalescence in Switzerland, her normal life was resumed, and the winter passed peacefully until yet another night when there came 'scratch, scratch, scratch' upon the window, and the same 'hideous brown face'. This time the brothers arrived as the creature scuttled across the lawn and shot it in the leg. The next day a trail of blood was followed to a nearby family vault which was opened. There, brown and mummified, was the same face that had looked through the window, on a body with recent pistol shots in the leg. They burnt it.

I have heard people recount this story as gospel truth, read in some newspaper, though they have forgotten the date.

There seems to be no country that has not had its own case of vampirism, but the natural home of the species was Eastern Europe, where they abounded. Vampirism was a part of life and death. A distinguished Victorian surgeon and expert on the subject, Dr Herbert Mayo, wrote that vampirism 'spread like a pestilence through Slavia and Wallachia in the middle of the 18th Century – causing numerous deaths and disturbing all the land with fear of the mysterious visitors against which no one felt himself secure.'

Don Calmet, one of the great historians on the subject, wrote the following in 1746:

> We are told that dead men ... return from their tombs, are heard to speak, walk about ... injure both men and animals whose blood they drain ... making them sick and finally causing death ... Nor can the men deliver themselves unless they dig the corpses up ... and drive a sharp stake through these bodies, cut off the heads, tear out the hearts; or else they burn the bodies to ashes. It seems impossible not to subscribe to the prevailing belief that these apparitions do actually come forth from their graves.

In spite of this last remark, Calmet remained sceptical. Montague Summers opened *The Vampire his Kith and Kin* with this line: 'In all the darkest pages of the malign supernatural there is no more terrible tradition than that of the Vampire, a pariah even among demons'. Then there is the surprising statement by Jean Jacques Rousseau:

'If ever there was in the world a warranted and proven history, it is that of vampires: nothing is lacking, official reports, testimonials of persons of standing, of surgeons, of clergyman, of judges; the judicial evidence is all-embracing.'

Even today, writing in *Crime* (1974), Colin Wilson agrees:

'There *must* have been a reason that these vampire stories suddenly caught the imagination of Europe. Obviously *something* happened, and it seems unlikely that it was pure imagination.'

Much of the confusion is due to the looseness of the definition which embraces two types of vampire – the live man who drinks the blood of others, and the 'living, mischievous and murderous' dead body. It is the idea of the vampire as the *living* dead that is so incredible. Yet there is a weight of apparent evidence that seems to support it. A typical 'case history' was recorded in Yugoslavia in 1732, when a deputation was sent from Belgrade to investigate the report of a vampire who was attacking a family in a remote village. The qualifications of this deputation are formidable: it consisted of civil and military officials; a Public Prosecutor; a lieutenant of Prince Alexander of Wurtemberg's regiment; twenty-four soldiers, and various 'respected persons'. Prince Alexander even paid a visit himself.

The deputation discovered that the vampire had killed three of his own nieces and nephews and one brother in the last fortnight. He had started on his fifth victim, a beautiful young niece whose blood he had sucked twice, when he was interrupted.

As dusk fell, the deputation went to the grave accompanied by a crowd of villagers. The vampire had been buried three years earlier; now they opened his grave and found the man apparently as healthy as anyone present – his hair, his fingernails, his teeth, and his eyes (which were half-open) were all still attached. His heart was beating – a detail which is mentioned casually but is surely sensational.

As the heart was pierced by an iron bar, a white fluid burst out – mixed with blood. The head was cut off with an axe and after the body had been buried with quicklime, the girl who had been attacked began to recover.

Another familiar story, recorded by Augustin Calmet in that same period, concerned a Hungarian soldier who was billeted in a house near the border. One evening at supper he saw a stranger join them at table and noticed that his host and the rest of the family seemed frightened. The next morning his host was dead and the soldier was told that the stranger was the man's father, dead for ten years, who had sat down beside him and had both announced and caused his death.

He reported this to his regiment and the family were questioned by officers, a surgeon and an auditor, to whom they confirmed the soldier's story. The corpse of the vampire was exhumed and he looked like a man who had just died – 'his blood like that of a living man'. The Count de Cabreras, captain of the regiment, ordered the vampire's head to be cut off, after which the body was laid to rest again in its tomb.

While admitting that the apparitions he described might have been a delusion, Augustin Calmet consistently quoted men of repute:

I have heard from the late Monsieur de Vassimont, Chief Financial Adviser in Bar, that when he was sent to Moravia, by the late Duke Leopold of Lorraine to mind the affairs of his brother, Monseigneur Prince Charles, Bishop of Olmutz and Osnaburgh, he was told that it was common knowledge in these parts that a man, dead for some time past, might suddenly make an appearance at a meal and sit down among his friends without a word, nodding his head perhaps at one of the company, who would then invariably sicken and die a few days later. This occurrence was confirmed by several persons, among them a priest, who had seen it happen more than once.

The bishops and priests of the country consulted Rome about these singular occurrences, but they received no reply, for it was held that they were delusions or popular superstitions. Later they were advised to exhume the bodies of the men who had haunted them and to burn them, or destroy them in some other manner. Thus they were delivered from the importunities of the apparitions which are now much less common in these parts; so said the priest.

Calmet referred to a book about the apparitions, printed in 1706 and written by an 'expert in law' who examined 'the facts of the case scrupulously'. He described how a woman was buried with the normal procedure in a remote village. Four days later, the villagers heard an uproar and saw an apparition that took the form first of a dog, then of a man: 'striking them, catching them by the throat, squeezing them in the stomach till they nearly suffocated; they were bruised all over and reduced to a pitiable condition, pale, thin and exhausted. The apparition attacked animals as well, and cows were discovered bruised and half-dead; sometimes they would be tied together by the tail. The horses would be found lying as though they were weak with exhaustion, heated, sweating, and gasping, covered with lather as though they had run a hard race. These calamities lasted for several months.'

As no vampiric exorcism was needed before the 'calamities' ceased for good, this suggests an outbreak of some epidemic unknown at the time.

Another case concerning a Hungarian soldier, Arnold Paul, was investigated and witnessed by regimental surgeons and 'respected local inhabitants', and was reported to the Imperial Council of War in Vienna. Paul was killed when a cart fell on top of him but he returned from the dead thirty days later, attacking four people who died immediately 'in the manner that was traditionally ascribed to vampirism'. Then it was remembered that the soldier had spoken of a vampire near the Turkish Serbian border which had attacked him earlier in his military service. Believing the superstition that victims become vampires themselves after death, he thought he had cured himself by eating earth from the vampire's grave and rubbing himself with its blood. Evidently this precaution failed, for when his body was exhumed 'he showed all the marks of an arch-vampire. His body was flushed; his hair, nails and beard had grown, and his veins were full of liquid blood that splashed all over the winding-sheet.' The governor of the district, who knew the 'drill', ordered that a stake be thrust through the body, whereupon it uttered the familiar shriek. Then the head was cut off and the body burnt, and the same procedure was applied to his four recent victims, in case they had become activated too. Unusually, all these precautions failed: five years later, within the space of three months, seventeen people died of vampirism. One woman woke shrieking in the night to say that her son Millo, who had died nine weeks earlier, had tried to strangle her in her sleep. She died three days later, but her accusation was followed up and Millo's body exhumed. He was found to be a vampire and the governors of the district demanded an inquiry into why the previous precautions had failed. It was discovered that Arnold Paul had attacked animals, as well as his four human victims, and that the 'new vampires had eaten' them. All the recent dead were exhumed and found to show familiar signs of vampirism. They were staked, decapitated, burnt, and their ashes were thrown into the river. This seems to have been the end of the outbreak.

Calmet quotes another, 'most remarkable,' case which was vouched for by Michel Raufft, the German author of *De Masticatione Mortuorum in Tumulis*. This concerns a Hungarian who returned ten weeks after his burial and shook some villagers so violently by the throat that they died within twenty-four hours. He claimed nine victims in eight days and his widow declared that he had appeared in front of her and demanded his shoes, which frightened her so much that she left the village.

The remaining villagers applied to the Emperor's representative for leave to have the body exhumed and burnt, and when he showed some reluctance they threatened to abandon the village. The official granted their request and arrived at the village with the curé. When the body was exposed there was no overpowering smell and it seemed intact, apart from the tip of the nose, which was withered. Hair was abundant; new fingernails had grown; and new skin appeared beneath the old. Blood was noticed on his mouth, which convinced the villagers that he had sucked his victims to death, so they seized a sharp stake and plunged it into his breast, whereupon 'a quantity of fresh scarlet blood issued, and from the nose and mouth as well; more issued from that part of his body which decency forbids me to name.'

In quoting such cases, Calmet does not confirm them. He was sceptical compared with the credulous Raufft or Summers, and is one of the few historians to show sympathy for the innocent victims of the superstition, those who recovered after their burial, a logical explanation as I shall show. Calmet concludes:

It suffices to explain how vampires have been dragged from the grave and made to speak, shout, scream and bleed: they were still alive. They were killed by decapitation, perforation or burning, and this has been a great wrong; for the allegation that they returned to haunt and destroy the living has never been sufficiently proved to authorize such inhumanity, or to permit innocent beings to be dishonoured and ignominiously killed as a result of wild and unproved accusations. For the stories told of these apparitions, and all the distress caused by these supposed vampires, are totally without solid proof. I am not surprised that the Sorbonne has condemned the bloody and violent retribution wrought on these corpses; but it is astonishing that the magistrates and secular bodies have not employed their authority and legal force to put an end to it.

Ever impartial, Calmet adds:

This is a mysterious and difficult matter, and I leave bolder and more proficient minds to resolve it.

⁶ It is obvious that Bram Stoker learnt of such stories during his research; he could hardly have envisaged that they would persist into the twentieth century.

I have spoken to both the Coroner and the policeman involved in a most unusual case. It took place in January 1973 in Stoke-on-Trent; it is hard to imagine a place more distant from the forests of Transylvania, for it is a blasted landscape of rubbish and rubble in the foreground and slag heaps and chimneys beyond, a landscape devoured greedily by man and then discarded.

Yet there is one avenue of houses with a hint of former grandeur, known simply as The Villas, and it was to Number Three of these that a young, fresh-faced policeman called PC Pye was summoned one night to investigate the death of a man. The house was, and still is, used as lodgings for East Europeans and the man in question was a Pole, Demitrious Myiciura, who had come to England after the last war in which he lost everything, including his family. PC Pye was bewildered when he entered the man's bedroom. There was no electric light bulb so the scene was gradually revealed by the beam from his torch.

Frederick Hails, the City Coroner, adjusted his monocle and read me PC Pye's report of 'a sudden death of which the cause was unknown'. The pathologist said the man had swallowed a pickled onion, 'which I thought was rather unusual. Never mind, these things do happen, people do bolt their food and die.' PC Pye was unconvinced; he had examined the room and suspected that 'this man believed in vampires and was frightened of vampires and took various precautions to stop the vampire from getting at him. He had the room strewn with salt, in what the PC described as a ritual fashion. He had a bag of salt between his legs resting on his testicles, he had garlic round the room and, in addition, he had outside on the window-sill an inverted bowl covering human excreta and also garlic in the middle of it. Anyhow this man believed thoroughly that these vampires existed and therefore he took his way round it.' Mr Hails lowered the report and removed the monocle: 'Now, as you probably know, salt and garlic are vampire repellants. He mixed salt with his urine in various containers and outside, with his excreta, garlic – the idea being that the vampire would be attracted to this magnificent feed and would then swallow it, on the principle of rat-bait, and would be poisoned by the garlic.

'To make assurance doubly sure he put his garlic into his mouth and unfortunately he choked on it. And died.'

'So it wasn't a pickled onion after all?'

'At first the pathologist thought it was, but we had a little talk about it. It was quite obviously a clove of garlic. After all, my wife was half French, and I can recognise garlic.'

'Would you say this is the most unusual case you have come across?'

'I've been a lawyer for a long time dealing with courtroom cases. I've seen all sorts of depravity, all sorts of nonsense, but I can visualise what was behind this man. He was back there in Poland, he'd had a lot of evil happen to him. All right, I'll cling to the evil, I will cling to *something*. He happened to believe in vampires. I am convinced after this inquest that this man was genuinely afraid of vampires.'

And, in a macabre fashion, they *did* get him in the end.

In 1849, a crowd of soldiers and policemen waited in the Paris cemetery of Montparnasse to catch 'Le Vampyr', as a persistent intruder had become known. In the darkness they heard the sound of a coffin being opened, a shape was seen and shots fired. 'Le Vampyr' escaped over the wall, but a trail of blood was traced to a Sergeant Bertrand, who claimed that he assaulted the corpses of women when he was in a trance. In spite of the widespread panic he had caused, Bertrand was sentenced to only one year's imprisonment because there was no murder of any *living* person.

A startling modern parallel took place in the early hours of 13 March 1970, when a crowd of a hundred vampire hunters assembled outside the gates of Highgate Cemetery. They were led by a Mr Blood, described as a 'vampire expert and history teacher', abetted by David Farrant who spoke to the newspapers of his plan 'to stake the vampire through the heart with a wooden cross'. Farrant, who was twenty-eight years old and the self-styled high priest and President of the British Occult Society, was eventually brought to trial. The jury at the Old Bailey heard of naked girls who danced on desecrated graves, which prompted the judge to remark that it must have been extremely chilly, in October. They listened to reports of an alleged seven-foot vampire hovering over the graves and were told that iron stakes had been thrust through mutilated corpses after the tombs had been smashed in. A police inspector visited the home of one of the witnesses and found salt strewn around the windows and the doorway, and a wooden cross under the pillow. Voodoo dolls with pins through their chests had been sent to people who were going to testify for the prosecution.

Farrant was charged with interfering and offering indignity to the remains of a body 'to the great scandal and disgrace of religion, decency and morality'. He was sentenced to four years and eight months' imprisonment.

His obsession sounds paranoiac. Yet just around the corner from Highgate Cemetery, at St Saviour's Vicarage in Eton Road, there is a man who takes reports of vampires seriously. I asked him how he would describe a vampire.

'A sort of half-animal, half-human – if one could put it like that,' replied the Rev. Christopher Neil-Smith.

'Now most people would say that it's all in the mind, wouldn't they?'

'Yes, but I think that's a very naïve interpretation.'

'But it could be, couldn't it?' I pressed him.

'Well, I suppose it could be, but then there's all the evidence which points to the contrary.'

I asked Neil-Smith, who is the author of *The Exorcist and the Possessed*, if he had experienced a specific case of vampirism.

'Oh yes, more than one,' he replied calmly. 'The one that particularly strikes me is that of a woman who showed me the marks on her wrists which appeared at night and definitely showed where blood had been taken . . . the marks were there in the morning. And there's no apparent reason why this should have occurred.'

'What sort of marks?'

'Well,' and he spoke with deliberation,' the marks were almost like those of an animal. Something like scratching.'

I asked if she could have done this herself.

'Well, she was a married woman and there was no evidence that the husband . . . such things *did* occur at night.'

'And she came to you for help?'

'She came when she felt her blood was being sucked.'

Neil-Smith performed an exorcism and the marks cleared up afterwards.

He gave another example of a man whose brother had died as a young boy and who had always felt as if his life-blood had been sucked from him after his brother's death, as if the spirit of his brother was feeding on him, literally feeding on his life-blood; but when an exorcism was performed he felt a release as if new blood was running in his veins. I suggested this was psychological and that the man felt guilt or some other strong emotion regarding his brother. Neil-Smith was firm that there was no disharmony; at first it had not even been clear to him that it was his brother, there was just this sense of having his whole life sucked away.

Neil-Smith told me of a third case, a businessman from South America who had shown him the marks where blood had been sucked from him at night. I suggested that the South American might have had an exciting sexual night out somewhere, but Neil-Smith stressed that the man was intelligent enough to recognise the abnormal, 'He thought he had been attacked by a vampire.'

'And did you believe it?' I asked.

'I must admit at that time I was a bit suspicious, I'll be quite honest. Then when he showed evidence I came to realise this was obviously correct.'

'Then you would say you do believe there is such a thing as vampirism?'

'Yes.'

Christopher Neil-Smith is an interesting man to talk to. I have no doubt that he is sincere when he insists that it is 'not all in the mind'.

CHAPTER TEN

Tears from a Dead Man's Eyes

In the spring of 1974, I spoke to a handsome gipsy woman known as Tinka in the valley of Curtea de Arges in Romania. Her father had died when she was a young girl and when the family came to dress his body for the funeral they found it was still soft and assumed that *rigor mortis* had not taken possession. This news raced through the village and the fear of a vampire in their midst was so real that the villagers protected themselves by plunging a wooden stake through her father's heart. In fact, *rigor mortis* is only a temporary state, but it may well have been that the wretched man was still alive: one of those innocent victims of superstition pitied by Dom Calmet.

There are several logical explanations for belief in vampires. Legends proliferated in times of ignorance, when people seized on any explanation for things they could not understand, when medical knowledge was scant and there was no electric light to dispel the shadows.

Dennis Wheatley has told me of a time when beggars were so destitute that they broke into graveyards and slept in tombs and mausoleums by day, emerging at night to scavenge for food and rob unsuspecting people. It is not surprising that rumours of vampires spread rapidly and with wild exaggeration if they were glimpsed in the darkness, rising from their sepulchral homes.

But of all the explanations for vampirism, premature burial is the most convincing. It is not uncommon for people to be buried alive. Early in 1973, people were shocked by the report from a Birmingham hospital of a 'corpse' which was being dissected for a kidney transplant when it was discovered that the man was alive. If we can make such mistakes today, imagine the confusion a hundred and more years ago. It has always been difficult to certify the state of death – it has been said that decomposition of the body is the only certainty. Lyall Watson has stated that there is only one reliable sign of death, putrefaction: 'When the bacteria and fungi begin to proliferate in the intestines, they produce a discoloration on the abdomen which starts as grey spots that gradually turn to green and produce a foul smell. Not even this however is foolproof, because certain diseases of the skin produce markings exactly like these signs of final decay.' He comes to the conclusion that 'It is biologically possible for an individual, in some form and at least for a short while, to survive death.'

Wilkie Collins, and many others, left instructions that every possible precaution should be taken before they were declared dead; they had good reason to do so. At the beginning of this century it is claimed there was one premature burial a week in the United States. One of these was a young lady near Indianapolis who revived after fourteen days of suspended animation. Six doctors had signed her death certificate after making the usual tests. Her young brother was convinced that she was not dead and clung to the body as she was finally removed for burial. In the confusion a bandage around her jaw was loosened and it could be seen that her lips were quivering. 'What do you want, what do you want?' cried the boy. 'Water.' The woman revived and lived to a good old age.

Another American, head matron of a school for orphans, was twice declared dead and each time her body was shrouded until she was resuscitated by friends. The second time, though special precautions were taken, the mistake was only discovered when the undertaker happened to pierce the body with a pin and a drop of blood oozed from the puncture.

A famous thought-reader, Washington Irving Bishop, often relapsed into a cataleptic state for hours on end and once was considered dead until the surgeon's knife at the autopsy revealed that he was alive. There was a similar occurrence with a Grand Inquisitor of Spain while he was being embalmed: his heart was actually brought into view and was seen to beat. At this moment the Cardinal regained consciousness and 'even then had sufficient strength to grasp with his hand the scalpel of the anatomist' before he died for ever.

In Moravia, a postmaster was thought to have died of epilepsy but some years later, when it became necessary to transfer various bodies in the graveyard and this man was disinterred, it was discovered that he had been buried alive. The appalled doctor who had signed the certificate lost his reason.

When coffins were broken into by body-snatchers and grave-robbers, it might be discovered that the body had moved. Sometimes there would be blood around the mouth where the wretched person had bitten himself in anguish. Occasionally the shroud, or even the body itself, seemed to have been eaten in a last desperate attempt to stay alive. More likely it had been gnawed by rats or devoured by insects, but again it is understandable if such revelations gave rise to wild stories.

As for the remarkable preservation of the body, which was frequently reported, this was largely a matter of soil conditions. On the Greek island of Santorini the earth was so volcanic and naturally antiseptic that bodies were found to be intact years after burial, giving rise to the saying 'Send a vampire to Santorini' as we say 'take coals to Newcastle'. Even the length of the teeth is explicable – they do *look* longer after death because the rest of the flesh has shrunk around them.

Graveyard conditions in England were so appalling by the beginning of the last century that the Victorians created their great landscaped cemeteries, like Highgate, with tombs designed by the leading architects of the day. Nunhead was another, referred to in verse in the *Burial Reformer*:

> There was a young man at Nunhead,
> Who awoke in his coffin of lead.
> 'It is cosy enough,'
> He remarked in a huff
> 'But I wasn't aware I was dead.'

If the belief in vampires was a form of mass hysteria, it explains why the legend was particularly strong in times of plague, when people were anxious to dispose of bodies as quickly as possible owing to their fear of infection. Even those who collapsed in a drunken stupor ran the risk of waking to find themselves incarcerated in breathless darkness. After a plague epidemic the country would be weak and nervously depressed, like Germany after the Black Death, when the epidemic of

St Vitus' Dance swept across the country until the dancers dropped from exhaustion.

As early as 1196, William Newburgh recorded a story of a 'lecherous husband', the familiar outcast of society and scapegoat, who returned from his grave to terrify his home town:

> The air became foul and tainted as this fetid and corrupting body wandered abroad, so that a terrible plague broke out and there was hardly a house which did not mourn its dead, and presently the town, which but a little before had been thickly populated, seemed to be well nigh deserted, for those who had survived the pestilence and these hideous attacks hastily removed themselves to other districts lest they also should perish.

Two young men, braver than the rest, traced the living corpse to its grave and cut its head off with a spade so that the red blood gushed out. The time-honoured destruction of the vampire succeeded:

> No sooner had that infernal monster been thus destroyed, than the plague, which had so sorely ravaged the people, entirely ceased, just as if the polluted air was cleansed by the fire which burned up the hellish brute who had infected the whole atmosphere.

There is an obvious parallel with the cholera epidemic described by Charlotte to her young son. This is coincidental, but aspects of Charlotte's experience keep recurring. Two of her stories dealt with typical cases of premature burial. She told Bram of a soldier, Sergeant Callan, who was such a giant that his coffin could not hold him. The undertaker took a hammer to break Callan's legs in order to squeeze him in, but at the first blow the corpse came back to life and the risen Sergeant was seen frequently by Charlotte afterwards.

Another of her stories concerned a man who carried his wife to the hospital on his back, with a red handkerchief tied round her waist to relieve the pain. When he returned to see her, they told him she was dead. It was the practice during the emergency to throw forty or fifty corpses into a large trench and cover them with lime. Searching for his wife to give her a proper burial, he noticed a corner of the red handkerchief and when he removed her body found that she was alive. 'He carried her home and she recovered and lived many years.'

So, in the web of superstition, there is this rational explanation for people rising from their coffins. It is even conceivable that they sought out their relatives, who had put them there in the first place, to gain revenge. There is a flaw in the theory: why would they wish to return to their coffins at the break of day? Surely they would be determined to remain with the living, having made their escape? Even so, ignorance grasped at superstition: anaemia, leukemia, epilepsy, catalepsy were all liable to be misinterpreted as vampirism. Anyone different, be it by reason of a birth-mark, a hare-lip, red hair, even blue eyes – almost any permutation – was suspected as a vampire. And as such they ran the danger of being buried alive, like this man referred to by Dr Herbert Mayo:

When they opened his grave ... his face was found with a colour, and his features made natural sorts of movements, as if the dead man smiled. He even opened his mouth as if he would inhale fresh air. They held the crucifix before him, and called in a loud voice, 'See, this is Jesus Christ who redeemed your soul from hell, and died for you.'

After the sound had acted on his organs of hearing, and he had connected perhaps some ideas with it, tears began to flow from the dead man's eyes. Finally, when after a short prayer for his poor soul, they proceeded to hack off his head, the corpse uttered a screech, and turned and rolled just as if it had been alive – and the grave was full of blood.

Incredibly, in view of the accuracy of his descriptions, Bram Stoker never set foot in Transylvania. His knowledge was gleaned from a Baedeker's guide and hours of research in the library of the British Museum: 'I read that every known superstition in the world is gathered into the horseshoe of the Carpathians, as if it were the centre of some sort of imaginative whirlpool.' One other source might have been *The History of Magic* by the German, Joseph Ennemoser, published in 1854, which referred to Wallachia 'where the blood sucking vampire hovered the longest, a superstition of the most revolting kind'.

There is no doubt that Bram knew of the particular relevance of vampirism to Eastern Europe, and he had the personal advantage of help from another source with undoubted authority: a Hungarian professor with the Stokerish name of Professor Arminius Vambery. I suspect there is a touch of Vambery in the character of Van Helsing.

Vambery was an adventurer. As a young man he travelled through the Middle East in disguise, showing considerable courage, as he was the first to acknowledge. He was accused of a 'desire for vainglory' and was a man of undoubted pomposity. When he took the chair of Oriental Languages at the University of Pesth, he did so 'as a fit reward for my extraordinary struggles in life'. And in *His Life and Adventures, written by himself*, published by Fisher Unwin in 1884, there are delightful moments of self-satisfaction when he describes his success after addressing the Royal Geographical Society:

> No wonder, therefore, that a few weeks sufficed to make my name familiar over the whole of the United Kingdom. London society vied in the manifestations of all kinds of acknowledgement. Invitations to dinner parties and to visit in the country literally poured in upon me, even from persons whom I never saw or met in my life; and it happened frequently that I had to write thirty letters of refusal and acceptance in one day. Infinite was the number of those letters in which I was asked for my likeness or my autograph.

Despite his vanity, his reports were received with the greatest respect. Recognised as taking 'an active part in the defence of British interests in Asia', he came into contact with leading politicians who sought his advice: Palmerston greeted him with the remark, 'You must have gone through nice adventures on your way to Bokhara and Samarkand;' Lord Strangford spoke to Vambery in Hungarian – 'nay, even the language of the Gipsies; and what struck me most was his vast information concerning the various literatures and histories of these people. No wonder, therefore, that I felt from the beginning a particular attraction to the learned Viscount, and that he also, as I afterwards had ample opportunity to learn, took a fancy to me and became my most zealous and disinterested supporter in England.'

Vambery had the percipience to point out that the British would insist on treating Eastern problems in European terms and that the Russians achieved greater results with smaller use of men but more skilful diplomacy. For his advice he was awarded with the Commander of the Royal Victorian Order and was received by Edward, Prince of Wales, on 29 September 1888 during the Prince's visit to Pesth.

As a social lion, it was inevitable that Vambery would be entertained by Irving in the Beefsteak Room. This was a revival of the 'Sublime Society of Beefsteaks' started by Sheridan; the room itself had become one of the Lyceum's lumber rooms. Irving had it redecorated, stocked it with fine wines, champagne and brandy, brought in his own chef, and made it the pivot of his social life. There is a happy portrait by Bastien Lepage showing the young Irving as host, raffish and exuberant Ellen Terry, who acted as hostess for the more elaborate dinners, arranged the lighting, making the room dignified but cosy. It was hung with Whistler's portrait of Irving as Philip the Second, and Sargent's of Ellen Terry as Lady Macbeth. The smells and chatter must have tantalised the other actors as they passed by. Martin-Harvey described it as a fine old Gothic Hall – the Gothic of Pugin, no doubt. 'I liked to picture the great man here, seated at the head of the long table, lighted with candles and loaded with good things supplied by Gunter, a great fire crackling . . . his clear-cut alabaster profile outlined against the sombre oaken panelling . . . But I must fly these hallowed precincts before I am caught by the ubiquitous Stoker.'

The Beefsteak Room was one of Stoker's perquisites, though the all-night dinners eventually left him exhausted. Sometimes it was the scene for discussions until dawn between Irving, Stoker and Loveday on present and future productions. As I have mentioned, they entertained the leading personalities of Europe – the Prince of Wales; Lord Randolph Churchill and his 'beautiful wife'; Sarah Bernhardt; Alfred Gilbert, who took the whole Beefsteak party to drink at the fountains of Piccadilly before his statue of Eros. Irving, able to relax after the performance, was alive with mischief: when someone repeated an unflattering comment he replied, 'Ah yes. But they were *friends*. One must not expect too much from friends.' And, as always, Stoker basked in Irving's reflection. It was here that he met the explorer Richard Burton, who had written *Vikran and the Vampire* and shared many of Bram's enthusiasms.

Vambery was entertained at the Beefsteak Room on 30 April 1890, after a performance of *The Dead Heart*. Irving was 'delighted with him' and Bram asked if he had ever felt fear:

'Fear of death – no; but I am afraid of torture. I protected myself against that, however!'

'However did you manage that?'

'I had always a poison pill, fastened here, where the lappet of my coat now is . . .'

Bram saw him again, two years later, when Vambery received a degree from Dublin University, and enthused: 'He shone out as a star.'

There is good reason to assume that it was the Hungarian professor who told Bram, for the first time, of the name of Dracula.

CHAPTER ELEVEN

Dracula the Impaler

There have been a number of human monsters in history who may be described as 'vampires': among the most notorious were the Marshall of France, Gilles de Rais, and the Hungarian Countess Elizabeth Bathory.

De Rais (or de Retz) was brought to trial in 1440 for the torture of more than two hundred children, most of them boys. He was obsessed by the idea of blood, and used to order his servants to stab the children in the jugular vein so their blood would shoot over him. At his civil trial, one of his servants testified that while the children were bleeding to death 'he would sometimes masturbate on them until they were dead, and sometimes he did this after they had died while their bodies were still warm'. He was accused of sitting on the bowels of a boy and drinking his blood as he was dying.

Elizabeth Bathory was a lesbian counterpart with a blood fetish that accounted for the murder of six hundred and fifty girls, who were tortured in the dungeons below her castle. Her vain excuse was the hope that her complexion would be improved if she bathed in their blood. The macabre beauty baths had little effect. Finally, there was such an outcry over the disappearance of so many local girls that she was brought to trial in 1611. Because of her eminence, she was imprisoned in her castle, where she died three years later. The Lord Palantine described her as 'the blood thirsty and blood sucking Godless woman'.

Dracula was their equal.

There *was* such a person. Dracula, Prince Vlad Vth of Wallachia, lived from 1431 to 1476. It is possible to imagine Bram Stroker's relish as he seized upon the name, exploring the menace as it rolled off his tongue – *Drac-ula* – the only one of his eighteen books with a single-word title.

Vlad was bloodthirsty, even for his own time. He made mothers eat their babies; when his mistress claimed she was pregnant, he had her split open to prove it; he invited the beggars of one town to a sumptuous feast, then locked the doors and set fire to the place with the justification that this prevented plague and eliminated inferior stock. When some visiting ambassadors neglected to doff their turbans in his presence, he ordered that they should be nailed to their heads – a lesson in good manners that was emulated by Ivan the Terrible.

He was known as Vlad Tepes (*tzepa* meaning spike), owing to his penchant for impaling his enemies on tall stakes – an excruciating torture as the man was thrust downwards on to the sharp, oiled point. Gradually, his own weight would force this upwards, slowly splitting him apart until, after several hours, the stake pierced so deeply that he died. Seldom can death have been so welcome.

A print shows Vlad eating a meal beneath the impaled, with a nonchalance that is almost admirable. When one of his boyars dared to comment on the surrounding screams and smells, Vlad had him impaled also, on a taller stake – 'You live up there, yonder, where the stench cannot reach you.'

Admittedly, impalement was an effective warning to his enemies, and was a practice learnt from the Turks themselves when Vlad was their prisoner as a boy. There is a story that he bribed his guards into bringing him small birds which he would mutilate and then impale on sticks in neat rows. If true, this was echoed by Stoker in his powerful characterisation of the lunatic Renfield, who caught flies to feed spiders to feed birds which he devoured himself.

Undoubtedly, Vlad was a great warrior. It is claimed that after one battle in 1456 he impaled 20,000 Turks. After another victory over the Infidel Turk, the bells of Christendom rang out in celebration as far off as the Island of Rhodes.

In Romania, Vlad is regarded as a national hero; it is said that he made Wallachia so safe that it was possible to leave a purse in the middle of the road and no one would touch it. With Vlad hovering around, it is surprising that anyone *dared* to walk in the middle of the road. His cruelty is justified now as the necessity of 'a political genius' and 'the only way of rendering his opponents defenceless', and it is said that he became 'the victim of the intrigues of a clique, after which he was defamed for ever'.

In 1458, Vlad Dracula built the citadel of Bucharest, one reason for the special respect he receives today. In his time there was no such country as Romania. The land consisted of the three states of Transylvania, Moldavia and Wallachia. The latter were united in 1859 and joined by Transylvania after the First World War to form the new country of Romania. Mention has been made already of Wallachia as the land 'where the blood sucking vampire hovered the longest'. But Vlad Dracula was no vampire. Blood-thirsty in the extreme, capable of appalling sadism, he was nevertheless *not* a vampire. The present, incorrect identification of the historical and fictional Draculas is the cause of much confusion in Romania today.

There is just enough resemblance to the factual truth in Stoker's novel to complicate matters and blur the difference. It has been suggested that Stoker based the Count on his historical namesake, and there is indeed a resemblance between the early woodcuts, the Innsbruck portrait of Vlad, and Stoker's description of the fictional count:

> His face was strong – very strong – aquiline, with high bridge of the thin nose and peculiarly arched nostrils; with lofty domed forehead, and hair growing scantily round the temples, but profusely elsewhere. His eyebrows were massive, almost meeting over the nose, and with bushy hair that seemed to curl in its profusion. The mouth, so far as I could see under the heavy moustache, was fixed and rather cruel looking, with peculiarly sharp white teeth . . .

Stoker might have seen the Lubeck print of 1485; possibly it was included in the exhibition on Eastern Europe, displayed in London at that time; even the white, sharp teeth seem to be showing.

There is controversy over the name of Dracula, which some claim means 'Son of the Devil'. But *Dracul* also means dragon, which is more convincing, as Vlad's father was a member of the Order Draconis founded by the Holy Roman Emperor Sigismund (also King of Hungary), which sported a crest with a

E

cross and a dragon below. Tyrant though he was, even Vlad was more likely to describe himself as 'Son of the Dragon' than 'Son of the Devil'. Dracula simply means son of Dracul.

People have accused Stoker of 'getting his geography just a bit wrong' and of being 'far from accurate'. The late Professor Nandris wrote: 'Bram Stoker fused the historical information and confounded it in such a way that it is not possible to unravel the various sources.' However, these critics are assuming that Count Dracula is based literally on Vlad Tepes.

In a short historical passage in *Dracula*, the Count does refer to his ancestry: 'We Szekelys have a right to be proud, for in our veins flows the blood of many brave races who fought as the lion fights.' Again, referring to the moment of shame 'when the flags of Wallach went down beneath the Crescent', the Count mentions his great ancestor: 'One of my own race who as Viovode crossed the Danube and beat the Turk on his own ground! This was a Dracula indeed!' The next passage, with a reference to a further Dracula – 'that other of his race who in a latter age again brought his forces over the great river into Turkey land' – is confusing only if you expect to find it historically accurate. Count Dracula dismisses the charges of cruelty: 'They said he thought only of himself. Bah! what good are peasants without a leader? Where ends the war without a brain and heart to conduct it?'

Even a cursory assessment will show that Stoker seized on the name of Dracula, together with a vague impression of the background, and that was all. The confusion of fact with fiction is aggravated by the so-called 'Dracula Tours', on which horror addicts land in Romania, eager to follow in Jonathan Harker's footsteps, and are directed instead to the ruins left by Vlad Tepes. They are being shown the *wrong* Dracula!

'It is a delicate affair,' said the Romanian Minister for Propaganda, when I arrived in Bucharest for the first time in 1972. The other men round the table sighed, and nodded their heads in grave agreement. It was eleven o'clock on a Monday morning and the streets outside were shimmering already with the heat that would descend all too heavily in the afternoon. The walls of the office, in the *Carpati* headquarters of National Tourism, were decorated with maps and photographs hung there for my benefit. I was being welcomed, with true Romanian hospitality, as Stoker's great-nephew, even though the name of Stoker was comparatively new to them. *Dracula* has never been published there, apart from extracts in a magazine serial in 1928.

The Romanians were only then beginning to realise the immense tourist potential inherent in the Western obsession with *Dracula* – and they were dismayed. They sensed the danger of exploiting Count Dracula at the risk of labelling and libelling their hero Vlad as a vampire; and their fear was justified, as I discovered when I joined the first British 'Dracula Tour', organised by BEA's Sovereign Holidays, in 1974.

BEA's Dracula Tour starts gently with a visit to Lake Snagov, a few miles to the north of Bucharest. Crossing by boat, the tourists land on a small island and are led into the cool shadows of a monastery where Vlad Dracula is supposed to be buried. Inevitably, there are conflicting reports of his death: after his victory over the Ottoman army in 1461 he was defeated by the Turks, who installed their own favourite in his place – his treacherous, effeminate brother, known as Radu the Handsome. Vlad later regained power but it seems that in 1476, after he had been defeated as ruler of Wallachia for the second time, he made a raid behind the Turkish lines disguised as a Turk himself. This final burst of bravery was fatal, for his disguise was all too effective and on his return he was killed by his own men, who failed to recognise him in time.

When Vlad's tomb was opened in 1931 it was found to be empty and rumours spread of a headless skeleton, which would have been correct, for Vlad's head had been severed and sent to the Sultan in Constantinople as proof that the great Impaler was destroyed at last. In fact, the archaeologist Dinu Rosetti found little more than a few rotting bones, but he did unearth a crown of white porcelain with blue stones and golden claws of a type that was awarded to Vlad at a Nuremberg tournament.

Curiously, the 'Dracula Tour' ignores Vlad's main head-quarters in Tirgoviste, a hundred or so kilometres to the West. Today, Tirgoviste displays the typical surging progress of most Romanian towns: building, excavations, new roads in prepara-tion, industry and mud on the outskirts; a couple of rough look-ing restaurant bars, with the usual tables outside, in the centre; and then, unexpectedly, the ancient part of the town which has been scrupulously preserved. Ruinele Palatului, the ruined battlements of Dracula's former palace, is dominated by a sixteenth century tower which overlooks the town and the flocks of children below in cool school uniforms of blue and white, listening to their teacher recounting the glories of Vlad Tepes – though not the gore.

Instead, the travellers mount their coach for the valley of Curtea de Arges and the remains of Poenari Castle, to the north. This is a beige-pink relic when the sun is right, a mountain retreat over a deep gorge. Vlad used to order his noblemen to drag stones to the top which they could hurl at the enemy below, thus starting an avalanche to engulf them. This is echoed in the novel, when the Count tells Jonathan Harker that it was ground

fought over for centuries by the Wallachian, the Saxon and the Turk. Why, there is hardly a foot of soil in all this region that has not been enriched by the blood of men, patriots or invaders. In old days there were stirring times when the Austrian and the Hungarian came in hordes, and the patriots went out to meet them – men and women, the aged and the children too – and waited their coming on the rocks above the passes, that they might sweep destruction on them with their artificial avalanches.

This does not mean that Bram Stoker was trying to retell Vlad's story, but is rather an historical detail gleaned in his research, and included to lend conviction.

Though the fortress proved safe from attack, it was isolated also from supplies and help, as Vlad discovered. Although there was a secret route to another mountain Vlad was captured, this time by Mathias, King of Hungary, and imprisoned for twelve years in what must have been a friendly sort of 'house arrest', since he married the King's sister, Helen Corvinus.

Today's tourists gallantly climb the 1,450 steep steps to the top to find the castle restored, with artificial rock at the base that might have been delivered straight from a set for Hammer Films, and this is as close as they get to the wrong Dracula, let alone the right one. The exploitation of the Dracula image is an understandable gimmick by tour operators to encourage people into visiting Romania; but it has nothing to do with Stoker and not much with Vlad either, ignoring as it does the magnificent old Saxon town of Sighisoara where he was born. The brochure claims that the inspiration from Bram Stoker's novel ... was based on the life of Dracula Vlad (there is no lie so successful as the lie repeated).

The Romanians have built a large hotel in Bistrita, referred to in the novel as Biztritz, where Jonathan Harker stayed overnight before he left for Castle Dracula. This is the setting for the tremendous opening of the book, when the landlady of the Golden Krone implores Harker not to leave, warning him that it is St George's Day, Walpurgis Nacht when 'all the evil things in the world will have full sway' as the clock strikes midnight. But Harker is a Victorian gentleman with his duty to perform and no time for such nonsense, though he accepts the old lady's crucifix which she hangs around his neck, because it would seem churlish to refuse.

Even the Romanians can be guilty of brochure overstatement:

Today more than 100 years after the fantastic occurrences related in the pages full of owls, bats, monsters and vampires, the traveller who comes to Bistrita to track down Count Dracula will spend his first night at the same Golden Crown. It has changed a bit, it is a modern hotel built in architectonic style which suggests a mediaeval burgh.

In 1974 it seemed closer to one of those rapidly erected hotels in Majorca with a lot of disconnected wires and bathroom taps that fall off when you turn them on. On my first visit, I was assured that the modest Hotel Cerbul was the original; and indeed it was the only old-fashioned, wooden hotel I found in Romania, with a coffin maker's opposite for good measure.

Now a most ambitious scheme has been proposed to meet tourists' needs: with the construction of a special Castle Dracula. The original sprang from Stoker's imagination alone, though the Borgo Pass remains remarkably as he described it, with white mists interrupted by a solitary stone cross or the black figure of a shepherd. Until now, the tourists' substitute has been Bran Castle, on the way to Brasov. It is impressive, with its small high windows in the battlements and its turrets and courtyards, and was a favourite resting place of Queen Marie; but it has little to do with Vlad Dracula, though he may have stopped there as he stopped everywhere, and no connection at all with Bram Stoker. This does not prevent the guides from repeating the name 'Dracula' in various foreign tongues as the tourists shuffle through the corridors in the canvas slippers provided at the entrance. The Romanian officials are alarmed, yet again, that a respected national monument has become a horror attraction. This is why they propose to invest a really vast sum of money in building a castle somewhere along the Borgo Pass, where the fictional Castle Dracula might have been. A startling miniature model which is more reminiscent of Snow White has been made in Bistrita. Evidently, the Romanians are conceiving the project in stylish terms as a blend of Disney and Diaghilev, with taped wolves howling along the Borgo Pass; a caleche with four coal-black horses to take the passengers on the final stage of their fearful journey; befanged waitresses to serve the appropriate food and wine, blood-red of course; screams in the night, bats and strange happenings. Carried out with panache, the Castle Dracula Hotel could be fun.

Hopefully this will be opened within the next few years, and Stoker's fantasy will become reality of a sort.

'Welcome to my house! Enter freely and of your own will!' He made no motion of stepping to meet me, but stood like a statue, as though his gesture of welcome had fixed him into stone. The instant, however, that I had stepped over the threshold he moved impulsively forward, and holding out his hand grasped mine with a strength which made me wince, an effect which was not lessened by the fact that it seemed as cold as ice – more like the hand of a dead than living man. Again he said:

'Welcome to my house. Come freely. Go safely. And leave something of the happiness your bring!'

'Count Dracula?'

He bowed in a courtly way as he replied: '*I am Dracula.*'

Such was Count Dracula's courteous first greeting, in the darkness of the night. This is followed by passages when the great vampire figure is almost sympathetic. But seen in the light of day, as one of the living dead, replete and sated, he presents a different appearance:

There lay the Count, but looking as if his youth had been half-renewed, for the white hair and moustache were changed to dark iron grey, the cheeks were fuller, and the white skin seemed ruby-red underneath; the mouth was redder than ever, for on the lips were gouts of fresh blood, which trickled from the corners of the mouth and ran over the chin and neck. Even the deep, burning eyes seemed set amongst swollen flesh, for the lids and pouches underneath were bloated. It seemed as if the whole creature were simply gorged with blood; he lay like a filthy leech, exhausted with his repletion.

CHAPTER TWELVE

Vampirism in Literature

At the turn of the nineteenth century, there was a rash of literary vampirism: Goethe's *The Bride of Corinth*; Burger's poem *Lenore,* published in England in 1796, translated by Sir Walter Scott; Robert Southey's vampire ballad *Thalaba the Destroyer*, described as High Gothic.

In 1816 Lord Byron set out for Switzerland, accompanied by his doctor friend John Polidori, to meet the Shelleys. Polidori was the uncle of Dante Gabriel Rossetti and translated Horace Walpole's *The Castle of Otranto* into Italian. He had been commissioned by Byron's publishers to chronicle their journey, but the two men quarrelled from the outset and Polidori was virtually excluded from the circle of Shelley's friends, though not before that historic evening when they relieved the tension with a literary game.

'We will each write a ghost story,' said Lord Byron. The others joined in readily: Byron started on a novel about a modern Greek vampire; Shelley began a story in verse; and Mary Shelley, who was then seventeen, 'dreamt' of *Frankenstein,* and wrote it.

It would be surprising if *Frankenstein* (1818) had *not* cast some influence over Stoker. With *Dracula,* it is the great English horror novel; only *Dr Jekyll and Mr Hyde* can compete. It would be silly to claim that one is better than the other: they stand together. All three books have given names to our language. Each has an eternal theme: Mr Hyde reveals the ambivalence in all of us; Baron Frankenstein creates life; Count Dracula perpetuates it.

A weird flight of the imagination, the original novel of *Frankenstein*, like *Dracula,* is more powerful than any cinematic presentation, though *Dracula* is the more entertaining. In her introduction to the second edition, Mary Shelley wrote:

> Poor Polidori had some terrible idea about a skull-headed
> lady, who was so punished for peeping through a keyhole –
> what to see I forget – something very shocking and wrong,
> of course; but when she was reduced to a worse condition
> than the renowned Tom of Coventry, he did not know what
> to do with her, and was obliged to dispatch her to the tomb
> of the Capulets, the only place for which she was
> fitted. The illustrious poets, also, annoyed by the plati-
> tude of prose, speedily relinquished their uncongenial
> task.

This would seem to dispose of 'poor Polidori'. Indeed, after
further quarrels, he was dismissed and later imprisoned in Italy
for disorderly conduct, where Byron had to bail him out; he
eventually died of an overdose of drugs at the age of twenty-six.
However, on his return to England he had contributed a long
story called *The Vampyre* to Colburn's *New Monthly Magazine*
in 1819. A preface hinted that Byron was the author, but in
fact Polidori had written it himself, basing the plot on Byron's
original idea of the Greek vampire. Because Byron was widely
accepted as the author, in spite of, or perhaps all the more
because of his protestations, *The Vampyre* became a sensation
throughout Europe. Various versions were presented on the
stage, including two adaptations by Alexandre Dumas and Dion
Boucicault.

Professor Leonard Wolf says, 'Polidori gave us the prototype
vampire as, at least in English literature, we will get him ever
after. That is to say, as a nobleman, aloof, brilliant, chilling,
fascinating to women, and coolly evil.' E. F. Bleiler confirms
this assessment in *Three Gothic Novels* (1966): 'In the history
of the English novel Polidori's *Vampyre* has interest beyond its
literary merits. It is probably the first extensive vampire story
in English, and it served as the model for many later develop-
ments.'

One of these was *Varney the Vampire, or, The Feast of
Blood*, published in 1847. The author, Thomas Preskett Prest,
had a previous claim to fame: *Sweeney Todd, the Demon Bar-
ber of Fleet Street*, published the year before. Two extracts

from the torrent of words from this prolific writer, who turned to music-hall songs at the end of his life, indicate Prest's style and his possible influence on Stoker:

> The figure turns half round, and the light falls upon the face. It is perfectly white – perfectly bloodless. The eyes look like polished tin; the lips are drawn back, and the principal feature next to those dreadful eyes is the teeth – the fearful looking teeth – projecting like those of some wild animal, hideously, glaringly white, and fang-like. It approaches the bed with a strange, gliding movement. It clashes together the long nails that literally appear to hang from the finger ends. No sound comes from its lips. Is she going mad?

In due course, 'it' pounces:

> The glassy, horrible eyes of the figure runs over that angelic form with hideous satisfaction – horrible profanation. He drags her head to the bed's edge. He forces it back by the long hair still entwined in his grasp. With a plunge he seizes her neck in his fang-like teeth – a gush of blood, and a hideous sucking noise follows. The girl has swooned, and the vampire is at his hideous repast.

There are hints of *Dracula* here: the white face; the fang-like teeth; the angelic victim; the male vampire at his 'hideous repast'.

On a higher level is *The Horla*, a disturbing story by Guy de Maupassant that indicates a growing fear of his own impending madness. It starts happily with the narrator, living near the Seine, noticing a fine schooner from Brazil. 'The sight of her gave me so much pleasure that for some reason or other I saluted her.' Later, he realises that he has drawn the attention of an evil influence, a 'Being', which takes possession:

> There is no doubt about it. It has seized upon me again. My former nightmares have come back. Last night I felt that there was someone squatting on my chest. His mouth was on my mouth and he was drinking my life from between

my lips. He was draining my vitality like a leech. Then, when he had had his fill, he rose and left me, and I awoke.

Have I lost my reason? he asks, when he discovers that his water jug is empty in the morning. 'I must be going mad. Again the contents of my water bottle have been drunk by someone during the night. Was it myself? Was it I? Who else could it be? Who indeed? Oh my God! I am going mad. Who will deliver me?

I wait for sleep as one might wait for the executioner.

Finally, in an attempt to destroy 'Man's new master', he sets fire to his house. Afterwards he realises he has not destroyed the Horla and there is nothing left but to kill himself.

The Horla is included in the paperback anthology *The Vampire*, presented by Roger Vadim. Unlike so many collections of 'horror', this offers the reader some of the finest stories of this genre. *The Beautiful Vampire*, by Theophile Gautier, and Gogol's *Viy* are balanced by two modern stories, *The Man Upstairs*, by Ray Bradbury, and *The Cloak* by Robert Bloch. The threat of death was a favourite theme of Edgar Allen Poe and *Berenice*, 1835, is included also, though unfortunately it is one of his most far-fetched ventures. Berenice, apparently a victim of premature burial, drives the narrator mad with the perfect appearance of her teeth, all thirty-two of which are scattered around the floor at the incredible climax.

The Parasite, by Sir Arthur Conan Doyle, was published as a companion volume to Stoker's *The Watter's Mou*, so it is virtually certain that Stoker would have known of it. Anthony Masters describes it as a battle 'against a soul-sucking vampire in the shape of an insignificant spinster'. Certainly it has a curiously compelling atmosphere. It is basically the story of a sceptical professor and a crippled clairvoyant, Miss Penelosa. Rashly the professor agrees to act as guinea pig in one of Miss Penelosa's experiments and gradually her post-hypnotic influence takes hold of him. When she reveals her infatuation with him he responds with revulsion and her love, predictably, turns to hate and persecution. There is a touch of Jekyll and Hyde, with undertones of guilt that may have appealed to Stoker, but the story lacks the style of Sherlock Holmes who had no time for vampires, as he made clear to Doctor Watson in *The Adventure of the Sussex Vampire*:

> 'Rubbish, Watson, rubbish! What have we to do with walking corpses who can only be held in their graves by stakes driven through their hearts? It's pure lunacy.'
>
> 'But surely,' said I, 'the vampire was not necessarily a dead man? A living person might have the habit. I have read, for example, of the old sucking the blood of the young in order to retain their youth.'
>
> 'You are right, Watson. It mentions the legend in one of these references. But are we to give serious attention to such things? This agency stands flat-footed on the ground, and there it must remain. No ghosts need apply.'

Watson's reference to 'the old sucking the blood of the young' illustrates one of the great appeals of the vampire: the elixir of life. 'The blood is the life,' wrote Stoker, and there have been several attempts at rejuvenation made in this century – particularly by Voronoff, who injected testicular extracts from chimpanzees, and by the late Dr Niehans, who used extracts from young animals.

With his medical knowledge, Doyle knew that doctors discourage the habit in old people of sleeping alongside children, because they drain their vitality. Conversely, I have noticed that if a puppy is introduced into a household, the old family dog ages quickly.

Bram Stoker and Conan Doyle knew each other through the Lyceum production of *Waterloo*. When Stoker published *The Mystery of the Sea* in 1902, Doyle sent him a note of congratulation: 'My Dear Bram – I found the story admirable . . .'

Another vital influence was the narrative style employed so successfully, and so startlingly then, by Wilkie Collins in the marvellous *Woman in White*, published in 1860. His story is taken up by different characters, with extracts from their diaries, and this style was adopted by Bram Stoker with reference to the latest recording devices such as 'Dr Seward's Phonograph Diary, spoken by Van Helsing'. This was Bram's contribution to the vampire novel, to plunge it straight into the placid contemporary Victorian setting, which made it infinitely more alarming. Borrowing from the skilful precedent of Wilkie Collins, Bram Stoker heightened suspense with such cliff-hanging comments from Harker's Journal as: 'I now know the span of my life. God help me!', and such dramatic entries as the horrifying moment when he sees the Count's head looking out of a castle window.

I was at first interested and somewhat amused, for it is wonderful how small a matter will interest and amuse a man when he is a prisoner. But my very feelings changed to revulsion and terror when I saw the whole man slowly emerge from the window and begin to crawl down the castle wall over that dreadful abyss, *face down,* with his cloak spreading out around him like great wings. At first I could not believe my eyes. I thought it was some trick of the moonlight, some weird effect of shadow; but I kept looking, and it could be no delusion. I saw the fingers and toes grasp the corners of the stones, worn clear of the mortar by the stress of the years, and by thus using every projection and inequality move downwards with considerable speed, just as a lizard moves along a wall.

What manner of man is this, or what manner of creature is it in the semblance of a man? I feel the dread of this horrible place overpowering me; I am in fear – in awful fear – and there is no escape for me; I am encompassed about with terrors that I dare not think of . . .

There, his entry for 12 May comes to an alarming close.

Stoker introduces letters between Lucy Westenra and Mina Murray, the phonograph diaries and a newspaper report of a shipwreck, taken from the *Daily Telegraph*; and Harker even produces his Kodak snaps of Carfax, the house near Purfleet for which his employers are negotiating on Count Dracula's behalf.

Dracula's library includes *Whitaker's Almanac* and *Bradshaw's Guide,* as well as English periodicals. Mundane details provide further deceptive reassurance, details like the meal of excellent roast chicken which is laid on for Harker after his arrival, though no servant is seen. Dracula's hairbrush and comb are noticed in the house he has bought in Piccadilly. Sometimes there is a pleasing touch of total incongruity, such as Count Dracula's jaunty straw hat which 'suit not him or the time', as Van Helsing remarks. Telegrams and letters arrive at a speed that is inconceivable today.

This contemporaneous background lends an extra dimension to *Dracula*. It is described frequently as a Gothic novel – 'In the tradition of Walpole, Lewis, Radcliffe and Maturin' (Wolf), but *Dracula* succeeds partly because it is *not* Gothic; to the Victorian reader it must have seemed daringly modern.

Carmilla, however, published in 1872, could be described as Gothic, and this book above any other, inspired Stoker's obsession. The influence of his compatriot Sheridan Le Fanu, who wrote this story about a beautiful 'Styrian' Countess who was really a vampire, can be traced directly in 'Dracula's Guest'. This was the chapter that Stoker deleted from his finished novel, though it was published after his death by Florence and stands as an effective story in its own right. Jonathan Harker has lost his way as he sets out for Castle Dracula on Walpurgis Nacht, 'when the graves were opened and the dead came forth and walked. When all evil things of earth and air and water held revel'. A thrust of moonlight reveals that he is in an overgrown graveyard, a great marble tomb in front of him, as white as the snow that covered the ground:

> With the moonlight there came a fierce sigh of the storm, which appeared to resume its course with a long, low howl, as of many dogs or wolves. I was awed and shocked, and felt the cold perceptibly grow upon me till it seemed to grip me by the heart. Then while the flood of moonlight still fell on the marble tomb, the storm gave further evidence of renewing, as though it was returning on its track. Impelled by some sort of fascination, I approached the sepulchre to see what it was, and why such a thing stood alone in such a place. I walked around it, and read, over the Doric door, in German:
>
> COUNTESS DOLINGEN OF GRATZ
> IN STYRIA
> SOUGHT AND FOUND DEATH
> 1801
>
> On the top of the tomb, seemingly driven through the

solid marble – for the structure was composed of a few vast
blocks of stone – was a great iron spike or stake. On going
to the back I saw, graven in Great Russian letters: 'The
dead travel fast'.

A tornado of huge hailstones makes Harker press himself
against the bronze door, which swings open:

The shelter of even a tomb was welcome in that pitiless
tempest, and I was about to enter it when there came a
flash of forked-lightning that lit up the whole expanse of
the heavens. In the instant, as I am a living man, I saw,
as my eyes were turned into the darkness of the tomb, a
beautiful woman, with rounded cheeks and red lips, seemingly sleeping on a bier. As the thunder broke overhead, I
was grasped as by the hand of a giant and hurled out into
the storm.

There is a remarkable description as Harker recovers consciousness:

There was an icy feeling at the back of my neck and all
down my spine, and my ears, like my feet, were dead, yet
in torment; but there was in my breast a sense of warmth
which was, by comparison, delicious. It was as a nightmare
– a physical nightmare, if one may use such an expression;
for some heavy weight on my chest made it difficult for me
to breathe.
    This period of semi-lethargy seemed to remain a long
time, and as it faded away I must have slept or swooned.
Then came a sort of loathing, like the first stage of sea-
sickness, and a wild desire to be free from something – I
knew not what. A vast stillness enveloped me, as though all
the world were asleep or dead – only broken by the low
panting as of some animal close to me. I felt a warm rasping
at my throat, then came a consciousness of the awful truth,
which chilled me to the heart and sent the blood surging
up through my brain. Some great animal was lying on me
and now licking my throat. I feared to stir, for some instinct of prudence bade me lie still; but the brute seemed

to realise that there was now some change in me, for it raised its head. Through my eye-lashes I saw above me the two great flaming eyes of a gigantic wolf. Its sharp white teeth gleamed in the gaping red mouth, and I could feel its hot breath fierce and acrid upon me.

Rescue arrives, in the form of several soldiers on horseback, and the animal rises from his breast and makes for the cemetery. The wolf, as you might have guessed, was either Count Dracula himself or else under his command, and has kept Harker alive in the freezing night, warming his blood with the warmth of its own animal body. It is a powerful scene, though its inclusion would have delayed the splendid introduction to Castle Dracula with Harker's departure from the Golden Krone Hotel as the peasants cross themselves. The echo from *Carmilla* is found in the inscription on the tomb – COUNTESS DOLINGEN OF GRATZ IN STYRIA. This is taken directly from Le Fanu's story, which opens: 'In Styria, we, though by no means magnificent people, inhabit a castle, or schloss.' Bram cannot be accused of plagiarism, as suggested, for he did little more than borrow a name. Nevertheless, the climax of Le Fanu's story is so attuned to *Dracula* that Bram must have remembered it deeply, or returned to it again.

The next day the formal proceedings took place in the Chapel of Karnstein. The grave of the Countess Mircalla was opened; and the General and my father recognised each his perfidious and beautiful guest, in the face now disclosed to view. The features, though a hundred and fifty years had passed since her funeral, were tinted with the warmth of life. Her eyes were open; no cadaverous smell exhaled from the coffin. The two medical men, one officially present, the other in the part of the promoter of the inquiry, attested the marvellous fact, that there was a faint but appreciable respiration, and a corresponding action of the heart. The limbs were perfectly flexible, the flesh elastic; and the leaden coffin floated with blood, in which to a depth of seven inches, the body lay immersed. Here, then, were all the admitted signs and proofs of vampirism. The body, therefore, in accordance with the ancient practice, was raised, and a sharp stake driven through the heart of the vampire, who uttered a piercing shriek at the moment, in all respects such as might escape from a living person in the last agony. Then the head was struck off, and a torrent of blood flowed from the severed neck. The body and head were next placed on a pile of wood, and reduced to ashes, which were thrown upon the river and borne away, and that territory has never since been plagued by the visits of a vampire.

This was written twenty-five years before *Dracula,* and one year before Le Fanu's death.

Green Tea, another powerful story by Le Fanu, was the history of a clergyman haunted by the evil presence of a small, black monkey, visible only to himself for the simple reason that 'it' is a guilt-ridden part of himself. This is recounted by a German physician, Martin Hesselius, and it has been suggested by Maurice Richardson in 'The Psychoanalysis of Ghost Stories' that Hesselius might have been the basis for the character of Van Helsing. Equally, *The Roses and the Key,* 1871, included scenes in a madhouse which might have prompted Stoker's private asylum to which Renfield was committed. Le Fanu was a master of the macabre but he spread his skill more evenly than Bram, with such books as *Uncle Silas,* without achieving the solitary classic.

There is a curious postscript to vampiric literature. In the spiring of 1975, Dennis Wheatley included *The Horror at Fonenay* in his Library of the Occult, with the glowing recommendation: 'Here is a wonderful discovery; a novel by the great Alexandre Dumas *père,* never before translated into English – which hardly tallies with the cover's description of it as 'immortal'. In fact this was a totally forgotten book until a battered copy was found in Paris by Alan Hull Walton, the translator of Baudelaire and De Sade, who has now translated and adapted the novel for English readers. Wheatley acknowledges the 'honour' of presenting it to the British public.

Its relevance to *Dracula* lies in the last chapter, 'The Carpathian Vampire', which describes Kostaki, splendidly dressed in the traditional costume of the Magyars. He bows to the heroine and mutters something in his own tongue. 'It was then

I noticed a curious thing. The gold light from the fire was casting our shadows, and those of the furniture, on the smooth
pavement of the floor – but Kostaki had *no* shadow at all!'
He returns to her *after* his death:

I felt heavy and weak, and sitting on the edge of my bed
I fell backwards in a half-fainting state. Yet I retained
sufficient consciousness to hear a slow and heavy footstep
approaching the door of my room. After that I heard nothing more, not even the opening of the door if it ever *did*
open! Yet, before fainting into complete oblivion, I felt a
sharp stab of pain at one side of my naked throat...

With some effort I slowly dragged myself to the long mirror on the wall opposite my bed; and, holding a candle
close, examined my neck. A puncture, somewhat larger than
a pin prick, was apparent over the caratoid artery, and a
thin trickle of blood was still flowing from it.

The mirror figures again when she remembers that Kostaki
stood with his back to it, '... and I could swear that his image
was not reflected in it!'
This is echoed by Stoker in the effective scene when Count
Dracula approaches Jonathan Harker as he is shaving.

I started, for it amazed me that I had not seen him, since
the reflection of the glass covered the whole room behind
me. In starting I had cut myself slightly, but did not notice
it at the moment. Having answered the Count's salutation,
I turned to the glass again to see how I had been mistaken.
This time there could be no error, for the man was close
to me, and I could see him over my shoulder. But there was
no reflection of him in the mirror!

The Count is aroused by the sight of the blood trickling down
Harker's chin. 'His eyes blazed with a sort of demoniac fury,
and he suddenly made a grab at my throat. I drew away, and
his hand touched the string of beads which held the crucifix.'
The fury passes instantly, and Count Dracula hurls the
offending shaving-glass to the courtyard below, where it
shatters.

This is no reason for assuming that Stoker knew of *Une Journée à Fontenay-aux-Roses*, as it was titled in 1849. But the passages do show the astonishing prevalence of the vampire legend in literature. Bram Stoker's triumph was that he managed to co-ordinate the most interesting themes and present them more compellingly than before.

CHAPTER THIRTEEN

Count Dracula Makes his Entrance

To refer to Bram's 'genius' for research is not putting it too strongly. Not only could he conjure up atmosphere from musty books in the British Museum, but also he utilized every place he *did* visit, exploiting every detail. He did this at Boscastle and Cruden Bay and, above all, at Whitby. It was here that Count Dracula arrived in England.

It is fascinating to go to Whitby today and find it unchanged. It is one of the few towns in the north of England that have not been scarred by tall towers or reduced to rubble. It is still the port for small fishing boats, built on both sides of the valley divided by the river Esk; still dominated by the ruins of Whitby Abbey.

The work of the great Victorian photographer, F. M. Sutcliffe, has recorded Whitby as it was in Stoker's time. He was an artist who composed his scenes carefully, but it is possible to chance on a view of boats and fishermen that is much the same today. Give or take a few cars, it is like placing a negative over a print. The only serious difference is of sound rather than sight – the loudspeaker Bingo calls that drift across the harbour on summer days.

There is one photograph by Sutcliffe of a great sailing-boat washed up on the Whitby sands in 1885 which may have given Bram the idea for his shipwreck of the *Demeter*, hurled ashore in another of his favourite storms – 'One of the greatest and suddenest storms on record . . . with results both strange and unique.' The inhabitants were appalled by what they found: no sign of the crew, apart from the dead Captain lashed to the wheel; the boxes of Dracula's earth in the hold below; and then they saw a vast black dog which leapt on to the land and raced up the cliff towards the church at the top. Dracula had arrived!

The churchyard where Dracula found Lucy Westenra and claimed his first victim in England is exactly as Bram described it. Perhaps the stones are more weathered; they stand like lines of dark surf in the high grass for, unlike most graveyards, which are a haphazard mixture of crosses and stones of different shapes, this one has uniform stones. Many record death at sea: 'John Storr coxwain drowned with eleven others by the upsetting of the lifeboat at Whitby Feb. 9 1861' or 'William Scoresby born 1760 many years successfully engaged in the arctic whale fishery died Whitby 1829' or 'Charles Summerson Dalton drowned on his passage to Trinidad 1829'. I could not find the exact inscriptions of the novel but there is a low gravestone with a fossilised skull and crossbones which might have inspired Stoker's reference to the fictitious 'Edward Spencelagh, master mariner, murdered by pirates off the coast of the Andes'.

Even the interior of St Mary's Church has a nautical air, making me think of the Whaleman's Chapel in *Moby Dick*.

'No such thing,' said the old woman shrilly who sat near the door collecting money for postcards, 'there's no such thing as Dracula.'

'I know,' I said gently, having mentioned his name, 'but he landed here, in the book.'

'What book?' she asked suspiciously.

As I went outside I overheard a couple who were looking rather blankly at the graves.

'Dracula's supposed to be buried here,' said the woman vaguely. The man grunted, unimpressed, '*He's* supposed to be buried all over.'

Bram described the churchyard as 'the nicest spot in Whitby, for it lies right over the town, and has a full view of the harbour and all up the bay to where the headland called Kettleness stretches out into the sea.' This is from Mina Murray's journal but plainly echoes his own feelings. 'There are walks, with seats beside them, through the churchyard; and people go and sit there all day long . . .'

I did so myself, for seats are still there though the originals must have been replaced, and looked across to 7 East Crescent where Stoker is thought to have lodged. I suspect this is local confusion, because in the book it is the house where Lucy and Mina stayed. It is in a residential crescent, with large windows on the ground floor, a balcony with a white ironwork balustrade above. It was from here that Mina thought she saw Lucy in the churchyard:

> As the cloud passed I could see the ruins of the Abbey coming into view; and as the edge of a narrow band of light as sharp as a sword-cut moved along, the church and the churchyard became gradually visible. Whatever my expectation was, it was not disappointed for there on our favourite seat, the silver light of the moon struck a half-reclining figure, snowy white. The coming of the cloud was too quick for me to see much, for shadow shut down on light almost immediately; but it seemed to me as though something dark stood behind the seat where the white figure shone, and bent over it. What it was, whether man or beast, I could not tell.

Mina flew down the lanes to the pier and along by the fish-market to the bridge, which was the only way of reaching the East Cliff. She hurried up the 199 steep steps, known as the Church Stairs, so that she was exhausted when she reached the top – as any hurrying visitor would be now. But she was too late. As she neared the seat 'something' raised a head and she saw a white face and two gleaming red eyes bent over Lucy's lovely white throat. Count Dracula had struck. There is a touching scene as Mina gives her shoes to Lucy and the two girls run back in the darkness, Mina barefoot, Lucy in her nightdress, down the steep steps, across the bridge, and up the narrow lanes, desperately afraid they will be seen. The next day Mina is distressed to see the marks of a safety-pin which she had used to fasten her shawl round Lucy's throat the night before: 'The skin of her throat was pierced . . . there are two little red points like pin-pricks, and on the band of her nightdress was a drop of blood.' But *we* know it was no safety-pin.

Why Whitby? It is a curious destination for a ship from the Black Sea. Obviously Bram fell in love with the place as a location, and he was right. I have not been able to discover when or why he stayed here, but there is evidence that Henry Irving stayed at the Hotel Metropole (*after* the publication of *Dracula*, admittedly), and went on to Scarborough to see George Gros-

smith 'doing poor business at the Spa Theatre', and they performed at The Grand Theatre, Hull, in the 1890s. Whitby would
have been a perfect haven to escape to on a northern tour of
their own. Also, it was a family resort – known absurdly as the
'English Engadine' – and, on at least one occasion, Bram brought
his son Noel here on holiday, and tried to teach him to swim.

CHAPTER FOURTEEN

The Dracula Game

Bram wrote *Dracula* as if he was inspired. Apart from all the influences mentioned, why this one glorious exception? What prompted him to write *Dracula* at all? There have been many bizarre explanations. It is widely accepted that Bram 'dreamt' the idea after a late night supper of dressed crab, but though Whitby is famous for its crab, I have not been able to establish the source of this story. I suspect there is some confusion with Mary Shelley's dream of *Frankenstein*.

The late Professor Nandris suggested that Bram Stoker was influenced by the murders of Jack the Ripper in 1888, but there is no hint in the novel or any of his writings of either the Ripper's violence or the subsequent panic. Even less convincing is Nandris' further claim that Bram was influenced by the downfall of Oscar Wilde, comparing the dancing of the harlots, when Wilde was sentenced, to the gloating of the vampire women at Castle Dracula.

Anyone who wishes to play the Dracula game can bend the most surprising pieces of evidence to fit the puzzle. A number of distinguished American professors have done so with relish. One of the most astounding interpretations comes from Dr Joseph S. Bierman, of Baltimore, who argues that Bram's subconscious wanted to eat my grandfather Tom. In his work *Dracula: Prolonged Childhood Illness and the Oral Triad*, he bases this on the 'oral triad: the wish to eat, be eaten and sleep', and stresses the importance of Bram's childhood illness. Stoker was able to walk for the first time at the age of seven: apparently the number seven is the clue, and Bram's book of children's stories is the key. As I have mentioned, *Under the Sunset* was dedicated to 'My Son Whose Angel Doth Behold the Face of the King', which Dr Bierman explains as revealing 'some death wishes towards his son'. For him, the crucial story in *Under the Sunset* is 'How 7 Went Mad', with examples of 'blood-letting, madness and sleep disturbances'. Arithmetic apart, everything in the story has significance for Dr Bierman: 'The parallels and similarities of this story to parts of *Dracula* are very apparent.' These are some of his deductions from 'How 7 Went Mad' – 'another tale of medical detection'.

1. Number seven represents Stoker as a child with his near mortal illness, his inability to stand on his own two feet, and the feeling of being different from his siblings.

2. ... this parallel between No. 7 and Stoker, gives a hint as to the kind of medical treatment which might have been instrumental in laying the groundwork for Stoker's dreaming about a vampire.

That is, Stoker might have been bled just as No. 7 was bled. This was a practise that was extremely common in Ireland in the 1840's. The association in the story between madness and bleeding would then suggest that Stoker became 'mad' when he was bled. Certainly in DRACULA the 'zoophagus mania' combines madness and blood.'

3. There is another theme in addition to the one of Stoker as the sick, different child that is furnished by an analysis of the slip in the multiplication of seven to the fourth power in which a three is substituted for a four.

The swelling and shrinking in size of the raven, the stress on kith and kin, and on the horoscope suggest very strongly that the powers of seven represent the birth order of the seven Stoker children.

After the third power the raven swells, and then starts to shrink to his natural size after the fourth seven is dropped. In oral terms this sequence suggests his mother's pregnancy with the fourth born Tommy who was delivered when Stoker, the third born, was twenty months old.

The mathematical error by a man who had received honors in mathematics at Trinity College implies not only that he felt Tommy was a mistake, who should have been 'wrong multiplied' as No. 7 was, but also that Tommy, number four, should not have been the product of the multiplying, i.e., should not have been born, but that he, number three should have taken his place.

4. At age twenty-one months, Tommy was born and Stoker would have seen him nursing at the breast. This would have aroused great feelings of rivalry and the wish to get rid of Tommy, the wish that he would die.

Because of being bed-ridden, Stoker would not have had the usual outlet of motility for his aggression but would have had to express it orally. Killing would have been seen as eating up, as was the case in HOW 7 WENT MAD.

5. . . . when we look at the original sum that causes Tineboy to wish that number seven had never been invented, we find that it is seven to the seventh power which would represent George, the youngest brother, who was born when Stoker was seven. Stoker *must have wished*, as Mr Daw did, that *George would croak, a word which in Victorian England, also meant 'die'*. This wish is carried out by eating and swallowing and is undone by regurgitation.

The death wishes towards his baby brothers, Tom and George, may be found in *Dracula* in the form of three instances of infanticide by eating and sucking and the frequent usage of the names Tom and George for different minor characters and events. For example, Harker arrives at Dracula's castle on St. George's Eve. Even the novel itself is dedicated to *a Tommy* – to *Thomas* Hall Caine, a novelist friend of Stoker's.

My grandfather was never called Tommy, as far as I know, but always Tom, and Hall Caine was seldom called Thomas: in fact, Bram's dedication uses a favourite nick-name – 'To my dear friend – Hommy-Beg'. Though 'Hommy' might have been a babyish pronounciation of 'Tommy', the link is too feeble to take seriously. In his conclusion, Bierman returns to the much quoted meal of dressed crab, and adds some remarkable dressing of his own:

6. WE are now in a position to analyze the association to the vampire dream – that it was caused by eating too much dressed crab. The two stories THE WONDROUS CHILD and HOW 7 WENT MAD furnish us with a basis for this analysis

by combining the fantasy of the baby coming from over
the sea and being found on a bed of parsley with the stress
on the horoscope. Dressed crab was classically served in
England at that time on a bed of parsley. Crab, when
viewed horoscopically for this horror tale, is that sign of
the Zodiak that covers the period between June 23 and
July 23. George, Stoker's youngest brother, was born under
the sign of the crab on July 20th. *Eating the dressed crab
meant, unconsciously eating up and killing baby George.*'

A further permutation involves Irving because he was 'known
to his intimates as The Crab'. Dr Bierman claims that Bram was
obsessed with Cain's fratricide of Abel. Quoting his entry in
Who's Who, under 'recreations', as 'pretty much the same as
those other children of Adam'. Also, that Renfield compares
himself to Enoch, Cain's son; and that Mina has a scar on her
forehead, the mark of Cain.

He comes to the triumphant verdict: 'Parts of the novel and
the two stories that are associations to it suggest that DRACULA
concerns itself with death wishes towards his younger brothers,
nursing at the breast, and primal scenes expressed in nursing
terms.'

From correspondence and personal diaries, it is plain that
Bram remained on excellent terms with my grandfather, sending
him his books with the affectionate inscription: 'Tom Stoker
C.S.I. with Bram's love'. As for George, he was a constant
visitor to Cheyne Walk, where he attended the man who had
thrown himself into the Thames, and also to the Lyceum
Theatre, where he promptly lanced Ellen Terry's thumb when
he realised she had a serious case of blood poisoning. Bram was
so proud of him that he asked Richard Burton to let George
accompany him on an expedition to re-open the old Midian
gold mines. Burton was favourably impressed by George's record
and asked him to join his party as a doctor, but the plan fell
through after an Arab revolt. Of course, Dr Bierman might say
that to encourage such an expedition, with the dangers involved,
was a death wish on Bram's part, but there is no denying
George's own relish for excitement. He had served in the Russo-
Turkish war as a surgeon for the Turks and was Chief of
Ambulance of the Red Crescent, bringing all the Turkish

wounded to Philippopolis after the battle of Schipka Pass. When there were problems over carrying the body of Paris across the stage in *Romeo and Juliet,* Bram boasted to Irving that his brother had ample experience of handling dead bodies and George demonstrated on Bram, throwing him over his back like a butcher carrying the carcass of a sheep. Irving laughed and decided the best way, after all, was to *drag* the body into the tomb.

Always generous to others, except at the cost of Irving's interests, Bram had encouraged George to write down his experiences in the Turkish war, which were published in 1878 under the title *With the Unspeakables.* Their fraternal relationship seems to have been exceptionally warm.

Though an enthusiast, Dr Bierman is no crank; he is an intelligent man, as I discovered when he visited me England in the spring of 1973, with his wife and two children. He was delighted when I showed him a letter from William Fitzgerald, part-illustrator of *Under the Sunset,* who had written to Bram pointing out his mathematical mistake ($2,301 \times 7 = 16,107$ and not $16,807$) and asked in his postscript: 'Was this an oversight, or has it any deep significance?' To Dr Bierman it is all too significant, but his death-wish interpretations make my mind boggle. With that sort of reasoning, you can prove *anything.*

While Dr Bierman dreams of fratricide, Royce MacGillivray, of the History Department in Waterloo University, Ontario, implies, though he does not specifically claim, that Bram had thoughts of parricide. He quotes Maurice Richardson's statement that Count Dracula was the 'father-figure' personified.

To be fair, his interest in Dracula, like Dr Bierman's, stems from admiration:

Stoker created a myth comparable in vitality to that of the Wandering Jew, Faust, or Don Juan. This myth has not, so far, been crowned with respectability by its use in great literature, yet is it too much to suggest that in time even that may be achieved? While the idea of scholarly study of a horror novel may initially seem ridiculous, I think I can show that *Dracula* is substantial enough to deserve the attention of scholars. Even if the novel should seem to most others less impressive than it has seemed to me after a number of readings, I suggest that historian and sociologist will find it worthwhile to pay attention to the novel that has been so influential in our century.

Pursuing the theme of parricide, Royce MacGillivray explains:

The theme of Dracula as a father-figure is less overt than the theme of alienation, and one feels that in inserting it in the novel Stoker was not fully conscious of his own feelings. Dracula is the patriarch of his castle, for as a little sifting of the evidence will show, the three female vampires who share it with him are his wife and two daughters, perhaps by another marriage, or his wife and two sisters. [Surely it makes a difference? In fact, there is so little evidence that they have been described also as his three daughters, and even his three wives.] Rather more importantly for the emotional undercurrents of the novel, Dracula even aspires to be, in a sense, the father of the band that is pursuing him. Because he intends, as he tells them, to turn them all into vampires, he will be their creator and therefore 'father'.

The theme of Dracula as father figure gains psychological interest from the framework of references to the death or murder of parents in which it is inserted. One of Dracula's earliest victims in the novel is a mother who comes to the castle to demand the return of her abducted child. In a horrifying scene which Harker watches from a castle window she is torn to pieces by the wolves who are at Dracula's call. An old man, another father figure, is found dead with a broken neck in the churchyard at Whitby shortly after Dracula's landing at that port. Then there are the deaths from natural causes of Arthur Holmwood's father; of Harker's employer and patron, who had been a father to him and Mrs Harker; and of the mother of Lucy Westenra. It is suggestive of the emotional significance the parricide theme seems to have had for Stoker that the last three of these deaths are incidental to his narrative, which would be improved by their omission.

When I suggest that there is indeed reason to suppose that Dracula was partly based on Stoker, I am not attacking Stoker's character. The popularity of the Dracula myth in this century suggests that many people find a resemblance between themselves and Dracula and between themselves and Vampires in general.

Again there is stress on Bram's bed-ridden childhood and his sudden recovery:

In his own development Stoker must have found clues for his depiction of Dracula as someone who developed in the tomb, slowly groping his way toward the full mastery of the possibilities open to him. Similarly, Stoker's migration from Dublin, where he must have felt isolated with his youthful literary ambitions, to London, the intellectual capital of the British Isles and the hub of a vast empire, parallels Dracula's migration from his thinly populated Transylvanian feeding-grounds to the same city and its teeming human life. In his isolation in Dublin and in his later role as an Irishman in England, Stoker *must* have picked up clues for his depiction of Dracula as an alienated figure. Even the cumbersome train of baggage that Irving and his acting company carried with them as they toured the provinces and America may have been in his mind when he described Dracula's movements with his boxes of earth.

I emphasize that 'must' because it is another example of false assumption misinterpreted as fact. Dublin was less isolated then than now, and though Bram's literary ambitions may have been frustrated, he was undeniably a leading light in Dublin's intellectual circles – already an author, editor and dramatic critic. The 'Anglo-Irish' were more Anglo than Irish; Trinity was a university for Protestants, a supreme example of their arrogance; and the lack of 'isolation' is shown in the frequency of Irving's visits. How often has Olivier played there in the last twenty-five years? To compare Dublin of the last century to the remoter forests of Transylvania stretches the point too far. But Royce MacGillivray does, intriguingly, relate the novel to the Victorians:

While the novel's parent-child conflicts are presumably
rooted in Stoker's private feelings, one can see interesting
parallels with the twentieth-century revolt against the Victorian father and the whole Victorian heritage as expressed,
for instance, in Butler's *The Way of all Flesh* and Gosse's
Father and Son. The novel also reflects the foreboding
with which some Victorians faced the new century. Surely
some ill-fortune would take away the good things which
had been so unstintingly poured upon Victorian England?
Dracula may have partially symbolised for contemporaries
this nameless threat.

These points, though hardly specific, are more convincing
than Bram's apparent obsession with a father figure. Abraham
Stoker seems the last paternal figure to arouse such loathing; a
'mother fixation' would be more believable.

Bram's childhood illness is raised once more by the American
psychiatrist Seymour Shuster in his paper *Dracula and surgically induced trauma in children*, published in the *British Journal
of Medical Psychology* in 1973. Shuster claims that *Dracula*
springs straight from Stoker's early hospitalisation; that the
surgeon could appear, to a child's fertile imagination, to be a
blood-sucking villain surrounded by nurses who turned into
vampires.

Shuster also finds a connection between 'the creation of
monsters like the Frankenstein monster, Dracula, and Dr
Jekyll's evil counterpart, Mr Hyde, and surgically induced
trauma' and suggests that *Dracula* was inspired by a nightmare which 'resulted from the emergence of long-repressed anxiety relating to the childhood experiences with doctors – I suggest that the character Stoker came to call 'Dracula' basically
represents a child's perception of the surgeon who operates upon
him.'

To plead his case, Shuster has to presume 'that Stoker had
been hospitalised as a child'. Having made this assumption,
'despite the lack of details of Stoker's medical history', he goes
on to show 'that the sense of terror and helplessness that Stoker
was trying to evoke in his reader in the castle portion of the
book is that of the child who has been left by his mother in a
hospital to undergo surgery and/or blood-letting'. He proposes

that 'Harker's ordeal in the castle represents Stoker's terrifying experiences in a hospital. I say it was the reinforcement of his psychosexual fantasies by these experiences that compelled him to write *Dracula*.' Already, the hospitalisation has become *Terrifying*, and Dr Shuster goes several steps further: the novel is described as a 'distorted and disguised autobiography'; the baby in Dracula's bag, which he brings for his women, 'represents not only a fellow child victim in the hospital, but Stoker as well'; the bite of the vampire is compared to the jab of the nurse's needle; and 'Harker's miraculous avoidance of a vampire attack was simply Stoker's defence against the still terrifying doctors'.

Shuster finally proves his case to his own satisfaction:

Bram Stoker identified with the doctor by writing *Dracula* ... In private life, Stoker often referred to Dracula as 'Drac' (It is difficult to overlook the similarity of the common shortening of the word 'doctor' to 'doc', and the first two letters of the name Dracula are the common abbreviation for the word doctor) ... I believe we now know the identity of Dracula.

Dr Shuster is misinformed, or the flaw in his theory has eluded him. Of course the stress on Bram's childhood illness is valid, but Bram was always comfortably at home in Clontarf. There were no prolonged 'terrifying' experiences with a twilight Dracula-surgeon making his rounds at dusk, nor any vampire-nurses. The primitive conditions of a hospital in the 1850's would have been a last resort for a respectable middle-class family, only risked in the case of surgery – but for Bram no surgery was involved. The impression made by his childhood illness may well have been deep, but too little is known about its nature to carry supposition so far.

Playing the Dracula Game is fun, but too easy. The simple explanation, that Bram Stoker sat down to create a first-rate story, is not acceptable to the interpreters who frequently credit the artist with meanings that never occurred to him: Bram would have been astonished, and probably outraged, at their ideas. For in dragging *their* fantasies from the subconscious, they deny the power of Bram Stoker's imagination which, ultimately, was alone responsible for his masterpiece. Even the influence of Vlad Dracula can be exaggerated. Replying to an American correspondent in 1906, he thanks him for his 'interesting memorandum' and makes the revealing comment 'you know a lot more about *Dracula* than I do', suggesting his comparative ignorance of and indifference to the historical background.

CHAPTER FIFTEEN

The Dracula Industry

Dracula was published in 1897 and though it was well received, it was not the great success that people imagine.

The *Daily Mail* was enthusiastic: 'In seeking a parallel to this weird, powerful and horrible story, our minds revert to such tales as *The Mysteries of Udolpho, Frankenstein, Wuthering Heights, The Fall of the House of Usher,* and *Marjery Quelher.* But *Dracula* is even more appalling in its gloomy fascination than any of these!' The comparison is high praise, but other critics made unflattering reference to Wilkie Collins. *Punch* was lofty, though there is an interesting reference to the Devil in its review: 'This weird tale is about vampires, not a single, quiet creeping vampire, but a whole band of them, governed by a vampire monarch, who is apparently a first cousin to Mephistopheles. It is a pity that Mr Bram Stoker was not content to employ such supernatural anti-vampire receipts as his wildest imagination might have invented without venturing on a domain where angels fear to tread.' *The Athenaeum* was scornful: '*Dracula* is highly sensational, but it is wanting in the constructive art as well as in the higher literary sense. It reads at times like a mere series of grotesquely incredible events ...'

Curiously, the highest praise came from his mother Charlotte. Curious, not because she was his mother – praise from her would be naturally expected – but rather because her comments were shrewdly prophetic: 'My dear it is splendid, a thousand miles beyond anything you have written before, and I feel certain will place you very high in the writers of the day ... No book since Mrs Shelley's 'Frankenstein' or indeed any other at all has come near yours in originality, or terror – Poe is nowhere. I have read much but I have never met a book like it at all. In its terrible excitement it should make a widespread reputation and much money for you.' This confident encouragement suggests that Bram owed much to her influence when he was growing up.

Apparently the most damning comment of all came from Irving. There was a read-through of a swiftly dramatised version of *Dracula* presented on the stage of the Lyceum at ten in the morning of Tuesday 18 May, the month the book was published. This was purely for copyright purposes, to protect the novel from piracy, or so I thought until I saw the poster, which was printed especially and was worthy of a commercial production. Bold black letters on a green background proclaim: 'On Tuesday, May 18 at 10 o'clock a.m. For the first time. A Drama, in prologue and five acts DRACULA or, The Un-Dead By Bram Stoker Admission One Guinea.'

It is that charge of a guinea that seems so startling, as does the discovery that two different programmes were printed for the occasion – though at first sight they appear identical, with an attractive decoration at the top, and the name of the Royal Lyceum Theatre underneath. Ironically, Irving's name looms large as 'Sole Lessee and Manager', while there is no mention of Bram Stoker under the title *Dracula or The Un-Dead*. A closer examination reveals that the lettering of *Dracula* is infinitesimally smaller in one programme, which gives the time inside as 'a quarter past ten o'clock a.m.' instead of ten. There are two changes in the cast list: Miss Yeoland replaces Miss Gurney as 'Mrs Westenra', and Miss Holland becomes the 'servant', instead of Miss Cornford, in the 10 a.m. version. Otherwise the casting remains unchanged, with Mr Jones as 'Count Dracula' and Miss Craig, Ellen Terry's daughter, as 'Mina Murray'.

In both cases the synopsis is the same, starting with: 'Prologue: Transylvania', which is followed by five acts with such locations as: 'Outside the Castle', 'the Churchyard, Whitby' and 'Outside the tomb' – a staggering forty-seven scenes altogether. A final difference in the second programme is the omission of Loveday as stage manager, Meredith Ball as musical director and Bram himself as acting manager. Neither were there any of the usual management notices on the back, though these are included in the 10.15 version.

It seems a curious affair: the charge of a guinea to attend a lengthy read-through at ten in the morning cannot have been encouraging to the playgoer who would normally pay seven shillings for a seat in the Dress Circle to witness Irving in one of his classic portrayals. In fact the audience consisted of Lyceum staff, friends, and Maria Mitchell, Bram's cook.

Presumably the public were discouraged deliberately, for posters were only put up that same morning, and the charade of a proper production was undergone for the copyright reason suggested. Bram felt so strongly on this subject that he gave evidence two months later to a Select Committee of the House of Lords on the Copyright Amendment Bill. He explained that: 'It had been part of his duty since 1878 to express an opinion to Sir Henry Irving with regard to various plays, and he had considerable acquaintance with contemporary dramatic literature. In his experience it was a common and increasing practice for dramatists to take plot, dialogue, and incidents from copyright novels ... He was in favour of the right of the author to say who should dramatise his work.'

Fair enough; Bram had good reason to know and fear the rampant piracy that flourished in America. But the very fact of his anxiety to protect *Dracula* from an unauthorised dramatisation, and the two programmes and poster, suggest that he took such a dramatisation seriously. All the more hurtful, therefore, was Irving's reaction.

Legend has it that Sir Henry entered the theatre during the reading and listened for a few moments with a warning glint of amusement. 'What do you think of it?' someone asked him unwisely, as he left for his dressing room. *'Dreadful!'* came the devastating reply, projected with such resonance that it filled the theatre.

Orson Welles told me a parallel story in Paris in 1950, when he was appearing in his one-act plays *Time Runs* and *The Unthinking Lobster* with his young discovery Eartha Kitt. 'Stoker,' he declared expansively, 'told me this extraordinary story – that he had written this play about a vampire especially for his friend Henry Irving, who threw it aside contemptuously. But – you know' – his voice deepened and he leant forward – 'Stoker had his revenge! He turned the play into a novel and if you read the description of the Count you will find it identical to Irving!' Welles gave a great roar of laughter and I was impressed at the time, but there are two flaws in the theory: firstly,

Count Dracula has a big white moustache in the book, and secondly, Stoker died three years before Welles was born.

Ironically, however, it was the presentation of *Dracula* on stage that accounts for the Dracula industry today. The first dramatisation was produced at the Grand Theatre in Derby, in June 1924. This was confirmed in a letter from Jack Howarth, famous on television as Albert Tatlock in 'Coronation Street'. The producer was Hamilton Deane, an Irishman. Mr Howarth was the original stage manager and played the 'Warder' in the second act – 'a small part that Deanie wrote especially for me'. The part of the Comedy Maid, opposite him, was played first by Nancy de Silva, then by Betty Murgatroyd who became Mrs Howarth, later by Diana Wynyard, and later still by Vera Raven, who also married her 'Warder'.

Hamilton Deane possessed the sole dramatic rights, acquired from Florence Stoker, and made his own adaptation from Jack Howarth's copy of the book. They sensed the potential popularity of the play after the first few weeks, 'though it was difficult to tell as Deanie was such a Provincial Idol and played to 98 per cent capacity everywhere we went'. *Dracula* started as a single performance in the repertoire, without a special programme, but by 1926 it had replaced most of the other plays and Deane was able to boast: 'We never had a poor house with *Dracula*. By that time I was simply coining money with the play. I could not go wrong with it, anywhere.'

The part of Count Dracula was played for the first time (apart from Mr Jones' read-through at the Lyceum) by a well-known provincial actor, Edmund Blake, who sported a gold front tooth and a black cloak especially designed for him by Deane. He left the company and was replaced by Raymond Huntley who, at the age of twenty-two, introduced Count Dracula to London. Deane himself backed this production, with a Lancashire impresario, after West End managers had turned it down. *Dracula* opened in London for the first time at the Little Theatre on 14 February 1927 and, though it was scorned by the London critics, it captured the imagination of the public and ran for 391 performances after being transferred to two other theatres. Deane added to its success with the gimmick of placing a uniformed nurse in the theatre to scare the audience even more. One night, twenty-nine people fainted.

Raymond Huntley has written to me that he played the part 'at an absurdly young age because I played it in a touring rep company in which I was gaining experience. For various reasons, I declined the offer to play the part on Broadway, but I did subsequently join the N.Y. company for a Nationwide tour.' Dracula was played on Broadway by a Hungarian actor, born in Lugos – Bela Lugosi Blasko.

Meanwhile, Hamilton Deane was allowed no rest; audiences were so demanding that he was forced to present *Dracula* year after year. Some productions had a casting that is tantalising in retrospect, with, for example, Wilfred Lawson as Renfield. In 1939, Deane took the part of Count Dracula himself for the first time, in the American version, and though the play's impact was lessened by the greater threat of a new World War, it was transferred from the Winter Garden, most appropriately, to The Lyceum. One night Bela Lugosi walked on stage and embraced Deane's Dracula with a kiss on both cheeks while the audience cheered. *Dracula* was followed by *Hamlet*, the Lyceum's closing production and again an appropriate one, for this was the play that had introduced Bram to the West End.

Jack Howarth remembers 'Deanie' as an actor of genius – 'But like all stars, personality was the main thing. The outstanding moment was the curtain speech.' This was another brilliant piece of theatricality, when he addressed the audience: 'Just a moment, ladies and gentlemen! Just a word before you leave. We hope the memories of Dracula and Renfield won't give you bad dreams, so just a word of reassurance. When you get home tonight, and the lights have been turned out, and you are afraid to look behind the curtains, and you dread to see a face appear at the window, why, just pull yourself together and remember that after all – THERE ARE SUCH THINGS!'

Deane gave this warning in his role of Van Helsing which he had to accept because no one else in the company was suitable for the part. He had been looking forward to the relaxation of portraying Count Dracula himself, for surprisingly, this was only a small part in his production. The Count is seldom seen and his entrance as he greets the maid is so muted as to be almost unintelligible: 'I have sorrow if I have given to you the alarm – perhaps my foot-fall sounds not so heavy as that of your English ploughman.'

Though Deane's adaptation seems lugubrious today, his stage-craft must have carried conviction then, judging by the response. A reason for this is suggested by Jack Howarth's reply when I asked whether he believed in vampires: 'No. But Deanie did.'

It has been stated that *Dracula* is *always* being shown on stage somewhere in the world. This is one of those convenient statistics that are almost impossible to refute, but it seems to be true today. A parody, at the Theatre Royal, Stratford (in London's East End), was so popular that the season was extended into 1975. After touring the provinces, Peter Wyngarde reached Wimbledon in March in the title role of his own adaptation, which he was pleased to acknowledge as 'Bram Stoker's *Dracula*'. Billed as '*Pleasantly frightening*', this version was not sufficiently pleasant, while the most frightening moment was the apparent 'escape' of one of the white rats from the stage into the audience. With long flowing wig and droopy moustache, Wyngarde presented a surprisingly contemporary figure, though his appearance was deliberately based on the print of Vlad Dracula. His portrayal of the Count as a vampire was romantic and sensual. 'It is a totally sexual thing,' was his explanation for the perennial public fascination with Dracula. 'All the blood sucking and the girl's apparent orgasm when he kisses her – a form of the sex act. There is an attraction for girls in his impeccable manners and mesmeric quality. He is described as fifty but is ageless and actually grows younger during the play, an effect I should have liked to convey on stage, though I could do so on film. He has that sinister, almost violent look that men have who are extremely sexually attractive to women.'

'Will the public ever tire of seeing Dracula on stage or screen?'

'Never. He represents the evil in all of us.'

Few dramatisations are faithful to Stoker's original. Wyngarde's *Dracula* is set, inexplicably, in an English country house in the 1920s. In 1970, *Dracula: Sabbat*, by Leon Katz, was presented in New York with a moaning Lucy Westenra as part of a Black Mass. Dracula mounts her, wearing a dildo. Another American dramatisation, written by Ted Tiller and presented in Massachusetts in 1971, employed the old trick of borrowing Stoker's names, Harker, Van Helsing and Renfield, and ending the resemblance there. Apparently set in the thirties, with a

giddy succession of 'high-balls', the play introduces a new
character, Sybil Seward, short-sighted, middle-aged, and dipso-
maniac. She is a social snob: 'He's the only Count in twenty
miles and his visits lend us tone.' When she tells her husband she
has second sight, he replies calmly: 'Of course you have, dear,
but sometimes it gets blurred through your bifocals.'

Two years before Deane presented *Dracula* on stage, a silent
film called *Nosferatu* was made in Germany. This version was
pirated to avoid paying Florence Stoker any fee for the copyright. She brought an injunction, the company went bankrupt,
and the prints were ordered to be destroyed. Fortunately, one
negative, at least, escaped and *Nosferatu* was shown in British
'Art' cinemas recently. It is revealed today as one of the silent
classics, directed by F. W. Murnau and with Max Schenk pro-
viding some exceptional moments as Dracula, especially when he
rises from his coffin on board the ship taking him to Bremen.

But it was Tod Browning's brilliant film version in 1931 that
started the deluge. Bela Lugosi went on from Broadway to play
the Count in this and seized the part so effectively that he made
it his own. *Dracula* was billed as the first 'Horror Film' and is
still on release, standing up to the tests of time. Bela Lugosi
strikes the right note of cultured menace, and is delightful as
he listens, head tilted, to the howling of the wolves outside the
Castle: 'Listen to them – the children of the night. What music
they make!' His greeting to Jonathan Harker, also echoing
Stoker's words, reverberates: 'Welcome to my house. Enter
freely and of your own will. *I am Dracula!*'

Lugosi's Hungarian accent is crucial, for we must believe that
the Count is East European; the vampire women are surprisingly convincing, and the film is closer to the book than one
would expect.

There have been scores of Draculas ever since; it has been
estimated that more than four hundred films have been made
on and around the subject, Spanish, Mexican, Turkish and
Japanese. The Count has been portrayed by John Carradine;
Bill Tilden the tennis player; David Niven; Jack Palance, with
echoes of Vlad the Impaler; and by Donald Pleasance in *Barry
Mackenzie Holds His Own*. There have been such permutations
as *Billy the Kid Versus Dracula, Old Mother Riley Meets the
Vampire*, and *Blacula*; with today's tastes it is surprising there

hasn't been a *Dragula*, though the *Rocky Horrow Show* comes close.

Sometimes the effect is meant to be hilarious. In *The Blood of Dracula's Castle* the cellars are filled with captive girls whose veins are tapped for 'wine' to be served upstairs. This time, the distinguished actor John Carradine plays the moon-worshipping butler rather than the title role, and brings the blood in champagne glasses:

'I think you'll enjoy this . . . the type is rare.'

'Hm, beautiful!' says the Count after a sip.

'Pure?' asks the Countess.

'Oh, that is too much to hope for,' he replies.

The latest version, as I write, is by Paul Morrisey and Andy Warhol; in this one the Count has to drink the blood of a virgin or die in a fortnight – a challenge, these days. *Dracula* films seem to go on for ever; audiences will not allow him to die. One man who refuses to play the part further, and has resigned from the Presidency of the Dracula Society because he is tired of the association, is Christopher Lee. Lee is the one actor since Lugosi whose name has become synonymous with the part, giving it a grandeur which made his series of vampire films so successful for Hammer and earned them a fortune. It is understandable that he feels trapped in Count Dracula's embrace, but he has told me that he might be prepared to return in a version which is strictly true to Stoker's original.

Christopher Lee gave me his explanation for the Dracula obsession one afternoon in his apartment in Cadogan Square, referring to the figure's 'strange, dark heroism'.

'He offers the illusion of immortality,' he told me, 'the subconscious wish we all have for limitless power . . . a man of tremendous brain and physical strength . . . he is either a reincarnation or he has never died. He is a superman image, with erotic appeal for women who find him totally alluring. In many ways, he is everything people would like to be – the anti-hero, the heroic villain. Like the much maligned Rasputin, he is part saint, part sinner.

'Men are attracted to him because of the irresistible power he wields. For women there is the complete abandonment to the power of a man.'

Commenting on Stoker's phrase 'Blood is the life', he suggested that there is a physical appeal for someone who is being drained: 'It's like being a sexual blood donor. What greater evidence of *giving*, than your blood flowing from your own blood-stream.'

Maurice Richardson also sees Count Dracula as a tragic figure: 'The vampire is so orally obsessessed that he cannot love because he's too greedy. But in fact, of course, he has a great need for love. And I'm not at all sure that the vampire isn't really a great lover in a sense.' Universal shrewdly advertised the 1931 Lugosi film as 'the strangest love a man has ever known'.

When Denholm Elliott portrayed the Count on television, the programme happened to coincide with a national poll for the 'most dreamt-of person in Britain' that week. 'And I,' Elliott told me with suitable surprise, 'was the most dreamt-of person in my role of Dracula. And the second, just to show you how corny the subconscious can be, was the Saint. So you had the devil and the saint.'

Bram Stoker struck a chord that vibrates even more strongly today. Dracula has astounding staying power: his image has leapt into the twentieth century to become a household name alongside Mickey Mouse and Tarzan. Perhaps it is significant that our folk heroes have become steadily less innocent: from Mickey and the morality of Sherlock Holmes, to Superman, James Bond, the recent infatuation with Jack the Ripper, and Dracula. Who will be next? I suspect Hitler.

With the aimlessness of our values, it seems as though we *need* Dracula today, just as there is a growing relish for disaster, fire, inferno, and earthquake, in our films. But one can be too serious. There is also the healthy release from the mundane. Virginia Woolf wrote: 'The preternatural has both great advantages and risks: the former, because, no doubt, it eliminates the blows and cuffs that real life deals.'

Meanwhile, the Dracula obsession accelerates, justifying the Romanian reference to a 'psychosis'. A Marvel Comic *Dracula Lives* was sold out within a few days; an ice-lolly manufactured by Wall's and advertised as 'Count Dracula's Deadly Secret – Eat one before Sunset!' – sold seven million in its first two months; and recently there has been a much-advertised crisp called 'Fangs!' that goes crunch in the night.

I am member number 0092 of the Dracula Society but they have more than two hundred members now. In the autumn of 1974, the Society organised a Dracula tour of Romania which managed to leave the tourist track and explore the Stoker landscape as well – a thousand miles covered in less than twelve days, but it was those extra few days compared with the usual eight-day tour that proved so profitable. Bernard Davies, the Honorary Secretary, wrote to me afterwards, 'The hospitality was terrific especially the Jonathan Harker luncheon at Bistrita which developed into the most gigantic binge lasting (I think) until about two in the next morning. Beautiful cloudless weather either end; just two days in the middle round the Borgo Pass appropriately dark and stormy, and when we picnicked up in the Calimani Mountains round a big fire, à la Mina and Van Helsing, it actually snowed on us. We even managed to have a fight with a band of gypsies – rather a one-sided affair albeit. It simply was the most amazing experience.' The Romanians were equally amazed by the Society members, especially the flowing black cloak of the Chairman, Bruce Wightman, and by Mrs Bernard Davies, who is beautiful and black: 'Coleen kept getting stroked and hugged by peasant women (vampires?),' wrote her husband. 'They'd obviously never seen a black person in the flesh in their lives. People broke off whatever they were doing to follow us around the streets in a crocodile in Bistrita. It was like a royal tour.' Wightman echoed the general enthusiasm: 'How Bram Stoker would have envied us the *actuality* of Romania.' A second tour by the Dracula Society left at the end of September, 1975.

A total of four million tourists are expected in Romania this same year, which is small by Western standards especially as the majority come from Communist countries, but this is one of their growth industries. Many thousands of Dracula fans will have arrived from Spain, and a Japanese agency offers a 'Dracula: Legend and Truth' visit, which heads straight in the wrong direction, as usual. There is also talk of a World Dracula Festival in 1976, to coincide with the 500th anniversary of Vlad Dracula's death.

A British architect is designing a 'Dracula Pub' for Bucharest, and there is talk of a Dracula Nightclub. One already exists in Switzerland, owned by the millionaire industrialist Gunther

Sachs, and the orgiastic climax of one cabaret act in a Copenhagen nightclub is a Dracula 'take off' in which the vampire and a naked girl are raised to the ceiling on a rope, dangling in mid-air 'in what could only be described as a compromising situation'.

In America there are Dracula Dolls, and a Dracula TV series.

When a Mexican entry was introduced at a film festival in Paris, the audience burst into wild applause and took up the chant 'Drac-ula, Drac-ula'. There are so many vampire films at the moment that a book is being written purely about the films. Count Dracula often appears in startling fictional form, such as in *Dracula's Brothers*, casting him in such unlikely roles as an adversary of the New York Mafia.

Apart from the fiction, there have been various learned investigations by distinguished men: *In Search of Dracula*, by Professors Florescu and McNally; *A Dream of Dracula*, by Professor Leonard Wolf, also responsible for the *Annotated Dracula*, published in America, 1975; *The Dracula Myth*, by the *Times* correspondent Gabriel Ronay.

There is a bookshop in Berwick Street which caters for science fiction and Dracula literature alone, and is more crowded than the surrounding Soho shops which concentrate on pornography.

As for Bram Stoker's original novel, published in 1897 with a plain, mustard-yellow cover and just the title in red letters, it has never been out of print. At the moment there are three separate paperback editions, including the honoured first place in Wheatley's 'Library of the Occult'.

'And where in all this, does the poor author stand?' asked *The Times Literary Supplement* in 1966. 'Nowhere very much; when a first biography appeared in 1962, on the fiftieth anniversary of his death, it was even titled *A Biography of Dracula*, a curious instance of the author apparently lost in his creation.'

It is true that in acclaiming Dracula we have forgotten Stoker. His novel must not be dismissed as a mere shocker. Re-examination proves that it is a classic, more rewarding than any imitation.

The reader who may *think* he knows Dracula, but has yet to discover Bram Stoker's own words, has a rare experience awaiting him.

Part Three

CHAPTER SIXTEEN

The Turn of the Tide

In the spring of 1895, Irving received a knighthood. In August, Stoker started work on *Dracula* at Cruden Bay. That year was a turning-point in both their lives: from then on, their good fortune slipped away.

It was late in the afternoon of 24 May, that Stoker had received a telegram from Irving: the usual summons, with a hint of emergency: 'Could you look in at quarter to six. Something important'. When Bram arrived at Grafton Street, he was shown two letters the actor had received that morning. One was from Lord Rosebery, announcing that the queen had conferred a knighthood on Irving for his services to art; the other, a note of congratulation from the Prince of Wales. As Laurence, his grandson, wrote later, this was the most sublime moment of Irving's life. It is hard to comprehend the accolade today, when Olivier is a lord, but Irving was the *first* actor to receive a knighthood and consequently the entire profession was honoured too.

After Stoker's emotional congratulations, they drove together to break the news to Ellen Terry. The Honours List was published the following day and by an odd chance, even though it was a Saturday, Oscar Wilde was sentenced at the Old Bailey as Irving's honour became public. A veiled lady had delivered violets during his trial and Laurence Irving suggests this was Ellen Terry and that the message of sympathy came from Irving as well, for violets were his favourite flowers. When Wilde was released two years later, one of the few greetings awaiting him came from Irving. Significantly, Wilde does not have a single mention in Stoker's reminiscences of Irving, though several pages are devoted to names alone. But at that particular moment, Stoker was too busy to worry about Wilde's tragedy. 'It seemed,' he wrote, 'as if the whole world rejoiced at the honour to Irving. The letters and telegrams kept coming literally in hundreds during the next two days and cables constantly arrived from America, Australia, Canada, India and from nearly all the countries in Europe.' It was Stoker, of course, who had to acknowledge them.

As for the great actor, Max Beerbohm glimpsed him in his carriage as he drove to Paddington Station on 18 July on his way to Windsor to receive his knighthood from the Queen, and gives a pleasing description of the change in him:

> Irving in his most prelatical mood had always had a touch –
> here and there – of the old bohemian. But as I caught sight
> of him on this occasion – a great occasion, naturally, in his
> career . . . he was the old bohemian and nothing else. His
> hat was tilted at more than his usual angle and his long
> cigar seemed longer than ever; and on his face was a look
> of such ruminant sly fun as I have never seen equalled.
> . . . I was sure that when he alighted on the platform at
> Paddington his bearing would be more than ever grave and
> stately with even the usual touch of bohemianism ob-
> literated now in honour of the honour that was to befall him.

'I am very, very pleased,' said the Queen when she greeted him.

At the very moment when a man has reached the peak of his career, fate seems to take a cruel delight in changing sides. Perhaps this is inevitable after so much glory. As Bram wrote, recognising the scent of trouble, 'the tide must turn some time – otherwise the force would not be a tide but a current. The turning came on the night of 19 December 1896.'

This was the opening night of *Richard III*, described, uncritically, by Stoker as an 'unqualified success'. Afterwards there was the usual first-night party on stage, this time for 500 guests, received by Irving, who had changed into evening dress. The tables were lavish with a cold supper from Gunter's and doubtless there was ample drink as well. When this was over, Irving moved on to the Garrick Club with a friend, then to the friend's rooms, and reached his own home at dawn. Stoker realised that the 'player was too high strung to rest' but no one is clear what happened next. Stoker said he slipped on the top stair and his knee struck an old oak chest on the landing. Rumour spread that Irving was drunk, slipped on the top of the stairs and fell right down them. This was exacerbated by Bernard Shaw's review a few days later, which suggested that Irving was actually drunk during the performance:

> He was occasionally a little out of temper with his own nervous condition. He made some odd slips in the text, notably by repeatedly substituting 'you' for 'I' ... Once he inadvertently electrified the house by very unexpectedly asking Miss Milton to get further up the stage in the blank verse and penetrating tones of Richard ... If Kean were to return to life and do the combat for us, we should very likely find it as absurd as his habit of lying down on a sofa when he was too tired or drunk to keep his feet during the final scene.

Irving's admirers seized on the last sentence as applicable to Irving, an interpretation which Shaw found regrettable, or pretended to. 'The murder is out!' he wrote to Irving, rather flippantly. 'They tell me that you consider that my criticsm of Richard III implied about you what it said about Kean. I reply flatly that it *didn't* .... The rest of his letter stood by his original adverse review. Irving's terse reply proved that he could hold his own in the art of invective: 'You are absolutely wrong in your polite insinuation of the cat out of the bag – as I had not the privilege of reading your criticism – as you call it of *Richard*. I never read a criticism of yours in my life. I have read lots of your droll, amusing, irrelevant and sometimes impertinent pages, but criticism containing judgement and sympathy I have never seen by your pen.'

Did Irving drink? Never on stage and not too noticeably off. But there was one night when he attended a dinner because he thought his absence would be misconstrued, and the boredom and champagne reduced him to such unintelligible grunts that his great rival Tree took him home and had a last view of him clinging to the railings with one hand while he waved a dramatic farewell with the other. Realising the story Tree might make of it, Irving was well-prepared a few days later when someone mentioned his name: 'Ah – a gud fellow. A – very – mm – gud fellow. A pity he drinks.'

The 'drunken' episode with Shaw put an end to a shaky relationship: they had been negotiating for the rights to *Man of Destiny* which Shaw was prepared to present on the condition that Irving would produce Ibsen at the Lyceum. But the main contention was Shaw's role as confidant to Ellen Terry, who was tactless enough to suggest bringing him to Irving's bedside. Now the play was returned with a curt rejection. What a wasted opportunity for the theatre as a whole! Like Wilde, Shaw does not receive a mention in Stoker's *Irving*, and soon afterwards was barred from the Lyceum on Stoker's instructtions – but talked his way in, nevertheless.

But Shaw was a mere irritant compared to the consequences of that fall. The ligatures under Irving's knee-cap had been ruptured, and for the first time in his life he found that he was an invalid, unable to appear on stage. Bram wrote out a 'Lyceum Special Notice', an eventuality he must have dreaded for years: 'The management regrets to announce that owing to a sprain Henry Irving will be unable to play for a few days. The Lyceum Theatre will therefore be closed for this evening and tomorrow and Wednesday evenings.' But a later bulletin had to be issued to the press, signed by Bram as the acting manager: 'In consequence of the sprain to his knee received on Sunday which will prevent Sir Henry Irving from appearing for a short time in his part of Richard III, the further performances of that play have been postponed. Due notice will be given of their resumption.' The Lyceum was closed until Boxing day, while Bram, realising there was little chance of Irving's early return, struggled to find a substitute production. On 2 January, he issued another statement: 'At the consultation on Sir Henry Irving's knee this afternoon it was found that progress had been as satisfactory as possible but that more time must be allowed for repair of the injury.' Stoker did his utmost to keep the Lyceum going with a new version of *Cymbeline* but the receipts were so abysmal, without the draw of either Irving or Ellen Terry, who was taking a cure in Homburg, that he closed the theatre after a week. The great machine ground to a halt. Even when Ellen Terry returned, the theatre failed to pay its way. ' 'I am not here to collect money,' Irving had once remarked contemptuously; now there was no money to collect. The season ended with a loss of £6,000 (according to Stoker; £10,000 according to Laurence Irving).

Later the profits of *Madame Sans-Gêne* helped to recoup some of the loss but Stoker wrote afterwards: 'The disaster of that morning was the beginning of many which struck, and struck, and struck again . . .'

First there was a personal one which a few will understand: the death of Fussie, Irving's dog. Irving might have 'preserved a barrier of mystery' to other people, as Beerbohm suggested, but his devotion to Fussie was as open as his grief. Fussie died in Manchester, where a stage-hand had thrown his jacket over a trap door. In search of a ham sandwich which he had scented in the pocket, Fussie fell through the trap and was killed instantly. Irving was found later staring into space for hours on end and took the plump remains to London the next day to be buried in the dogs' cemetery in Hyde Park. He loved his dog, said Ellen Terry, as much as his rehearsals.

On a February morning in 1898, Stoker was roused by the noise of violent knocking on his door at Chelsea. Stumbling downstairs, for it was ten minutes past five, he opened the door and the cabby gave him a letter from the police station at Bow Street. The Lyceum Storage, which housed all the scenery and props, was ablaze in Southwark.

The four-wheeler was waiting, and I was soon on the way there as fast as the horse could go. It was a dim, dank morning, bitterly cold. I found Bear Lane a chaos. The narrow way was blocked with fire-engines panting and thumping away for dear life. The heat was terrific. There was so much stuff in the storage that nothing could be done till the fire had burnt itself out; all that the firemen could do was to prevent the fire spreading.

Bram watched, appalled. He knew that 'All the scene painters in England working for a whole year could not have restored the scenery alone.' There were 260 scenes for 44 plays, 22 of them great productions. There were more than two thousand pieces of scenery and 'props'. Because the Storage House had been presumed fireproof, Stoker had only taken insurance for

£10,000, and only recently Irving himself, searching for econo-
mies, had reduced this to £6,000. Now it was estimated that
£60,000 would have been needed to replace the treasure-house
but even that would have been impossible, considering the
artistic effort involved. Irving had made a point of withdrawing
productions at the peak of their success, so that he could include
them, untarnished, in later seasons. In this night his resources
were destroyed, the glory of his repertory gone: *Hamlet; The
Merchant of Venice; Othello; Macbeth; Twelfth Night* ...

The story becomes melancholy, but it was a magnificent
melancholy: the ageing actor with the stamina of a man running downhill, thus able to continue but unable to stop. Every
set-back meant further exhaustion for Stoker, as the actor withdrew into himself. Ellen Terry noted, astutely, that 'For years
he has accepted favours, obligations to, etc., *through* Bram
Stoker. Never will he acknowledge them himself, either by
businesslike receipt or by any word or sign. He "lays low" like
Brer Rabbit better than anyone I have ever met.'

In spite of the extra strain all this involved, Bram was far
from pleased by the appointment of a press secretary which was
made without consultation. The man's name was Austin Brere-
ton, a reminder of that other rival, L. F. Austin, on the second
American tour. Even so, those had been happier times.

Honours cascaded from the great universities: Irving was
gowned and boarded from every side. Doctor of Letters in
Cambridge; Doctor of Laws in Glasgow. Stoker, as always,
applauded from the wings, even in his own city of Dublin,
where he failed to receive his own due – 'As Irving passed
to his place in the Examination Hall he was loudly cheered.
I was, of course, not close to him; I sat with the Senate,
of which I am a member.'

The first signal that Irving had exhausted his bodily strength
came on the provincial tour in the autumn of 1898, during their
first week in Glasgow. Before the curtain rose on the second act
of *Madame Sans-Gêne*, Stoker was called to his office where he
found Irving, 'his face drawn with pain', dressed for his part
as Napoleon. 'I think there must be something wrong with me.
Every breath is like a sword-stab. I don't think I ought to be
suffering like this without seeing someone.' At such an admission,
Stoker knew Irving was really ill and asked if he could dismiss

the audience. Irving refused. 'I shall be able to get through all right; but when I have seen a doctor we may have to make some change for tomorrow.' As Stoker hurried to fetch a doctor, Irving limped on to make his first entrance as Napoleon in the play.

The doctor diagnosed both pneumonia and pleurisy. Assigned two nurses, but tended by Collinson, Irving lay in bed in Glasgow for the next seven weeks while Stoker 'lived in trains', trying to keep things going. The northern tour continued, with another actor, on Irving's instructions because the livelihood of seventy people depended on it – always this reponsibility – and Stoker succeeded in leasing the Lyceum to Forbes-Robertson, the Carl Rosa Company, and Martin-Harvey – hampered by the need to retain options to break the tenancies if Irving recovered. At least he was able to tell his friend that everything was being taken care of. His eyes must have been red-rimmed from lack of sleep, but his one concern was the actor:

As I used to see Irving every few days I could note his progress – down or up. At first, of course, he got worse and worse; weaker, and suffering more pain. He had never in his life been anything but lean, but now as he lost flesh the outline of his features grew painfully keen. The cheeks and chin and lips, which he had kept clean shaven all his life, came out stubbly with white hair. At that time his hair was iron grey, but no more. I remember one early morning when I came into the sitting-room and found his faithful valet, Walter, in tears. When I asked him the cause – for I feared it was death – he said through his sobs: 'He is like Gregory Brewster! [the old soldier in *Waterloo*].' Walter did not come into the room with me; he feared he would break down and so do harm. When I stole into the room Irving had just waked. He was glad to see me, but he looked very old and weak. Poor Walter's description was sadly accurate. Indeed, he realised the pathetic picture of the dying Sir John Falstaff given by Mrs Quickly: 'His nose was as sharp as a pen.'

Descriptions by Ellen Terry show how Irving changed over the years:

In 1867 – everything was against him as an actor. He could not speak, he could not walk, he could not *look* ... He was really almost ordinary looking with a moustache, an unwrinkled face, and a sloping forehead. The only wonderful thing about him was his melancholy.

In 1878 – (he had lost) much of the stiff, ugly self-consciousness which had encased him as the shell encases the lobster. His forehead had become more massive. He was a man of the world, whose strenuous fighting now was to be done as a general – not, as hitherto, in the ranks.

He was far simpler than I in some ways. He would talk, for instance, in such an ingenuous way to painters and musicians that I blushed for him.

He never pretended.

He looked like a great famished wolf, weak with the weakness of an exhausted giant [in the final scenes of Macbeth].

In 1895 – a superb brow; rather small dark eyes which can at moments become immense.

He has an ugly ear! Large, flabby, ill-cut and pasty looking, pale and lumpy.

His hair is superb; beautiful in 1867 when I first met him, when it was blue-black like a raven's wing, it is even more splendid now when it is liberally streaked with white. It is rather long, and hangs in lumps on his neck, which is now like the neck of a youth of 20!

His skin is very pale, delicate, refined, and stretched tightly over his features.'

Never have I seen such hands ... he always makes them up for the stage, very brown.

In 1899 – his illness has made him look queer ... very grey, sly-looking and more cautious than ever. Bother!

She remembered one splendid dying fall when he turned to her and remarked, 'How strange it is that I should have made my reputation ... with nothing to help me – no equipment, My legs, my voice – everything has been against me. For an actor who can't walk, can't talk, and has no face to speak of, I've done pretty well.'

And Ellen Terry, looking at 'that splendid head, those won-

derful hands, the whole strange beauty of him, thought, "Ah,
you little know!"'

Her last description is fine: 'He looked like some beautiful
grey tree that I have seen in Savannah. His old dressing-gown
hung about his frail yet majestic figure like some mysterious grey
drapery.

'What a wonderful life you've had, haven't you?' she said
suddenly.

'Oh yes . . . a wonderful life – of work.'

'And there's nothing better after all, is there?'

'Nothing.'

'What have we got out of it all? . . . You and I are getting
on, as they say. Do you ever think as I do sometimes, what
you have got out of life?'

'What have I got out of it?' He smiled, 'Let me see . . .
well, a good cigar, a good glass of wine – good friends.' He
kissed her hand.

'That's not a bad summing-up of it at all. And the end
. . . how would you like that to come?'

'How would I like that to come?' He repeated her
question. He was silent for thirty seconds, then he snapped
his fingers decisively – '*Like that!*'

But there was another, less tender side of him which Ellen
Terry noted as well. Perhaps there was a tinge of resentment
at his friendship with Mrs Aria, a lady who was a newspaper
'diarist of gosssip', though she carefully avoided gossip about
herself. 'I think it is not quite right in him that he does not
care for anybody much (I think he has always cared for me a
little, very little) and has had passing fancies, but he really
CARES for scarcely anyone. Quiet, patient, tolerant, impersonal,
gentle, CLOSE, crafty! Crafty sounds unkind, but it is HI.' Two
years later, she wrote, 'Very odd, he is not improving with age.'
And in the year of his first serious illness, 'I wonder how his
other friends and lovers feel to him. I have contempt and affection and admiration. What a mixture!'

As for Stoker, she described him as one of the most kind and
tender-hearted of men, filling a difficult position with great tact,
never taking a mean advantage of the company but always being

straight with them: 'Stoker and Loveday were daily, nay hourly associated for many years with HI but, after all, did they or anyone else *really* know him. And what was HI's attitude? I believe myself that he never wholly trusted his friends and never admitted them to his intimacy, although they thought he did which was the same thing to *them*. From his childhood up, Henry was lonely.' Regarding that 'daily association', the only time that Stoker was not at Irving's side was in 1899, when the actor received his honorary degree at Glasgow. Stoker had pneumonia: 'It was the only occasion at which in twenty-seven years I was not present when honour was done to him.'

Apart from the strain on Irving's health, the worst consequence of this first illness was the increase in that 'furtive' and 'crafty' side of his nature that had been noticed by Ellen Terry. During his recovery at Bournemouth, admittedly when he was at a low ebb, he betrayed both her and Bram Stoker – the two people who had reason to think they were the closest to him of all. But, at this moment, she remained optimistic over the outcome: 'Poor old King H. is at his downest, and I'm amazed at the few in number of his useful friends. After a dreadful illness (the first in his life) he has to lie up for months, and is at Bournemouth, twiddling his poor thumbs and thinking out the best way to get to work again. He is ruined in pocket, heavily in debt, and I doubt not, will in spite of all and everybody, rise from his ashes like *the* Bird!'

CHAPTER SEVENTEEN

The Fall of the Lyceum

At no time, as treasurer of the Lyceum, was Bram free from monetary crisis. He could hardly have chosen a more hazardous enterprise than a theatre, whose success or failure depends so much on the tastes of the audience, on the unforeseen magic that creates a popular triumph from unpromising material, or conversely, on that 'something' lacking which plunges an expected hit into a lingering flop. Even a London fog could sway the balance.

These unpredictable factors, together with the constant need to adapt the theatre to both the convenience and safety of the audience, meant that Bram could never work to a set budget, though he did his best to resist unnecessary expenses. As early as January 1883, when Irving was asked to contribute £1,990 towards some 'recent alterations at the Lyceum', Bram replied by return:

My dear Sir,
Mr Irving who is just going on the stage and wishes there to be no delay, desires me to say for him in answer to your letter of today that with all willingness on his part to meet you in any way of mutual benefit he feels that he cannot in justice to himself join you in the cost of the requirements compelled by the Board of Works. He paid himself for structural alterations in 1881 for the permanent good of the building no less a sum than £7,000 this to the architect and the builders only and being quite exclusive of all decorations and other collateral matters which amounted to a more than equal sum in addition. Since taking his lease in 1878 the improvements which he has made have cost him over £24,000.

Mr Irving is very sorry that you have any misunderstanding in the matter as he had never any intention of being a part of the Board of Works expenses. He thinks if you will refer to his letter you will see that there is not anything leading to such a conclusion and he has no recollection of having said anything to that purpose.

Even when the going was good, as it was then, Bram had a yearly battle with his figures. By 1900, the pressure was so great that the battle had become a daily struggle. Bram was hardly helped by the prevarications of Horatio Bottomley, who owed bills for £800 and consistently defaulted. On 28 March 1900 Bram wrote to the Secretary of the Associated Financial Corporation:

Dear Sir,
Sir Henry Irving holds a bill for £800 drawn by Mr Horatio Bottomley accepted by the Assoc Financial Corp. It was duly presented by Messrs Coutts & Co on the 20th, the day of its maturity. It was not paid on that day and Mr Bottomley asked that it should be re-presented on 23rd as there had been a clerical error as to date. It was duly presented on 23rd but was not paid, the messenger being told that cheque was being sent by post to the holders! No cheque has been received yet.
As I have been told to recover from you the amount due on the bill I would be glad if you will send cheque at once as I am loth to send it to our solicitor. In the matter of a bill there should be no delay in taking it up if credit be good. I shall look to hear from you tomorrow before two o'clock.

Exactly a year later the same pattern was repeated with bills presented by Coutts and refused. Bottomley wrote to Bram at the Prince of Wales Theatre in Birmingham:

Dear Mr Stoker:
I find that by a foolish oversight in the office the bill drawn on the Associated Financial Corporation was entered as payable on the 23rd, that is to say allowing the three

days grace from the 20th. It appears, however, that it was actually payable today. You may be aware that the Company is in course of reorganisation . . .

And so on. Similar courteous but evasive letters followed.

Despite such unreliable creditors as Bottomley, Irving's reputation was so secure that he continued to receive, and rely on, sympathy from such eminent bankers as Alfred de Rothschild.

'Dear Bram Stoker,' wrote Louis Roche on 7 April 1903, 'I duly received your letter and at once spoke on the subject to Mr Alfred de Rothschild asking him if he had any objection to the Firm making the advance of £2,000 against Sir Henry's securities. Mr Alfred wishes me to say that he is pleased to oblige Sir Henry Irving . . .' The money was paid to Coutts that same afternoon, and Louis Roche ended with a personal request: 'And now, dear Mr Bram Stoker, may I crave a little favour at your hands, if it is possible for you to oblige me. I want 4 stalls (in two lots of 2 each) for the opening night of Dante. I have tried various agents, but am met everywhere with a "non possumus".'

A further £1,000 was paid to Coutts on 28 April and another £2,000 advance, free of interest as before, on 1 July, though by this time, Irving's credit was beginning to run dry.

The question remains: was Stoker an *efficient* business manager? To have run the Lyceum for so many years, he must have been. But success is another matter altogether. At first he and Irving basked in it; perhaps they persevered too long; certainly they over-reached themselves. But could any man have curbed Irving's largesse, the grandiose suppers, the insistence on real apples for the trees on stage, the abrupt destruction of scenery that failed to please? Not only did he enjoy spending money; he liked over-spending. When a cabby ran after him, thinking his gold half-sovereign tip was a mistake, Irving replied, 'Think yourself lucky, my man, that it wasn't a sovereign.'

When he played the Haymarket Theatre, so the story goes, he kept a brougham waiting outside the stage door, leapt into it and cried dramatically – 'To the Carlton, and drive like mad!' The Carlton was a few yards around the corner.

'Had it not been for his old friend Bram Stoker,' said Henry Labouchère, 'Irving would have been eaten out of home and

theatre very speedily.' Reginald Auberon endorsed this view in
his book on *The Nineteen Hundreds* referring to Stoker as
Irving's

> faithful watch-dog and right-hand man, to whose unswerv-
> ing fidelity and marked business aptitude the Lyceum chief
> probably owed a good deal more than he acknowledged or
> realized. When Irving was up in the clouds (and where,
> by the way, he habitually lived), Stoker was down in the
> box-office, doing unobtrusive, but uncommonly useful, work.
> As a matter of fact, if Stoker had not been on the bridge,
> the Lyceum ship would have foundered a lot sooner than it
> did. The trouble was, Irving – who, despite his general
> astuteness, was a pretty poor judge of character, and would
> believe any one who flattered him sufficiently – surrounded
> himself with a greedy host of third-rate parasites at the
> expense of the theatre's not inexhaustible revenues. These
> merchants called themselves 'literary advisers', or some-
> thing equally high sounding. They were, however, merely
> able hacks, whose sole business it was to write speeches full
> of classical quotations and historical allusions, which Irving
> delivered to awe-struck gatherings in the provinces and
> America, and prepare the profound articles which from
> time to time appeared under his signature in portentous
> monthly reviews. It was pure dope of course, but the
> public wanted it, and it went down.

Probably Auberon was unaware of Stoker's own readiness to
write these speeches in the early days, and how dismayed he
was when his position was usurped by Austin.

He quoted Stoker – 'who had more brains than the entire
pack put together' – as hating the sight of them, and telling him
that if he could have made a clean sweep of the lot the Lyceum
treasury would have been saved thousands a year. 'Irving,
however, would not listen to such a proposal for a moment. He
thought it enhanced his dignity to be surrounded by a courtier-
like crowd of sycophants.'

Appalled by the rising costs of *Dante* in 1903, which had
become an obsession with Irving but smelt of commercial failure
to Stoker, the latter warned that it was above the minds of the

audience and would not succeed. 'My dear fellow,' the actor replied, 'a play like this beats Monte Carlo as a hazard. Whatever one may do – about losing – you certainly can't win unless you play high!' This was the vanity of the gambler.

As for Stoker's honesty, that is not in doubt. Two million pounds passed through his hands. With so much under his control he would have been able to accumulate reasonable capital for his old age – but he did not.

Gordon Craig, Ellen Terry's son, referred to him as 'A man of feeling, of understanding, of integrity. This was a man of character.' But Laurence Irving, the actor's grandson, was critical: 'Stoker, inflated with literary and athletic pretensions worshipped Irving with all the sentimental idolatry of which an Irishman is capable, revelling in the patronage which, as Irving's manager, was at his disposal, and in the opportunities which this position gave him to rub shoulders with the great.' Hardly an accusation, but Laurence Irving suggests that this attitude was harmful to the Lyceum:

This weakness and his emotional impetuosity handicapped him in dealing with Irving's business affairs in a forthright and sensible manner. Irving needed, though he might not have tolerated, a partner of financial and executive ability who would keep a stern check upon the extravagances and irregularities to which a theatrical organisation of this kind was peculiarly prone. Stoker, well-intentioned, vain, impulsive and inclined to blarneying flattery, was perhaps the only man who could have held his position as Irving's manager for so many years; from him Irving got the service he deserved, but at a cost which was no less fatal because it was not immediately apparent.

By contrast, he praised Harry Loveday without reservation: 'Irving treated Loveday with a trust and affection which was never so apparent in his relations with Stoker. While he might have had a shrewder man than Stoker in front of the house, without Loveday's help he could never have realised all that he contrived upon the stage.' This is harsh; with a little more of that 'trust', the final calamity might have been averted.

The Comyns Carr affair was an underhand business. It began the day that Irving left for Bournemouth to convalesce. Before his departure, Stoker was recalled from Manchester to see him at once on urgent business. This proved to be a speculative offer which Stoker warned him against. It seemed that Irving accepted this advice and on the 21st Stoker received a further summons to visit the Bath Hotel, where Irving was staying, and found him looking stronger, self-possessed and 'evenly balanced'. Stoker arrived with a carefully prepared schedule: first the rental of the Lyceum, then a short provincial tour with a few plays in order to keep expenses at a minimum. Then a two months' holiday in which Irving could regain further strength before returning to a season at the Lyceum. Then a profitable tour of America with the Lyceum leased for £10,000 for which he had obtained a secure offer. It seemed they were back in harness and Stoker recorded 'Irving's judgement was at a high tide when with fresh hope and vigour he accepted this policy.' Stoker left the next morning to join the rest of the company, who were playing at Brighton until Christmas Eve. 'We were both in good spirits, hopeful and happy.'

With such reassurance, he was unprepared for the betrayal that followed only a few days later. Throughout his *Personal Reminiscences of Henry Irving* there is not a hint of criticism or malice or even affectionate mockery. This is both the weakness and yet the strength of the book. Even now, the bitterness has to be glimpsed between the lines. 'It was an unfortunate thing for his own prosperity that Irving did not adhere to the arrangement then made. When the offer made by the parent Lyceum Theatre Company was put before him he jumped at it; and before he had consulted with me about it, or even told me of it, he had actually signed a tentative acceptance.' Only three weeks had passed since their last meeting, and Stoker and Loveday had been busy preparing the tours; now they were called to Bournemouth where Irving broke the news. They had the formality of a discussion over the two plans – Stoker stressed that every advantage lay with the one already agreed on. But he could see that Irving's mind was made up. 'When a man of his strong nature makes up his mind to a course of action he generally goes on with it despite reasons or arguments . . . He listened, as ever, attentively and courteously and with seeming thoughtfulness, to all I had to say – and then shifted conversation to details, as though the main principle had been already accepted.'

Comyns Carr, on behalf of the new Company, came down to join them. Stoker fought for better terms but could gain only details. However, when it was suggested that Irving should be listed on the prospectus as a director of the new company, he gave such a vehement 'No' that even Irving was prepared to listen. Stoker explained that as Irving was selling to the company and sharing his profits with them, it was unthinkable that he could commit himself further. Irving agreed.

Stoker was in the middle of negotiating with Charles Frohman for the autumn tour of America. This required careful handling. An exhausting tour of seven months in 1896 had produced receipts of £116,500. Irving's share was £73,000, but as the expenses came to £70,000 this left him a meagre profit of £3,000. Now the new details had gone beyond the scope of cable and Stoker had to leave for personal discussions at the very moment of crisis. He sailed for America on the *Germanic* on 31 January 1899, through one of the worst storms ever recorded, and arrived on 11 February. He was back again in London on 1 March. He found that during his absence everything had been settled. 'There was not anything left to me to do in the matter.'

The Syndicate consisted of Joe Comyns Carr, a former dramatic critic, and his two brothers – a solicitor and a 'financier'. They knew their scheme was 'dangerously attractive', as Laurence Irving called it, to the actor, who was in a state of physical and financial depletion. Outwardly it looked reasonable. It floated the Lyceum Theatre Company, which would take on the next eight years of the Lyceum's lease and all its properties. Irving was to give a guaranteed 100 performances each year, on sharing terms. He was to bear 60 per cent of the production costs and he was to undertake a four-month tour yearly of either the provinces or America, giving a quarter of these profits to the company. In return, he was to receive £26,000 in cash and £12,500 of the total shares issued to the public – £100,000 preference and £70,000 ordinary. But on his return from America, Stoker was shocked to discover that a further £120,000 mortgage debentures, to the free-holders of the Lyceum, had increased the capital issue to £290,000, also that, against his urging, Irving had allowed his name to be used in the prospectus as 'Dramatic Adviser'.

It is possible to see that such a scheme, with £26,000 in cash, might have seemed 'dangerously attractive'. It is more difficult to understand why Irving's affairs were in such a mess. He was advised and helped on the one hand by the Baroness Burdett-Coutts, whose loan had launched the Lyceum, and by Alfred Rothschild who was now handling his affairs and apparently always ready to help out financially. Even so, Irving had been so hard-pressed that he sold his precious collection of theatrical books and prints for little more than a thousand pounds, to help pay off his debts. I have seen four £1,000 IOUs made out to Ellen Terry, around this time, and never redeemed.

When Irving saw Ellen Terry at Bournemouth he had told her that he was ruined. 'Well,' she replied gallantly, 'as long as you and I have health, we have means of wealth. We can pack a bag, each of us and trot round the provinces.' But when she asked him his plans he astonished her by mumbling that he was touring with *The Bells* and *Waterloo*.

'Where do I come in?' she asked.

'Oh well, for the present at all events, there's no chance of acting at the Lyceum. For the present you can of course – er –do as you like.' At this moment, she recorded, he looked extremely silly. Her sense of humour lessened the hurt, but 'I felt a good many feelings. At top of all came amusement. I had in plain terms what Ted would call the dirty kick-out.'

But when the Syndicate was formed, Ellen Terry was one of the conditions and she suddenly found herself of value again. She had been terrified in the previous October by Irving's feebleness, but as he got better – 'Anything so icy, indifferent and almost contemptuous I never saw.'

For the first time there was coolness between Stoker and Irving. Laurence Irving thought that his grandfather regretted 'the hasty surrender of his independence' and also 'the inevitable division of the loyalty of his associates between himself and the company. He was not a man to admit he had made a mistake. Yet the knowledge he had done so in the face of Stoker's earnest opposition – to say nothing of Stoker's natural pique at his Chief's disregard – clouded a little their relationship to one another.'

Inevitably, misunderstandings occurred under the new arrangement. This is shown by a terse letter sent by Irving to Stoker on 4 April 1899.

There has been the most astounding, stupid mistake about the Sunday papers, which have no advertisements. Tell them in future to show *me* an advt. list – which I will supervise – in fact it is *you* who ought to make advts. for which I am responsible for the biggest share. At all events you must *revise*.

He concluded with formal goodwill: 'I hope you're all right and not tired out.'

But if Stoker was piqued, it was a pique of loyalty. The decision made, he stood by his chief and continued to defend his interests. Ultimately he was proved right, but this was little satisfaction. When they returned from America, where poor houses had finally forced Irving to remove *Dante* from the bill, and the scenery was given away in Canada rather than incur duty charges, they found that the Lyceum Syndicate was doomed. Failure became irrevocable when the LCC insisted on new fire precautions at a cost of nearly £20,000. The company had lost consistently, except when Irving played there; the only other time was when they followed his single piece of advice as 'Dramatic Adviser' and presented William Gillette as *Sherlock Holmes*. Years before, Irving himself had refused this role when Conan Doyle offered to adapt it for him. What a Holmes, with Stoker as his Watson!

There were a few last attempts to continue. I have an undated letter from J. Comyns Carr from the New Gallery in Regent Street which indicates one plan:

My dear Henry, . . . Since I saw you in town I have heard (by cable) from Frohman that he did not feel himself able on his own account to make an offer for the lease of The Lyceum Theatre and upon receipt of that information I called upon Willian Great (I am not sure of the spelling

G

of the second name) who is as you perhaps know in partnership with Engelbach. I know them because I recently sold to them the lease of the Comedy Theatre on very good terms. I learned then by inquiry that they are both men of very substantial means a good deal of which was acquired by the large interest they possessed in *The Sign of the Cross*. I also came to know that they have made it their business to speculate in theatres and they are surrounded by a group of very wealthy men who follow their advice in theatrical speculations. I put it to Great whether he would entertain the combined scheme viz: to take over the lease of the Lyceum Theatre for £10,000 and to find the money to run you for a season beginning at Easter in such pieces as you wanted to produce. I think it most probable from what he told me that he would be willing and able to carry out such a scheme and he would be as he said most willing that until your season was concluded their names should in no way appear and that as far as the public was concerned it should be in every respect your own last season in your own theatre. It would also fit in with his arrangements that should you see fit you should in subsequent years have a date reserved for you for a series of performances.

Now all this seemed to me to accord with the expression of what you desired when we met in London and I believe it can be carried through. The only thing I want to be assured of is

(1) That I am acting in accordance with your wishes in setting these negotiations in train

(2) That there is no other scheme already settled which would interfere with this.

The last point is important. In order to be able to make a definite proposal Great has to consult with some of his friends and of course he does not want to go seriously into the matter if you already contemplate some other arrangement that would render his efforts idle. Let me know what you feel. My own strong advice would be unless you have some very good offer before you, to let me proceed with these negotiations and to do nothing in any other direction until Great has had time to see what he can do. I believe in the man's ability and in his good will to carry this matter through.

Yours J. Comyns Carr.

As the letter opens with good wishes for the New Year, I assume it was sent early in 1902. Another letter, from Irving to Loveday, quoted by Laurence Irving but also undated, shows that Irving was considering a last effort to keep the theatre going:

Mr Chas. Scotter, Director of SW Ry – with whom I was dining last night – says it should be seriously considered – as do many who joined the Company on the inducement of my name – whether it would not be well to do something for the shareholders' sake, for my own sake, and for the preservation of the theatre.

If certain liabilities of the Company could be wiped off – Company newly constructed, a sum of £50,000 subscribed – County Council alterations made – with a certificate of finality for certain period – theatre redecorated and brought up-to-date – and an *invitation* to me to undertake management – I should be inclined to accept it under certain conditions which we have already talked over – and the more inclined if we could baffle the pack of daylight robbers. I feel it now to be my duty. Show this to Stoker.   H.I.

As he was one of the 'daylight robbers', the machinations of Comyns Carr were unacceptable. As for Irving's own suggestion, it was not possible to raise such capital. The Receiver moved in.

For all his goodwill, properties and services, and a quarter of the profits he made elsewhere, Irving received £26,800 in cash and £12,500 in shares which now proved worthless. Meanwhile, he had made £29,000 for the company in earnings. He had given two years of his life, his theatrical properties, and £2,200 for nothing. At a meeting of the promoters he said bitterly, 'You think I don't know you've been robbing me, but I *do*.' He felt guilt and shame and responsibility towards the shareholders who forgot the triumphs and remembered the recent failures such as *Peter the Great*, written by his son Laurence. There was an ugly meeting in 1903 when the company directors were heckled and Irving himself blamed.

A newspaper reported that:

The chairman, Mr Eves, had a none too friendly audience for his opening speech, and a remark he made to the effect that the Lyceum would eventually turn out to be a veritable gold mine was received with a shriek of laughter. He reminded the meeting that if the shareholders did not take some action quickly they might lose their property altogether, as the Debenture holders would have it in their power to foreclose.

He proposed the formation of a new company to convert the Lyceum into a Music Hall.

Stoker had bought five shares through someone else in order to have the right to attend, and addressed the meeting angrily. 'I thought it necessary,' he wrote afterwards, 'to put a stop to such misconception [about Irving's responsibility] and gave the rough figures showing the results of his playing during the time the contract existed, my statement was received even by the disappointed shareholders with loud continuous cheers – the only cheers which I ever heard at a meeting of the Company.'

He then read a letter from Irving:

Dear Bram Stoker,

As you will be at the Lyceum meeting tomorrow, will you please read, if permissible, this letter to the shareholders?

It seems to me that it would be a pity to have the Lyceum diverted from its purpose as a theatre, and I have great doubts as to the success of such a scheme.

Holding the views which I do regarding the possible good influence of a theatre on the community, I could not honestly acquiesce in such a proposal as that set forth, and under ordinary circumstances should have voted against it, being willing rather to sacrifice my own holding in the company, which is to me no inconsiderable loss.

If, however, the great bulk of the shareholders are wishful to make such a change, and think it to their interest to do so, I am willing in deference to their wishes, to simply abstain from any participation in the movement, and content myself with this expression of opinion.

If an alternative scheme should be proposed to hold over the property, which will increase yearly in value, until a purchaser could be found, I shall be prepared to pay any share or proportion, say, for two or three years, of any sum which might be required to meet the expenses of Debenture interest, sinking fund, and other necessary motions.

Possibly the advances from Rothschild were related to last minute hopes of salvage, but the decline of the Lyceum had gone too far. One pound shares were quoted at 6d to 1s 6d, part of a total loss of £125,000. Formed in 1899, with Irving as the 'front man', the company had paid only one dividend to the Ordinary shareholders. Now they voted for the conversion of the great Lyceum into a Music Hall, and Irving was left in the very position Bram had dreaded – an actor without a theatre of his own to play in.

CHAPTER EIGHTEEN

𝔜𝔬𝔲, 𝔞𝔟𝔬𝔳𝔢 𝔞𝔩𝔩 𝔐𝔢𝔫 . . .

'You, above all men whom I hold dear . . .' I remember this startling phrase, scribbled on the back of an envelope in the bag of letters given me by Noel Stoker. It was written in indelible pencil in Irving's seismograph hand and was virtually indecipherable apart from this phrase. I had the impression it was written in haste after a serious disagreement. It may have been a pang of conscience during the dispute of the Lyceum Syndicate; I can only guess. But it does seem, in spite of their differences, as if the two men became closer at the end, if only because of the durability of their relationship.

They did not meet so often; Irving had to husband his failing strength. His entertaining was restricted to Sunday dinner parties. But when the play was over he would dress slowly, chatting in the dressing-room, lingering as long as possible before returning to his rather bleak apartment or hotel bedroom. 'All that while,' wrote Stoker, 'night by night and year by year, he would stick to his purpose of saving himself for his work – at any cost to himself in the shape of loss of pleasure, or any form of self-abnegation . . . Thus life lost part of its charm for him. He felt it deeply; and, all unknowing, was fostered that bitterness which had struck root already. He was sixty-one when he was stricken with pleurisy and had been working hard for forty-two years; now he looked older than his age.'

The greatest help that Stoker could offer was 'to take on my shoulders all the work I could', visiting Irving's new flat in Stratton Street every day; his visits to the Lyceum office became rare.

Presumably, the Beefsteak Room lay silent.

Stoker noticed 'a certain shrinkage within [Irving] during the last seven years of his life which was only too apparent to the eyes of those who loved him. To the outer world he still bore himself as ever: quiet, self-contained, masterful . . . Perhaps the little note of defiance which was added was the conscious recognition of the blows of fate. But outside his own immediate circle this was not to be seen.'

To the public it seemed a triumphal progress as they travelled from city to city and continent to continent, accepting the honours and the applause; they were deceived by the actor's camouflage. For a long time he had suffered from a complaint, known absurdly as 'clergyman's sore throat' because it was common among actors and public speakers. Stoker said that doctors classified it as follicular pharyngitis, an irritating and demanding disease, but Irving's condition seemed worse than that. His constant fits of coughing grew so bad that for the last three years he used *five hundred* pocket handkerchiefs a week to contain the phlegm. In February 1905 he fell fainting in the foyer of his Wolverhampton Hotel and the doctor discovered that for six years, ever since the attack of pleurisy, he had been coughing up pus from an unhealed lung. Lack of money forced him to continue. Stoker confirmed: 'For others there was rest; for him none.' And it was not just the performance he had to fulfil, but all the rigmarole of speeches and banquets held in his honour in every town. That was the worse ordeal. He developed the charade of pointing to some object of local interest and while his companion stopped to explain he had the chance to rest and recover.

They still had their triumphs. On 1 June 1904 he announced his retirement in Manchester; this enabled him to make a grand farewell tour in which he could say goodbye to his public in England, Canada and America. It would take two years. Learning this, George Alexander asked Stoker to join him as business manager of the St James's, an offer that must have been tempting, but Stoker stayed loyal. They started the farewell tour at Cardiff and Swansea, where the audience stayed in their seats and started to fill the theatre with their singing – 'Lead Kindly Light'. Irving returned to his dressing-room, his face wet with tears. At the Royal Hotel, Bristol, he made one of his finest speeches:

Without opening a book, or listening to music, or sitting

at the play, or meditating at a picture gallery, you can lead a blameless, prosperous and even energetic life. But it will be a very dry, narrow and barren life, cut off from some of the world's greatest treasures. It will be a life of defective growth on the imaginative side.

At the beginning of 1905, Stoker wrote in his diary – after the performance of *The Lyons Mail* at Boscombe – 'H.I. fearfully done up, could hardly play. At end in collapse. Could hardly move or breathe.'

He had to speak in the freezing cold to a vast crowd in Bath in the open street; at Wolverhampton he collapsed and the doctor told him he could not undertake both the speech to the town hall and the play at night – he chose *Becket*. The next day the doctor was adamant that he needed to rest for at least two months. The tour was abandoned.

There was a glorious moment on 10 June, the last night of a six week season at Drury Lane. The audience sensed this might be the last time they would see him and the house was the biggest he had ever played to in London. There was a roar when he made his entrance. At one point in the play there was the cry 'The King's Men, the King's Men'; a cry came from the gallery, 'Irving's Men', which was taken up by the whole house. Time after time the curtain fell at the end and had to rise again. At one moment, looking up, Irving smiled and wished his audience goodbye. 'NO *not goodbye*' came the cry. The audience refused to leave and, because a presentation was due on stage from the workmen of all the theatres in England, Stoker did something he had never done before – plunged the auditorium in darkness. Still they cheered. Irving ordered the lights to go up again and stepped before the curtain to ask the audience to join in 'a little ceremony of our own'. Apart from a benefit for a friend, this was the last time that Irving played in London.

As the provincial tour recommenced, the company watched him in the wings, gasping to catch his breath before he made his entrance, and then the old miracle would happen as he heard his cue. Why was he allowed to continue? 'He *could not* stop,' said Stoker. 'To do so would have been the final extinction. His affairs were such that it was necessary to go on for the sake of himself in such span of life as might be left to him, and for the sake of others.' The farewell tour 'would mean the realisation of a fortune'. Stoker was optimistic.

On 2 October, at Sheffield, the Lord Mayor gave a luncheon in Irving's honour, and Irving replied. The same ritual was followed in Bradford where the Mayor also gave a luncheon and made a presentation. In the evening, after a performance of *The Bells*, Irving collapsed. The company had come to dread *The Bells*, with its demanding role of Mathias, and the next morning, on 13 October, Stoker and Loveday planned to send back the scenery and delete the play from the next bill at Birmingham. To their surprise, Irving agreed readily and remarked that the tour of America would have to be abandoned. 'But time enough for that, we can see to it later. A kindly continent to me, but I will not leave my bones there if I can help it.'

That evening he played *Becket*. The young actor who played the King noticed that Irving brushed his hand with his lips as he made obeisance, something he had never done before. Other members in the cast noticed changes in his performance. Listening from the wings, they heard him say, 'God is my judge' instead of 'God's will be done'. Towards the end an actress heard him muttering, 'poor soul, poor soul'. At last they heard his final words: 'Into thy hands O Lord! into thy hands!' Yet he seemed all right afterwards and chatted cheerfully to Stoker in the dressing-room. Suspecting that *The Bells* had been haunting him, Stoker gave the assurance, 'Now you have got into your stride again, and work will be easy.'

Irving thought for a moment. 'I really think so.'

Stoker had to leave for supper with the advance agent who had come from Birmingham, and when he stood up Irving held out his hand to say goodnight, an unusual gesture between two men who saw each other daily. As Stoker left the room, Irving called, 'Muffle up your throat, old chap. It is bitterly cold tonight and you have a cold. Take care of yourself! Goodnight! God bless you!' An echo of 1876, when Irving handed his new friend a photograph of himself with the ink still wet, 'My dear friend Stoker "God bless you! God bless you! !" '

In the middle of supper, a carriage drew up at Stoker's lodgings. It is indicative that he could not afford to stay in Irving's hotel, to which he was now summoned. He arrived to find a group of men surrounding Irving's body, which lay full-length upon the floor. Collinson, his valet, was in tears beside him. Irving had died in his arms two minutes earlier. Stoker himself closed Irving's eyelids with the help of the doctor. They carried the body upstairs. Then Stoker returned to duty, dispatching the scores of telegrams – to family and friends and the Press of the world.

Returning to the hotel at seven-thirty in the morning, he waited for Irving's sons. In the evening he left with the undertakers and travelled with the coffin through the streets of Bradford to the station. A sea of faces, hats off as they drove through the assembled crowds, flags at half-mast, an astonishing silence apart from the bells.

'For a quarter of a century,' wrote Stoker later, 'I had been accustomed when travelling with Irving to see the rushing crowd closing in with cheers and waving of hats and kerchiefs; to watch a moving sea of hands thrust forward for him to shake; to hear the roar of the cheering crowd kept up until the train began to move, and then to hear it dying away from our ears not from cessation but from mere distance. And now this silence!'

CHAPTER NINETEEN

The Sexual Impulse

It was a great friendship.

When the pomp was over and Irving was laid to rest in Westminster Abbey, Stoker was bereft. Harry Ludlam states that 'He suffered a stroke which laid him unconscious for twenty-four hours, and which began a painful illness that dragged on for weeks, robbing his robust frame of much of its boundless vitality and leaving his eyesight impaired.'

Bram continued to write and read with the aid of a large magnifying glass. If proof was needed of his honesty, it lies in the poor state he found himself in now. Like Irving, he could not afford to stop.

There were a few diversions: a lecture tour in 1906 which seems to have fizzled out in Sheffield, and a disastrous return to the theatre as business manager for an American opera singer who was presenting a musical of *The Vicar of Wakefield*. It was one of those productions jinxed from the start; Stoker was greatly impressed by the audition of a fellow-Irishman John McCormack and fought on his behalf – then McCormack walked out; Laurence Housman, the adaptor, was so infuriated by the cuts that he refused to allow his name as 'author' and made a public scene on the first night. Severely shaken, the musical staggered onwards for two months and collapsed. For Stoker it was a humiliating return to the West End.

The following year, Lucy Clifford, a young authoress who referred to him as 'Uncle Bram', wrote confidentially for his help:

A certain young manager had two plays of mine lately, liked them, then wrote that he really could not risk production by an author who had only literary reputation.

If I had £500 or £800 to put in the venture it would be all right. I am not in a position to put in even 500 to 800 pence let alone pounds. As a matter of fact things are not going well with me of late; but do not say that to anyone for it is the last crime of all to which one should confess. – Well now I have been wondering whether you could and would see if you could place a play for me? I don't mean for fun, you work for your living, dear Bram, as I do for mine. I propose that it should be a business arrangement *between ourselves*. You could do me enormous service and I have sufficient literary reputation and I bear my husband's distinguished name so you need not be ashamed of me.

This was sent with the play from Viareggio on 28 February 1907, marked 'confidential'. Plainly Bram was unimpressed, possibly even piqued by the suggestion of such collaboration, for another letter followed, sent from Lake Maggiore in March: 'Dearest Uncle Bram, Your letter is a grief to me. I have the greatest faith in your judgement and just hope you are wrong.' Lucy Clifford then takes several pages to prove that he *is* wrong. But on another occasion she wrote to thank him for other advice: 'You are always a brick to take so much trouble with my work.' She added naïvely, 'I wish you had a theatre. I can't think why, after all the experience you have had, you can't get hold of a syndicate to start you in one.' Her naïvety lay in the failure to recognise that Stoker's theatrical peak had passed – he was too closely associated with Irving and the nineteenth century.

At the beginning of 1908, he organised the English section of the *Paris Theatrical Exhibition*, asking his friends for souvenirs. Their readiness to help reveals the esteem in which they held him. Genevieve Ward replied from Rome: 'Dear Brother Bram, it was very sweet of you to suggest *the* portrait, always thoughtful – Love to all – Please tell Florence I received her letter . . . Your affec old friend Genevieve Ward.'

But these were skirmishes, not battles. He concentrated on his writing above all, and could never be accused of laziness. His output over the years was indefatigable, even though so much coincided with his arduous work for Irving. There were eighteen books altogether, of which ten were written after *Dracula*.

Candidly, most of them might have been written by another author. There is throughout the most surprising contrast between florid romance and lurid horror.

Miss Betty, 1898, is dedicated to 'My Wife' and opens at Cheyne Walk where they lived – and that is the most intriguing part of it. The rest is an old-fashioned romance about highwaymen, with Miss Betty herself making Pollyanna look like Jezebel by comparison.

The Man, 1905, has a final flourish that would be hard to surpass in mawkishness:

> By the reading of his own soul he knew now that love needs a voice; that a man's love, to be welcomed to the full, should be dominant and self believing.
>
> When the two saw each other's eyes there was no need for words. Harold came close, opening wide his arms. Stephen flew to them. In that divine moment when their mouths met, both knew that their souls were one.

Before any reader leaps to the wrong (though more exciting) conclusion, let it be said that Stephen was a woman. Bram was able to match this passage with the climax of *Lady Athlyne,* 1908: Turning his eyes to hers he saw in them a look of adoration which made his heart leap and his blood seem on fire. The beautiful eyes fell for an instant as a red tide swept her face and neck . . .'

Bram's tales of horror had far more conviction. *The Lady of the Shroud,* 1909 concludes with a prophetic ariel attack, a foretaste of air-raids to come – and has a faint echo of *Dracula* in a Balkan princess who *pretends* to be a vampire. But Bram's interest in the supernatural went far beyond vampires. *Jewel of the Seven Stars* concerns the resurrection of an Egyptian Queen who ruled twenty-five centuries before Christ. I should place this book next to *Dracula* for suspense and readability. The climax is grand:

> The storm still thundered around the house, and I could feel the rock on which it was built tremble under the furious onslaught of the waves. The shutters strained as though the

screaming wind without would in very anger have forced an entrance. In that dread hour of expectancy, when the forces of Life and Death were struggling for the mastery, imagination was awake. I almost fancied that the storm was a living thing and animated with the wrath of the quick!

All at once the eager faces round the sarcophagus were bent forward. The look of speechless wonder in the eyes, lit by that supernatural glow from within the sarcophagus, had a more than mortal brilliance.

My own eyes were nearly blinded by the awful paralysing light, so that I could hardly trust them. I saw something white rising from the open sarcophagus. Something which appeared to my tortured eyes to be filmy, like a white mist. In the heart of this mist, which was cloudy and opaque like an opal, was something like a hand holding a fiery jewel flaming with many lights. As the fierce glow of the Coffer met this new living light, the green vapour floating between them seemed like a cascade of brilliant points, a miracle of light!

Then all goes wrong. The violent storm, Stoker's old device, breaks through the shutters and the blast of wind destroys the experiment, which ends in terror and death. It has been said Heinemann's were so shocked by the original ending that Stoker toned it down in deference to them. Even so, it is compulsive reading. 'The great stake' – the resurrection of a woman – is an immense theme, while the sincerity of the loyal band of fanatics has echoes of the avengers in their pursuit of Count Dracula.

Incidentally, the christian name of Trelawny, one of the main characters, is Abel, which supports Dr Bierman's claim that Stoker was obsessed by the conflict of Cain and Abel. Mr Trelawny is an eminent Egyptologist who has taken the mummy of Queen Tara to his house in London, where he is discovered near his bed bleeding from a wrist wound of seven parallel scratches – again the preoccupation with the figure seven. His daughter Margaret finally loses her individuality as a human being and becomes 'simply a phase of Queen Tara herself; an astral body obedient to her will!' Ironically, this makes her far more human as a character.

It has been stated unequivocally that Stoker was a member of The Hermetic Order of the Golden Dawn, a group of occultists headed by Liddell Mathers and W. B. Yeats which was eventually shattered by the intervention of 'The Great Beast', Aleister Crowley. The Order comprised both men and women and was devoted to ritual magic and astrology, with lodges in Edinburgh, Paris, London, and Weston-Super-Mare. At one point an actress called Florence Farr was put in charge and performed their 'Egyptian Rites' in Paris, charging admission. Conceivably, Bram might have known her professionally and been introduced to the Order by her. His membership has always been assumed by the 'cognoscenti' according to Francis King, the historian of ritual magic, who adds the surprising information that Constance Wilde was another member. But George M. Harper, another authority, tells me that to the best of his knowledge, which is extensive, Stoker did not belong to the Golden Dawn; a secret list of members which goes up to 1905 confirms this.

However, there were many splinter groups after Crowley's disruption of the original order, and it seems likely that Stoker was involved with an off-shoot called 'Alpha et Omega' which was run by the author J. W. Brodie-Innes. In 1915 Brodie-Innes published an occult novel, *The Devil's Mistress,* which he dedicated 'To the memory of Bram Stoker to whom I am indebted'.

It would be misleading to read too much into this, but if Bram was a secret member of one of the splinter groups it shows that he was involved with the supernatural more deeply than hitherto suspected: not merely an observer but a participant. Equally, there could be the explanation that this was an excellent way to gather research material.

Bram had a feeling for history and mystery. *Famous Imposters,* 1910, contains the intriguing theory of 'The Bisley Boy' – that Queen Elizabeth had died as a baby and a boy had been substituted by her terrified guardians, who were expecting a visit from King Henry.

Another piece of non-fiction, Stoker's most bizarre publication of all, was one of several articles contributed to the *Nineteenth Century Magazine* in 1908. Advocating the censorship of fiction, Bram revealed how deeply disturbed he was. The diatribe starts gently: 'There is perhaps no branch of work among the arts so free at the present time as that of writing fiction.' Stoker adds sadly that this means that the author's 'duty' to the state 'appears to be nil'.

His argument is age-old and all too familiar today: that there must be some sort of give-and-take rules, that 'freedom contains in its very structure the forms of restraint.' This could take the form of the writer's own 'reticence' which Stoker acclaims as 'the highest quality of art; that which can be and is its chief and crowning glory'. He admits that this is an attribute which is virtually undefinable. The other restraint is some sort of censorship, something to be avoided if possible. 'But if no other adequate way can be found and if the plague-spot continues to enlarge, *a censorship there must be.*' Conceding that one form of censorship already existed – the police – he is, at least, disinclined to support 'repressive measures carried out by coarse officials ... [though] ... it is the coarseness and unscrupulousness of certain writers of fiction which has brought the evil; on their heads be it.'

At one point, Stoker refers to stage censorship (which existed then under the powers of the Lord Chamberlain) and grew emotional as he did so, condemning those who catered for 'base appetites'; in 'the war between God and the Devil', the few who cater do so for simple reasons of avarice. 'For gain of some form they are willing to break laws – call them conventions if you will, but they are none the less laws. The process of this mutual ill-doing is not usually violent. It creeps in by degrees ... till a comparison between what was and what is shows to any eye, even an unskilled one, a startling fact of decadence.'

Officialdom wakes up too late. 'To prevent this, censorship must be continuous and rigid. There must be no beginnings of evil ... the more dangerous as it is a natural force. It is as natural for man to sin as to live ... But if progress be a good ... the powers of evil ... must be combated all along the line. It is not sufficient to make a stand, however great, here and there; the whole frontier must be protected.'

For once, and most revealingly, the 'fair sex' are included in the damnation of those with base appetites; indeed 'women are the worst offenders in this form of breach of moral law.'

Stoker's main attack concentrates on literature, or fiction as far his purpose is concerned: 'What use is it, then, in the great scheme of national life, to guard against evil in one form whilst in another it is free to act? In all things of which suggestion is a part there is a possible element of evil. Even in imagination, of whose products the best known and most potent is perhaps fiction, there is a danger of corruption.' At this point he makes an extraordinary admission: '*A close analysis will show that the only emotions which in the long run harm are those arising from sex impulses, and when we have realised this we have put a finger on the actual point of danger.*'

Stoker continues: 'Let not anyone with a non-understanding or misapplied moral sense say or believe that fiction, being essentially based on something that is not true, should be excluded altogether from the field of morals.'

After stressing that he has no wish to be vindictive, he succumbs to an outburst of rhetoric: 'They found an art wholesome, they made it morbid; they found it pure, they left it sullied. Up to this time it was free – the freest thing in the land; they so treated it, they so abused the powers allowed them and their opportunities, that continued freedom becomes dangerous, even impossible. They in their selfish greed tried to deprave where others had striven to elevate. In the language of the pulpit they have "crucified Christ afresh".'

Who are 'they'? He does not say. But his reason for this is explained, for it would give the writers the 'advertisement which they crave'. Wisely, from his point of view and unlike many of our puritans today, he was not going to play into the hands of the pornographer by drawing attention to the very product they were anxious to promote. But he condemned them, 'not merely with natural misdoing based on human weakness, frailty, or passion of the senses, but with vices so . . . opposed to even the decencies of nature in its crudest and lowest forms, that the poignancy of moral disgust is lost in horror. This article is no mere protest against academic faults or breaches of good taste. It is a deliberate indictment of a class of literature so vile that it is actually corrupting the nation.'

I have always felt that, when the Longfords of this world tell us what we should not read, they are more concerned with the danger of *their* corruption than our own. Most people can read pornography without such risk and can even benefit, but 'they'

H

recognise the temptation and in trying to resist it, involve us too to prove them right. The subject has a salacious appeal which they find irresistible.

It is depressing to have to place my great-uncle alongside Mrs Ormiston Chant, 'the prude on the prowl' and scourge of Marie Lloyd and music hall, in his own time, beside Lord Longford and Mary Whitehouse in ours.

Coming from the author of *Dracula* these views seem incredible. 'THE ONLY EMOTIONS WHICH IN THE LONG RUN HARM ARE THOSE ARISING FROM SEX IMPULSES.' Is it possible that Stoker did not realise he had written one of the most erotic books in English literature? Is it possible that he was unaware of the sexual implications it contained?

The passages in Dracula speak for themselves. I choose three. The first concerns the Dracula women who find Jonathan Harker in Castle Dracula:

The fair girl went on her knees and bent over me, fairly gloating. There was a deliberate voluptuousness which was both thrilling and repulsive, and as she arched her neck she actually licked her lips like an animal, till I could see in the moonlight the moisture shining on the scarlet lips and on the red tongue as it lapped the white sharp teeth. Lower and lower went her head as the lips went below the range of my mouth and chin and seemed about to fasten on my throat. Then she paused, and I could hear the churning sound of her tongue as it licked her teeth and lips, and could feel the hot breath on my neck. Then the skin of my throat began to tingle as one's flesh does when the hand that is to tickle it approaches nearer – nearer. I could feel the soft, shivering touch of the lips on the supersensitive skin of my throat, and the hard dents of two sharp teeth, just touching pausing there. I closed my eyes in a languorous ecstasy and waited – waited with beating heart.

After the virginal Lucy has become a vampire, the love of her suitor, John Seward, has turned to hate:

The thing in the coffin writhed; and a hideous, blood-curdling screech came from the opened red lips. The body shook and quivered and twisted in wild contortions; the sharp white teeth champed together till the lips were cut, and the mouth was smeared with a crimson foam. But Arthur never faltered. He looked like a figure of Thor as his untrembling arm rose and fell, driving deeper and deeper the mercy bearing stake, whilst the blood from the pierced heart welled and spurted up around it. His face was set, and high duty seemed to shine through it; the sight of it gave us courage so that our voices seemed to ring through the little vault.

And then the writhing and quivering of the body became less, and the teeth seemed to champ, and the face to quiver. Finally it lay still. The terrible task was over.

Finally, sex with Count Dracula:

With his left hand he held both Mrs Harker's hands, keeping them away with her arms at full tension; his right hand gripped her by the back of the neck, forcing her face down on his bosom. Her white nightdress was smeared with blood, and a thin stream trickled down the man's bare breast, which was shown by his torn-open dress. The attitude of the two had a terrible resemblance to a child forcing a kitten's nose into a saucer of milk to compel it to drink.

Having mocked at the interpretations of others, I realise the trap I set for myself by bringing Freud into it. Frankly, I would hardly recognise a Freudian meaning if I saw one, *except* in the case of Dracula and Bram Stoker, where it seems too obvious to ignore. In his *Psychoanalysis of Ghost Stories* (1959) Maurice Richardson writes that 'from a Freudian standpoint – and from no other does the story really make sense. It is a vast polymorph perverse bisexual oral-anal genital sado-masochistic timeless orgy'. I am sure that my great-uncle would have been aghast by this and, indeed, Richardson states: 'I doubt whether Stoker had any inkling of the erotic content of the vampire superstition.'

The vampire superstition is riddled with sexuality; indeed it is dependent on it, with all the sucking, the flowing of blood and the love-biting. He adds, 'Guilt is everywhere and deep'.

'Morbid dread always signifies repressed sexual wishes,' wrote

Freud. Ernest Jones in his chapter on the vampire, in *On the Nightmare*, writes, 'It may be said at the outset that the latent content of the belief yields plain indications of most kinds of sexual perversions.' Montague Summers concludes his book on vampirism with this statement: 'Consciously or unconsciously it is realised that the vampire tradition contains far more truth than the ordinary individual cares to appreciate or acknowledge.' Already he has noted that people find intense pleasure in the thought of blood during sexual intercourse – 'It has long since been recognised by medicopsychologists that there exists definite connection between the fascination of blood and sexual excitement.' Jones claims that, 'In the unconscious mind blood is commonly an equivalent of semen,' and in his book on the natural history of the vampire, Anthony Masters is explicit on this theme of blood-letting: 'There also existed in vampire belief a very strong love motive which involved the vampire in having intercourse with a living woman. This belief probably grew up via the occasional erotic stimulant of blood-letting in intercourse, the breaking of virginity, and, on a more mystic level, the medieval succuba, an erotic demon who preyed upon and destroyed man's virility.'

As for Stoker, his sexual life is something of a mystery. Colin Wilson refers to him as a *'faithful'* Victorian husband, but this must be guesswork. I know that he 'enjoyed' the reputation of being a 'womaniser', reputedly famous for his sexual exploits. Certainly he was obsessed by the ideal of the pure woman. In *Dracula: the Book of Blood* (*Listener*, 7 March 1963) Robert Dowse and David Palmer refer to Dracula's thirst for blood but wonder why he

seems to confine his appetites solely to young and innocent women. It is this single unexplained discrepancy which invites our suspicion that Bram Stoker was less than candid with himself; because the true horror of this story concerns the victims of Dracula. Legend gave its authority to the substance of Bram Stoker's tale, that the victims of the vampire themselves become vampires, and prey on those closest to them. So virtuous and respectable young ladies are gradually and inexorably transformed before the horri-

fied eyes of their adoring husbands or suitors into volup-
tuous creatures possessed with insatiable desire.

Do they mean that Stoker did protest too much in his tender
regard for the 'fair sex', as he would have called it? They go on
to refer to his fascination with the theme of the damsel in
distress: 'Maidenly purity is always ardently defended by the
chivalrous male. Similarly, in his private life, Stoker took great
pride in acting as the champion and protector of fragile woman-
hood; a role which he sustained for years in his relationship with
the actresses Ellen Terry and Genevieve Ward.'

Perhaps the answer lies in Florence Stoker – the cold, flirtati-
ous beauty in the fox-fur. Perhaps *Dracula* and the horror stories,
coupled with his contrasting attacks on sex in fiction, were a
much-needed release. Was he sexually frustrated? In his Ontario paper, Professor Royce MacGillivray describes the remarkable characterisation of Renfield the lunatic and concludes, 'Since
the quest of the vampires for blood seems often to be in some
undefined way a sexual quest, it is tempting to see Renfield, the
would-be vampire, as suffering from sexual frustration, and it is
not only tempting but plausible to suggest that sexual frustration
was one of the elements that Stoker drew on in creating him.'

Certainly the whole superstition is riddled with sexual guilt:

It is felt that because of this [writes Jones on the theme
of guilt] the dead person cannot rest in his grave and is
impelled to try to overcome it by the characteristic method
of defiantly demonstrating that he can commit the forbidden
acts. We are, of course, speaking of an unconscious guilti-
ness, which paradoxically enough, is most acute in the
presence of what is socially and legally the most permitted
love object, the married partner, manifesting itself here in
the form of marital unhappiness.

Florence Stoker was a beauty, and aware of it. This may
explain why she was a cold woman. My family, speaking of her,
gave me the impression of an elegant, aloof woman, more interested in her position in society than she was in her son. Her
granddaughter Ann, Noel's daughter, confirms this. She told me
that she doubted if 'Granny Moo', as Florence was called, was

really capable of love. 'She was cursed with her great beauty and the need to maintain it. In my knowledge now, she was very anti-sex. After having my father in her early twenties, I think she was quite put off.'

Ann McCaw remembers her as 'very vain ... I used to have to pluck her eyebrows, which I hated doing. She died in 1937 at seventy-seven, when I was twenty.'

A trickle from the Dracula fortune started to reach Florence in her final years, and in particular, the forty thousand dollars paid by Universal Pictures for the rights of *Dracula* in 1931. This enabled her to resume a life of comparative luxury: she was able to entertain at her home in Kinnerton Studios, and Ann remembers Ellen Terry at one of her teas as 'a very old, upright, large lady in a big hat. She had a big face she put near me, perhaps she was deaf? She wore a sort of lavender-grey flowing skirt and jacket to match. Another thing I remember is that "Granny Moo" had a sort of gallery built at one end of her bedroom, stairs up to it of course, used mainly for furniture and papers, but this wasn't put in before she had sold the film rights of *Dracula*.'The dollars also paid for the conversion of two cottages at Seaview: at least one Stoker was benefiting.

Noel had been put in the care of a wet nurse, and his daughter makes one statement that is remarkably revealing: she believes it is highly probable that Florence refused to have sex with Bram after her father was born.

This would confirm Bram's sexual frustration, forcing him to go elsewhere for satisfaction, which in turn created a sense of guilt. While Florence was in her early twenties, he was in his early thirties – chained to a beautiful but frigid wife for the years to come. This helps to explain his infatuation with the 'ideal' woman, so unnaturally feminine, so vulnerable to attack. There is a passage in *Lady Athlyne*, 1908, which is curious because it is completely out of place in the novel, as if Bram was trying to prove something to himself:

Joy was a woman in whom the sex instinct was very strong. She was woman all over; the type of woman who seems to draw man to her as the magnet draws the steel. Athlyne was a very masculine person and therefore peculiarly sensitive to the influence.

That deep thinking, young madman who committed suicide at twenty-five, was probably right in that wonderful
guess of his as to the probable solution of the problem of
sex. All men and all women, according to him have in themselves the cells of both sexes; and the accredited masculinity
or feminity of the individual is determined by the multiplication and development of these cells.

Thus the ideal man is entirely or almost entirely masculine, and the ideal woman is entirely or almost entirely feminine. Each individual must have a preponderance, be it ever
so little, of the cells of its own sex, and the attraction of
each individual to the other sex depends upon its place in
the scale between the highest and the lowest grade of sex.
The most masculine man draws the most feminine woman,
and vice versa; and so down the scale till close to the
borderline is the great mass of persons, who, having only
development of a few of the qualities of sex, are easily satisfied to mate with anyone.

What induced Bram Stoker to make such an assertion? That
'wonderful guess', which he considers so illuminating, is not only
naïve but inaccurate; had he never heard of the attraction of
opposites?

The ugly, squat or balding men who are irresistible to beautiful women?

The passage appears to be part of Bram's own search for the
unattainable, a search that began in 1879 after his son was born.
In retrospect, Noel's innate shyness, which I can remember,
seems clearer. Though he was devoted to his warm, motherly
grandmother, he was eclipsed by the beauty of his own mother,
who was indifferent to him, and by the bravado of his father,
who must have been a formidable personality with which to
compete. Bram was a boisterous father and when he took Noel
swimming at Whitby, he walked backwards after dump-
ing him into the sea at Robin Hood Bay while his son struggled
desperately to reach him. 'My father was very frightened,' says
Ann, 'and he never swam in my lifetime. I think that's why.'

Noel was registered at his birth as Irving Noel Thornley
Stoker, but his will stated that he was 'commonly called Noel
Thornley'. 'He seemed to dislike Irving,' says his daughter,

'both the man and name. He thought that Irving had worn Bram out.' Of course this was true; the actor always came before the family. Yet in spite of their closeness, Henry Irving remained as remote as Florence, apart from that scribble on the back of the envelope. There was also an unusually affectionate note from Irving to Florence, though he addressed her as 'My dear Mrs Stoker', sent on 25 March 1897, 'I am grateful for your letter. It came to me like drops of dew. I hope you will ever feel as kindly to me as I do to you and your husband. The accompanying little cake was sent to me yesterday from Lancashire – where the people are most hospitable – you will probably think so by the size of the article – and I am sure you will pardon my sending it to you when I tell you that I sometimes am excited with the thought of the terrible ravages made upon that dainty little cupboard of yours. Fill the monster with this –.' But for the most part his correspondence with Stoker was punctilious.

Writing from Torquay in 1905 about his final season at Drury Lane, he started his letter 'My Dear Stoker . .' and signed it 'H.I.' What formality, after thirty years of daily contact with Bram, apart from the occasional holiday or illness! Irving was incapable of supplying the warmth that Bram must have needed, he was too omnipotent, too like the characters he portrayed on stage: Kings and Emperors, Napoleon, Macbeth, Faust. What a perfect Count Dracula *he* would have made!

Noel was nearly twenty when *Dracula* was published, and Bram's guilt over Florence can be found seeping through its pages. By rejecting him, as it is said she did, she was also devitalising him. It is a coincidence, and cannot be more, that Rudyard Kipling wrote the following poem after seeing a painting by Philip Burne-Jones, the son of Sir Edward and a friend of the Stokers, shown at a London art gallery in that same year of 1897:

A Fool there was and he made his prayer
(Even as you and I!)
To a rag and a bone and a hank of hair
(We called her the woman who did not care)
But the fool he called her his lady fair
(Even as you and I!)

Oh the years we waste and the tears we waste
And the work of our head and hand,
Belong to the woman who did not know
(And now we know that she never could know)
And did not understand.

The fool was stripped to his foolish hide
(Even as you and I!)
Which she might have seen when she threw him aside
(But it isn't on record the lady tried)
So some of him lived but the most of him died
(Even as you and I!)

And it isn't the shame and it isn't the blame
That stings like a white hot brand.
It's coming to know that she never knew why
(Seeing at last she could never know why)
And never could understand.

Kipling titled this 'The Vampire', and his poem was included
in the catalogue. The picture, which was also called 'The Vampire', showed a woman in white leaning over her victim, his
chest bare and bleeding. It was shown in America and the two
vampires, poem and painting, became the inspiration for the
cult of the Hollywood 'Vamp' in 1913, with Nita Naldi, 'Queen
of the Vampires', and Theda Bara, whose name was an anagram
of 'Arab Death' and who was really called Theodosia Goodman.
She was photographed posing above a male skeleton and treated
men outrageously in *A Fool There Was*, which had the celebrated subtitle 'Kiss Me, My Fool'.

So some of him lived but the most of him died, and by
1911 the pressures were tearing Bram apart. That year marked
the publication of his last and strangest book: *The Lair of the
White Worm*.

It might have been written under the influence of drugs, a
'trip', along 'the high road to mental disturbance', to use a
phrase from the book. At one time I wondered if he was being
treated with drugs to alleviate the painful Bright's Disease which
corroded him in his last years.

At the very least, *The White Worm* is a literary curiosity. The plot is so bizarre, almost ludicrous, that it is hard to imagine anyone taking it seriously. But on a recent re-reading I became increasingly impressed by the way-out blend of Gothic surrealism; read on that level it is dazzling. Also, without a vestige of humour, it is immensely funny. Significantly, it is Stoker's most popular book after *Dracula* and has been revived in paperback over the years. It too could become a cult, with its rampant symbolism and powerful sense of hallucination.

Adam Salton, a wealthy young Australian, returns to the ancestral home in the cavernous Peak District. There is a sweet old uncle and a dear old friend, Sir Nathaniel de Salis, models of virtue. The other neighbours are downright evil: Edgar Caswall with a face 'so hard, so ruthless, so selfish, so dominant. "God help any," was the common thought, "who is under the domination of such a man!" ' (Could this be Irving again?) The other neighbour, anxious to ensnare Caswell as a rich husband, is Lady Arabella March, of Diana's Grove, who meets young Adam at the opening of the book when her carriage has broken down. He repairs it for her and notices several black snakes on the ground around him, but Lady Arabella, who slips from her carriage 'with a quick gliding motion' is already among them when he cries out to warn her: 'But there seemed to be no need of warning. The snakes had turned and were wriggling back to the mound as quickly as they could. He laughed to himself behind his teeth as he whispered, "No need to fear there. They seem much more afraid of her than she of them." '

He takes a good look at her, and her dress alone is enough to attract attention:

> She was clad in some kind of soft white stuff, which clung close to her form, showing to the full every movement of her sinuous figure. She wore a close-fitting cap of some fine fur of dazzling white. Coiled round her white throat was a large necklace of emeralds, whose profusion of colour dazzled when the sun shone on them. Her voice was peculiar, very low and sweet, and so soft that the dominant note was of sibilation. Her hands, too, were peculiar – long, flexible, white, with a strange movement as of waving gently to and fro.

Plainly, there is something odd about Lady Arabella. At a further meeting, Adam is carrying a mongoose which he has bought to get rid of the snakes; he sees Lady Arabella walking towards him:

Hitherto the mongoose has been quiet, like a playful affectionate kitten; but when the two got close, Adam was horrified to see the mongoose, in a state of the wildest fury, with every hair standing on end, jump from his shoulder and run towards Lady Arabella. It looked so furious and so intent on attack that he called a warning.

'Look out – look out! The animal is furious and means to attack.'

Lady Arabella looked more than ever disdainful and was passing on; the mongoose jumped at her in a furious attack. Adam rushed forward with his stick, the only weapon he had. But just as he got within striking distance, the lady drew out a revolver and shot the animal, breaking his backbone. Not satisfied with this, she poured shot after shot into him till the magazine was exhausted. There was no coolness or hauteur about her now; she seemed more furious even than the animal, her face transformed with hate, and as determined to kill as he had appeared to be. Adam, not knowing exactly what to do, lifted his hat in apology and hurried on to Lesser Hill.

On another walk, Adam notices the body of a dead child by the roadside: 'She was dead, and while examining her, I noticed on her neck some marks that looked like those of teeth.'

There are many such echoes of *Dracula*. The two heroines are Lilla and Mimi, as against Lucy and Mina. Lilla is the virtuous victim; Mimi becomes Adam's wife. Over tea, Lilla has staring-matches with Caswell, apparently tests of power between good and evil. Mimi comes to Lilla's rescue with her own flow of goodliness; Lady A. sides with Caswell. After one of these bouts, immense flocks of birds are summoned, presumably in response to Lilla's dove-like qualities. They arrive in tens of thousands, attracting ornithologists bewildered by this quirk of migration. The birds decimate the land, and so Caswell from his turret

flies an immense kite in the shape of a hawk and the land falls
quiet. The silence spreads to all the animals:

> The fear and restraint which brooded amongst the denizens
> of the air began to affect all life. Not only did the birds
> cease to sing or chirp, but the lowing of the cattle ceased
> in the fields and the varied sounds of life died away. In
> place of these things was only a soundless gloom, more
> dreadful, more disheartening, more soul-killing than any
> concourse of sounds, no matter how full of fear and dread.
> Pious individuals put up constant prayers for relief from
> the intolerable solitude. After a little there were signs of
> universal depression which those who ran might read. One
> and all, the faces of men and women seemed bereft of
> vitality, of interest, of thought, and most of all, of hope.

This strange though powerful theme of the birds is really
irrelevant, and Stoker soon tired of it. Adam compares notes
with Sir Nathaniel, who tells him the local legend of a monster
that lives underground, the great white worm. With a remarkable prophecy of the Loch Ness Monster, Stoker refers to the
original plains of England with 'holes of abysmal depth, where
any kind and size of antediluvian monster could find a habitat.
In places which now we can see from our windows, were mud-
holes a hundred or more feet deep. Who can tell us when the
age of the monsters which flourished in slime came to an end?'
Just imagine if such a creature could assume human form! Sir
Nathaniel tells Adam of an incident in Lady Arabella's childhood
when she wandered into a small wood at night and was found
unconscious, having received a 'poisonous bite'. To everyone's
surprise she makes a complete recovery, but it is noticed afterwards that she has developed 'a terrible craving for cruelty,
maiming and injuring birds and small animals – even killing
them'. It was hoped that her marriage to Captain March would
put a stop to that, but the poor fellow was found shot through
the head.

> 'I have always suspected suicide' [confesses Sir Nathaniel].
> 'He may have discovered something – God knows what!
> – or possibly Lady Arabella may herself have killed him.

Putting together many small matters that have come to my knowledge, I have come to the conclusion that the foul White Worm obtained control of her body, just as her soul was leaving its earthly tenement – that would explain the sudden revival of energy, the strange and inexplicable craving for maiming and killing . . . God alone knows what poor Captain March discovered – it must have been something too ghastly for human endurance, if my theory is correct that the once beautiful human body of Lady Arabella is under the control of this ghastly White Worm.'

'What was the real identity of the beautiful, reptile-like Lady Arabella March?' – asks the paperback cover. *She* is the great White Worm! They see, one night in the woods, an immense tower of snowy white, tall and thin, with the green light of her eyes above the trees, and vast coils of the serpent's body below. The white colour comes from the china clay in the cavernous soil. Like Count Dracula, the Worm moves with the vital protection of darkness.

Maurice Richardson, talking to me of Dracula, stressed that the mood of the manic depressive lifts as evening draws on: 'During the hours of light, the vampire is in his tomb. He's flat out. He's as near dead as can be. Evening comes on, night falls, suddenly he awakens and has magical power of every kind – he can climb down walls, he flies as a bat, and of course sexually he can have his will with anybody he wants.'

By virtue of his job at the Lyceum, Stoker himself must have been a night-animal, with discussions in the Beefsteak Room that lasted till dawn. It is wrong to press this too far, but there may have been something of the manic depressive in Stoker; certainly his night hours cannot have been conducive to regular family life.

Adam and Sir Nathaniel realise they have to destroy the White Worm: 'Such creatures may have grown down as well as up. They *may* have grown into, or something like, human beings. Lady Arabella March is of snake nature. She has committed crimes to our knowledge. She retains something of the vast strength of her primal being – can see in the dark – has the eyes of a snake. She used the

nigger, and then dragged him through the snake's hole down
to the swamp; she is intent on evil and hates some one we
love. Result . . .'

'Yes, the result?'

'First, that Mimi Watford should be taken away at once
– then –'

'Yes?'

'The monster must be destroyed.'

'Bravo!'

There is the obstacle of trespassing on private property.'Lady
Arabella, be she woman or snake or devil, owned the ground she
moved in, according to British law, and the law is jealous and
swift to avenge wrongs done within its ken.' Also, the monster
has the unfair advantage of being a woman.'I never thought this
fighting of an antediluvian monster would be such a complicated
job,' says Adam, exasperated.

'This one is a woman, with all a woman's wit, combined
with the heartlessness of a *cocotte*. She has the strength
and impregnability of a diplodocus [an extinct herbivorous
dinosaur]. We may be sure that in the fight there is
before us there will be no semblance of fair play. Also,
that our unscrupulous opponent will not betray herself!'

'That is so – being feminine, she will probably over-reach
herself. Now Adam, it strikes me that, as we have to protect ourselves and others against feminine nature, our strong
game will be to play our masculine against her feminine.
Perhaps we had better sleep on it.'

One of the delights of the book is its rampant snobbery. After
a wild tea-party during which Lady Arabella first tries to suck
Mimi into the well-hole and then attempts to imprison the
guests, Mimi's main objection is one of etiquette – 'As a social
matter, she was disgusted with her for following up the rich
landowner – throwing herself at his head so shamelessly.' The
landowner, meanwhile, is going mad in his turret. As the climax
is reached, there is another of Stoker's great storms: the lightning is attracted by the great kite he is still flying, with a wire
reel found in a chest that Mesmer had left to the family. He

disappears from the novel, raging against the elements: 'I am greater than any other who is, or was, or shall be. When the Master of Evil took Christ up on a high place and showed Him all the kingdoms of earth, he was doing what he thought no other could do. He was wrong – he forgot ME.'

The prevalence of sexual symbols cannot be denied. 'The dread of snakes,' wrote Freud, 'is monstrously exaggerated in neurotics – all this has a definite sexual meaning.' Chests correspond to 'the female organ, with the obvious symbolism of the lock and key to open it'. Revealingly, Mesmer's chest has *no* lock or key, though Caswell seems to open it in his sleep. Winding stairs 'are symbolic representations of the sexual act', and the rising kite is one of the most famous and familiar symbols of all. Finally, Stoker's disturbance over sexual intercourse can be seen in his revulsion from the snake's hole, which has to be destroyed. Adam has already laid charges of dynamite, but the whole of Diana's Grove is consumed by fire when lightning strikes the wire of the kite which Lady Arabella has brought to her home in order to ensnare Caswell and destroy him in the hole. That hole – the smell of which 'was like nothing that Adam had ever met with. He compares it with all the noxious experiences he had ever had – the drainage of war hospitals, of slaughter-houses, the refuse of dissecting rooms . . . the sourness of chemical waste and the poisonous effluvium of the bilge of a water-logged ship whereupon a multitude of rats had been drowned.'

The lightning explodes the charges of dynamite, the house collapses, and they can look down

where the well-hole yawned a deep and narrow circular chasm. From this the agonised shrieks were rising, growing ever more terrible with each second that passed. Some of these fragments were covered with scaled skin as of a gigantic lizard or serpent. Once in a sort of lull or pause, the seething contents of the hole rose, after the manner of a bubbling spring, and Adam saw part of the thin form of Lady Arabella forced to the top amid a mass of slime, and what looked as if it had been a monster torn into shreds. Several times some masses of enormous bulk were forced up and through the well-hole with inconceivable violence, and, suddenly expanding as they came into large space, disclosed sections of the White Worm . . .

Adam, Mimi and Sir Nathaniel return the following day but the turmoil is still not over:

At short irregular intervals the hell-broth in the hole seemed as if boiling up. It rose and fell again and turned over, Showing in fresh form much of the nauseous detail which had been visible earlier. The worst parts were the great masses of the flesh of the monstrous Worm, in all its red and sickening aspect. Such fragments had been bad enough before, but now they were infinitely worse. Corruption comes with startling rapidity to beings whose destruction has been due wholly or in part to lightning – the whole mass seemed to have become all at once corrupt! The whole surface of the fragments, once alive, was covered with insects, worms and vermin of all kinds. The sight was horrible enough, but, with the awful smell added, was simply unbearable. The Worm's hole appeared to breathe forth death in its most repulsive forms.

Surely his obsession with horror and this repetition of sexual symbols indicate that Stoker was disturbed.

'Bram Stoker eludes me,' says Professor Wolf. But, 'In Stoker's own writing a *person* occasionally shows through, or, better, is exposed. Particularly in his later novels (and of course *Dracula*) there obtrudes the raw, harsh presence of a man endowed with nearly inexhaustible energy who is writing over, around, or under what he knows about loneliness and – predominantly – sexual terror.' Referring specifically to *The Lair of the White Worm*, he concludes: 'There is no way to ignore the signs of confusion and loneliness the narrative obtrudes.'

The Lair of the White Worm was published three years after Stoker had written in the *Nineteenth Century* that 'the only emotions which in the long run harm are those arising from sex impulses.'

There is no deceiver like the self-deceiver.

CHAPTER TWENTY

'𝕿𝖎𝖒𝖊 𝖎𝖘 𝖔𝖓 𝖒𝖞 𝕾𝖎𝖉𝖊'

There is another, human though hardly admirable, explanation of his call for censorship – sheer *envy*. There are several references in his *Nineteenth Century* article to financial gain: 'The class of works to which I allude are meant by both authors and publishers to bring to the winning of commercial successes the forces of inherent evil in man.' He concludes with this sentence: 'The rewards of such – personal luxury and perhaps a measure of wealth – may be theirs but they must not expect the pleasures or profits of the just – love and honour, troops of friends, and the esteem of good men.'

In spite of the constant and prolific output, Stoker's books failed to make money. If he had little fame in his lifetime, he had even less fortune. His mother's prophecy of *Dracula*'s ultimate success was inaccurate only in her belief that in 'its terrible excitement it should make a widespread reputation and much money for you.' The reward for all his industry seems to have been pitifully meagre, for he did not inherit Irving's compulsive love of largesse. Conceivably, Florence's social climbing was crippling, though this seems unlikely.

They continued to entertain at home: Reginald Auberon, who 'saw a good deal of Bram Stoker' after Irving's death, described his visits to their home off the King's Road: 'as they knew everybody worth knowing, and were also exceedingly hospitable, one could always make sure of finding interesting people there.'

One of the regular lions was W. S. Gilbert. Auberon granted him his 'interesting' personality, but did not find it 'agreeable'. One afternoon a young actress asked Stoker to introduce them, but Gilbert shook his head fiercely – 'Don't want to know her,' he growled. 'Want to be left alone.' Auberon suggests that he had just overheard some tactless person praising Sullivan.

Auberon also detected financial cracks behind the social façade:

> Irving's untimely death must have been in many ways a great blow to Bram Stoker. Apart from the sudden severance of a close friendship between them . . . it meant the abrupt and entire cessation of his sole source of income. He had drawn a large (but well-earned) salary from the Lyceum treasury, and had lived up to every penny of it. Accordingly, on Irving's death, the problem of ways and means began to press rather hardly. Still despite the fact that he was getting on in years, Stoker had plenty of grit, and thrust himself into the rough-and-tumble anew, and with characteristic vigour. But he met with many rebuffs, for the Lyceum tradition was not wanted in the quarters where he offered his services. He even went after a five-pound a week job at a Manchester Exhibition . . .
>
> And was turned down.

These remarks suggest that Stoker's financial position was bad indeed, otherwise it is extremely odd that a friend should have put them on paper for all to see at a time when it was bad taste to discuss such personal matters.

My grandmother told me that Noel never recovered from the humiliation of being taken away from university. The dates are slightly puzzling here; Noel was at Winchester when *Dracula* was published, which implies that he was removed while Bram was still working for Irving. But the impression of Bram's growing financial difficulty was definitely conveyed to me.

There is sad evidence in the letters. When Irving died he was not penniless, as Laurence Irving claims, but the little that was left, about £14,000, was divided between the sons after a bequest to the valet Collinson. There was no souvenir for Stoker who became determined to buy the last picture drawn of Irving, a pastel by Sir Bernard Partridge: 'To me it is of priceless worth, not only from its pictorial excellence, but because it is the last record of my dear friend; and because it shows him in one of the happy moods which alas! grew rarer with his failing health. It gives, of course, a true impression of his age – he was then in his sixty-eighth year; but all the beauty and intelligence and sweetness is there.'

He acquired the pastel, but a letter from Bernard Partridge asking for his fee had that forced charm which characterizes letters from people demanding money that is due to them:

> I'm sure you'll acquit me of importunity if I say that if you can manage the cheque now I'd be very glad of it. In justice to myself I may say that you mentioned in your letter of June 5 1906 that you'd be glad if I wouldn't mind waiting for payment until 'I get some of my royalties': and your letter of June 14th same year says: 'I hereby agree to purchase the pastel which you have done of Henry Irving, together with copyright thereof for the sum of £30. I am to pay this sum within one year from today.' So I hope you'll see that it is in no Shylock spirit that I write, but simply because I rather want cash now; otherwise I would willingly have waited longer.

Anne Ritchie, Thackeray's daughter, wrote to Florence, 'My Dear Florence, Will you do me a very great kindness. Would you come twice a week in the evening to read an hour – are you by any chance free tonight and Monday say ... and would you let me send you 3/6 a time if you do not think it an outrageous proposal to trust on your good nature.' She knew of the Stokers' financial situation because she was involved in the attempt to enlist money for Bram from a literary fund, though she had second thoughts: 'I quite forgot when I said "my letter to the Sec. could count" that some short time ago I had written for a little known old friend and that my former letter might be coming up about this time so I don't want to appear twice and feel that it would be much better for anyone else independent ostensibly to support your claim. My note to the Sec. is in his hands but I will (with your approval) ask him to keep it back.'

This sounds suspiciously like a brush-off and must have been depressing to receive, but she does go on to suggest alternative sponsors of considerable distinction: 'C. Dickens is a most suitable person. Do you think Mr Barrie would be a good person ...' Rather than go the humiliating round, Florence turned to her old admirer W. S. Gilbert, who wrote, shortly before his death, as 'a very dear old friend', on 12 March 1911: 'I am delighted to learn from your husband that the Literary Fund has sent him a cheque for £100. This I fancy is as much as is ever given except under exceptional circumstances . . . Tell him that I shall be quite at his service if he decides to apply for a Civil List Pension.'

At least this was kindly meant, but considering Gilbert's fortune, it might have been less trouble if he had simply popped a substantial cheque in the post himself. Indeed, considering Bram's 'troops of friends', like the Baroness Burdett-Coutts, one of the richest women in England, and Henry Lucy the MP, it is odd that they never came to his assistance.

There was one man conspicuous in the absence of his help. This was his brother William, the successful Stoker brother as far as material possessions were concerned. Their mother, Charlotte, had died at the age of eighty-three, almost blind but content and proud in her sons' achievement. But Tom had become blind, and disillusioned, while Dick had vanished from the scene into the wilds of a remote lake in British Columbia where he lived with his wife as a recluse. William had been knighted in 1895, the same year as Irving, and preferred to be known as Sir Thornley, presumably because it had a grander ring. He was Surgeon to Richmond Hospital; Fellow of the Royal University; Inspector for Ireland under the Vivisection Act; Trustee and Governor of the Irish National Gallery, and so on – a public figure, respectable and responsible. He lived in one of the finest houses in Dublin, Ely House in Ely Place, described by Oliver St John Gogarty as 'one of the few remaining palaces of the spacious 18th century which exist in Dublin without having fallen long ago into decay. Sir Thornley Stoker, the famous surgeon, lives in Ely Place and in the 18th century, which he never really leaves, hence the house is filled with period furniture – Chippendale, Adam, silver candelabra match the silver jambs of the door, silver linings of great fireplaces under mantels of Siena and statuary marble.'

The novelist Henry Moore, a constant visitor and a constant thorn, would go over to an empty chair, tilt it, praise the 'excellent skin' of its Chippendale legs, and ask innocently: 'A cancer, Sir Thornley, or a gallstone?' – referring to his habit of buying a museum piece after an important operation.

One evening at a dinner party, the door burst open and a nude elderly lady ran in with the startling cry, 'I like a little intelligent conversation!' While the guests stood up formally, she ran round the table until two female attendants seized whatever napkins they could, to cover her, and led her screaming from the dining-room. According to Gogarty, Sir Thornley sat there with his knuckles on the table, his head bowed as if he were saying a silent grace. At last he broke his silence, imploring his guests to 'keep this incident, mortifying as it is to me, from any rumour of scandal in this most gossipy town. And now, Moore, I conjure you most particularly, as you are the only one who causes me misgivings.'

'But it was charming, Sir Thornley,' replied Moore. 'I demand an encore.' Of course the behaviour of Lady Stoker was known throughout Dublin the next day.

When they were young, the brothers were close. Irving stayed with Thornley when he visited Dublin; my grandfather stayed with him when he was courting my grandmother, and a letter to her in May 1891 refers to Mrs Thornley: 'She is better and is able to be down for a while but is not very vigorous yet and can't do much.' Perhaps this was an early symptom of the illness which took such possession later.

On 8 November 1910 the entire collection of Sir Thornley's fine arts had been sold by auction. The catalogue boasted that it formed 'one of the most valuable and comprehensive collections of Fine Art Property ever offered for public competition in this country, its merits bearing witness to the rare and varied taste and judgement of the owner.' Judging by the illustrated splendours, which would fetch many hundreds of thousands of pounds today, Sir Thornley must have received a small fortune, even if he *had* been obliged to sell due to financial pressures of his own. But only four months later, Bram was applying desperately for £100 from a literary fund. Perhaps pride came into it, but a rift seems more likely. His only child was named after Thornley but perhaps Thornley had become too 'posh' to care about Bram's misfortune.

The only man to offer his help readily was Bram's closest friend, Sir Hall Caine. He did so discreetly, in the form of a loan, though the amount is not disclosed. 'I know it may be just a little hurtful to you to take help like that,' Caine wrote tactfully on 11 March 1910, 'but in the first place no human creature need know anything about it except ourselves, and *I shall not even tell my wife, and you need not tell your wife.*'

This act of kindness was uncharacteristic, according to Samuel Norris who notes, in *Two Men of Manxland*, that 'many stories are told in the Isle of Man that even in small parochial and neighbourly efforts, the famous novelist, not to put too fine a point on it, was far from generous', though he concedes that Caine was more open-handed to widows of literary friends. Caine was proud of his extraordinary popularity, admitting his literary genius and his physical likeness to Shakespeare, which prompted a wit to claim that this settled the controversy over the authorship of the plays, it must have been Bacon. When he visited Sing Sing, on a visit to America, a condemned murderer fell on his knees and kissed Caine's hand.

'My poor man,' said Caine, 'why did you kiss my hand?'

'Because your face reminds of Christ's,' replied the demented man – a comparison which Caine reported dutifully in his subsequent interview with the Press.

Even so, Caine's attitude towards Bram was unstinting. In *My Story*, published in 1908 (two years before his confidential letter), he acknowledged Bram's help as the inevitable go-between when Caine was attempting to write a play with a suitable role for Irving: 'The pigeon holes of my study are still heavy with sketches and drafts and scenarios of dramas which either he or I or our constant friend and colleague Bram Stoker (to whose loyal comradeship we both owed so much) thought possible for the Lyceum Theatre.'

The failure of this project is revealing of Irving's implacability.

I think this result was perhaps due to something more serious than the limitations of my own powers. The truth is that, great actor as Irving was, the dominating element of his personality was for many years a hampering difficulty. He had created a character and assumed it for himself ... No man could sink a personality like that of Irving and towards the end of his life, with the ever increasing domination of his own character and the limitation of choice which always comes with advancing years, it was only possible for him to play parts that contained something of himself.

Caine was in a position, or felt he was, to make such criticism. He was the best-selling author of his day, the English editions of his books frequently selling more than half a million copies; *The Eternal City* sold a million. He claimed that his earnings were 'larger than those of Dickens and perhaps only less than those of Scott'. He left an estate worth £250,000, but that was years later, in 1931.

His most distinguished success was *The Manxman*, which Bram helped him to draft in 1891, making a list of the chapters on a sheet of notepaper headed *The Henry Irving and Ellen Terry Provincial Tour*. They encouraged each other with their writing; Bram advised him on contracts, and Caine shared Bram's enthusiasm for the supernatural, after a startling experience of looking into a mirror and seeing another man's reflection. Hall Caine dedicated *Capt'n Davy's Honeymoon* to Bram, and wrote emotionally:

When in dark hours and evil humours my bad angel has sometimes made me think that friendship as it used to be of old, friendship as we read of it in books, that friendship which is not a jilt sure to desert us, but a brother born to adversity as well as success, is now a lost quality, a forgotten virtue – then my good angel for admonition or reproof has whispered the names of a little band of friends, whose friendship is a deep stream that buoys me up and makes no noise; and often first among those names has been your own.

In return, Stoker dedicated *Dracula* to 'My Dear Friend Hommy Beg', a childhood nickname of Caine's. Ironic that his real name is now virtually forgotten, while thousands of new readers must be wondering who 'Hommy Beg' could have been.

There cannot be many people today with a vivid memory of Bram Stoker, though Lady Spencer Churchill may remember him at her wedding to Winston in 1906. I heard recently of one elderly woman who knew Florence and said that she used to be terrified when Bram wrote his horror novels because he '*became*' the personality he was writing about and behaved very strangely at home. Magnificent, if Dracula; distinctly odd if Lady Arabella.

My mother died in 1962, but she told me often how eccentric he was and how he took her to a royal procession, probably the Coronation of George Vth, when she would have been thirteen. Bram relished such occasions and went with Florence to 1 Stratton Street on 22 June 1897, as the guests of Mr and the Baroness Burdett-Coutts, to watch Queen Victoria go by on that 'never to be forgotten day' of her Silver Jubilee.

'He was rather dotty,' said my mother.

'How dotty?'

'Well, really very dotty. He had Bright's Disease, you know. I remember how his behaviour startled the crowd, when he handed out oranges from a large paper bag.'

In 1970 I was lucky enough to have the pleasure of meeting one person who remembered Bram well – Mrs Cruikshank, still sprightly in her nineties – at her home in Friockheim near Angus. Stoker refers to her by name in his story *The Watter's Mou* when she was the young postmistress at Cruden: 'Saw Bella Cruikshank hand ye the telegram as ye went by the Post Office.' She described him vividly: 'Reddish hair and beard, very jovial, never saw him in a bad temper though he could be sharp, dressed in tweeds, a round beret on his head, striding across the sands with a nice strong stick at seven in the morning before breakfast.' This was in the early days, when Bram and Florence had rooms in one of the hotel cottages. She waved to Bram and Florence as they passed the Post Office on one of their walks – 'a favourite was along the sands to the rocks near Whinnyfold, a small hamlet at the top of the cliffs where the story of *The Mystery of the Sea* was set.' Florence was known as 'Mrs Bram', 'one of the prettiest women who ever walked the Cruden Bay golf course'. She always called her husband 'Brammie'. Florence played golf while Bram wrote. They did not swim. When I asked Mrs Cruikshank if he spoke with an Irish accent, she said it was mild 'except on occasions when he was having an argument with someone, and then he spoke with a very strong Irish accent'.

Just as the London houses became smaller, there came the time when Bram was no longer able to afford the cost of the

Kilmarnock Arms to which he had returned so often. Instead, he rented a fisherman's cottage, known as 'Isie-leay's', overlooking the sea. He spent a month there; this was his last visit. After that, the wretchedness of his disease gradually confined him to bed, as feeble as when he had begun his life in Clontarf Crescent.

Bram Stoker died on 20 April 1912, at 26 St George's Square a year after the publication of *The Lair of the White Worm*. The quiet funeral at Golders Green was attended by Hall Caine, Genevieve Ward, and Laurence Irving. He left £4,723.

He was sixty-four years old.

POSTSCRIPT

There is a tragic postscript to this story.

I felt there was something peculiar about Bram's last years, as if a piece was missing. He had gone beyond sexual frustration into a sort of desperation.

Bram had gout, one of those diseases which, like mumps, are hilarious to others, though painful to the sufferer. Even so, gout would hardly account for any mental instability, though it could have been connected with his Bright's Disease – an illness named after Richard Bright, who wrote on kidney diseases in 1827. It is known commonly though less comprehensibly, as Nephritis, and is prevalent in 'large, white men' like Stoker. As high blood pressure is usual in extreme cases, I asked my doctor if Stoker might have been treated with drugs; he thought this unlikely.

It has been stated and repeated that Bram died from 'exhaustion'. It is a gratifying epitaph, with the implication that he wore himself out through overwork on behalf of others. But this is not the whole truth.

'Exhaustion' struck me as a curious expression for a death certificate, but when I received a copy I was no wiser from the other words I found there, until I showed them to my doctor. Bram died of tertiary syphilis. The medical terminology on his death certificate reads in full: 'Locomotor Ataxy 6 months Granular Contracted Kidney. Exhaustion. Certified by James Browne M.D.

My doctor was astonished that Dr Browne had not used a

customary subterfuge, such as 'specific disease'. 'Locomotor ataxia' is the equivalent of *Tabes Dorsalis* and *General Paresis*, better known as GPI – General Paralysis of the Insane. Various stages of the disease have been recorded in older medical books, which were more extensive.

> 'Preliminary stage: a change in character, marked by acts which may astonish the friends and relatives . . . unaccountable fatigue . . . mental restlessness . . . the patient may launch into extravagances and speculation of the wildest character. A common feature at this stage is the display of an unbounded egoism.
>
> *Second stage:* The intensity of the excitement is often extreme, acute maniacal stages are frequent; incessant restlessness, obstinate sleeplessness, noisy, boisterous excitement, and blind, uncalculating violence especially characterises such states.
>
> The patient becomes bedridden, death occurs from exhaustion.

I hesitated to include this until I was convinced that by revealing it, I would show Bram Stoker in a clearer light. It explains so much. The failing eyesight, for example, following his 'stroke', after Irving's death: Mott states that about 50 per cent of his asylum cases of tabo. paralysis had preceding optic atrophy. Its occurrence therefore is of grave significance. The mental symptoms may be delayed for several years.'

When his wife's frigidity drove him to other women, probably prostitutes among them, Bram's writing showed signs of guilt and sexual frustration. At a later stage, when the disease had taken possession, there was the revulsion from Lady Arabella's 'snake hole', and his statement that 'the only emotions which in the long run harm, are those arising from the sex impulse'.

He probably caught syphilis around the turn of the century, possibly as early as the year of *Dracula,* 1897. (It usually takes ten to fifteen years before it kills.) By 1897 it seems that he had been celibate for more than twenty years, as far as Florence was concerned. This would explain Bram's reputation as a 'womaniser'. Possibly the disease was contracted in Paris, where so many 'faithful' husbands, such as Charles Dickens and Wilkie

Collins, had gone for discreet pleasure before him. It is known that Bram did go to France on several occasions, and said the only words he needed there were 'pain', 'vin' and 'bain'. There is even the intriguing report that he brought money for Oscar Wilde, though this is not referred to in any of the Wilde letters.

Am I right in disclosing the real cause of his death? I believe so; there is no question of any hereditary taint, for all this happened many, many years after Noel, his only child, was born. And the knowledge brings a new sympathy for him. At least he was spared the last cruel madness of de Maupassant; even so, think of the anguish of the man as he limped across the sands of Cruden Bay with his 'nice, strong walking stick', broken in health and fortune, his mind devoured by the knowledge of the disease that was killing him and for which there was then no cure.

I hope he realised there would be triumph to come, and that he remembered the proud words of Count Dracula as he turned on his pursuers who were so bent on his destruction:

You think to baffle me, you – with your pale faces all in a row, like sheep in a butcher's. You shall be sorry yet, each one of you!

You think you have left me without a place to rest, but I have more.

My revenge is just begun! I spread it over centuries, and TIME IS ON MY SIDE.

Index